Real parenting for real kids

Enabling parents to bring out the best in their children

by
Melissa Hood

Practical Inspiration
PUBLISHING

First published in Great Britain by Practical Inspiration
Publishing, 2016

© Melissa Hood, 2016

All illustrations © Siobhan Barlow, 2016

The moral rights of the author have been asserted

ISBN (print): 978-1-910056-30-1

ISBN (ebook): 978-1-910056-31-8

Practical Inspiration
PUBLISHING

Praise for *Real Parenting for Real Kids*

"Most people learn how to be the parents they want to be only after their children have fled the nest. Parents say they are too busy with work, with getting by, with coping, to reflect deeply on what they really want for their children, and the values they want to implant. They unconsciously mimic the ways they themselves were brought up, or react strongly against it. This thoughtful book will help parents savour and enjoy to the full the greatest job that life will confer on them – bringing up the next generation".

– Sir Anthony Seldon, Vice-Chancellor, The University of Buckingham (former Headmaster of Wellington College) and author of *Beyond Happiness*

"With so much pressure and panic swirling around children nowadays, many parents feel overwhelmed and bewildered. *Real Parenting for Real Kids* slices right through that confusion. With clarity, rigour and wisdom, Melissa Hood reminds us what really matters in childhood – and shows us how to give it to our own children. She serves up step-by-step advice for tackling every parenting challenge under the sun, from bullying and screen time to exam pressure and figuring out what 'success' means. But she also goes beyond the tools and techniques to deliver a rare gift: a blueprint for building families that allow both parents and children to become their best selves. A wonderful book."

– Carl Honoré, author of *Under Pressure: Putting the Child back in Childhood*

"*Real Parenting for Real Kids* is an excellent and important book. Children are of course all unique and family dynamics will be correspondingly individualistic. Nevertheless there is something for every parent and potential parent to take from this book. An abundance of wise advice and counsel and a totally laudable absence of condescension or judgmental criticism. There is reassurance for the parent who is reaching the end of his or her tether that the problems they are dealing with are not unique to them, together with sound practical advice about how to move forward. There is also plenty of encouragement to continue and persevere with a sensible approach to parenting even if results are not immediately obvious. Children don't come with a manual but this book could easily be subtitled 'How to negotiate the pitfalls and navigate your way through the minefield of becoming a successful parent'."

– Michael Spens, Headmaster, Fettes College

"Melissa Hood's *Real Parenting for Real Kids* helps parents reclaim the leadership role in their homes, without resorting to shouting, bribes, threats or punishment. An easy-to-read yet comprehensive guide for any parent who has struggled to get her child to cooperate, loaded with concrete tools to help parents bring out the best in their children. Hood teaches the essential skills to raise wonderful kids, using stories every parent can identify with to illustrate better solutions for everyday parenting challenges, from squabbling and lying to screen time and schoolwork."

– Dr. Laura Markham, author of *Calm Parent, Happy Kid*

"*Real Parenting* is a real step-by-step guide to the nuts and bolts of being in the trenches with 'real kids' everyday. It is laid out in ways that actually help parents figure out their own plan of action with such helpful and positive advice, like 'chat throughs' and the many uses of role play. Unlike so many parenting books, *Real Parenting* is a great balance between not only what helps children do well, but what helps parents parent well."

– Bonnie Harris, author of *When Your Kids Push Your Buttons, And What You Can Do About It*

"*Real Parenting for Real Kids* is excellent – practical, thorough and crammed with wisdom gained from research-based psychology and professional and personal experience. Hood identifies our struggles as parents but always provides both explanation and potential solution. So for readers, every instance of cringing recognition – such as the pre-school breakfast-time narrative that has the adult resentfully asking their 7 year old, 'why does it take you so long to put on a sock?' – is balanced with insight and advice; meaning there are many light-bulb moments. It's enjoyable, informative, and inspirational. I think this book is invaluable – it has the potential to make a huge positive difference to families."

– Anna Maxted, journalist

Note from the author

Hello and welcome to *Real Parenting for Real Kids*. If you've popped your head in for a quick look around be my guest. I'm guessing you are a parent or someone close to you is a parent. So you probably know that for all its rewards, bringing up children can also be hard work. If you want some help with that, with insights to help you understand your child even better and family-tested strategies to bring out the best in them, you're in the right place.

I'm guessing one of the things you might like is for your children to do what you ask them without making a drama of it. Just to whet your appetite, would you like to know how to get your kids to follow instructions in 3 easy steps?

What parent wouldn't?

If you'd like to see a short video where I explain how to do just that, go to http://www.theparentpractice.com/book. And you can see the face behind the words in this book.

Enjoy! I hope this is the beginning of a fruitful partnership.

Best wishes,

Melissa

Table of Contents

the myths around discipline and using a problem-solving approach to behaviours you want to change.

Understanding why we get upset and respond ineffectively when things go pear-shaped and how we can keep calm.

Fostering harmony and resolving conflict between siblings and others; exploring friendships, bullying, social skills; being an only child.

Bringing out the best in your child at school, managing stress, handling homework, encouraging focus and organisational skills, fostering curiosity and passion and the role of non-academic activities.

Encouraging your children to have a healthy relationship with their bodies, positive body image and self-care; the role of sport; channelling energy positively.

Teaching children to be safe and kind online.

Understanding why lying, stealing, cheating, bullying, swearing and other 'bad' behaviours happen and what to do about it; the role of apologies; developing healthy attitudes to sex.

Introduction

My own story

Before I had children I thought I'd be a great parent. Of course. We're all experts before we have kids of our own. The things we were never going to do! Well in truth I didn't think about it much at all, I just *assumed* I'd be fine. I wanted to have children while I was young as I wanted to have lots of energy but apart from that I didn't give it much thought. That doesn't mean I was particularly conceited – I just thought it was easy enough and I had the right background to make me a good parent. I'd been a child, I'd had good parents, I'd looked after my much younger sister – how hard could it be? I thought all you needed to be a good parent was to love your kids. I *did* love my kids, but when it came to it I found I needed a whole lot more than that.

Parenting turned out to be quite different from what I'd expected. But not immediately. My first child, Gemma, came into the world easily and blissfully quickly and was, of course, adorable. Although I was tired she was lovely and caring for her was a new game. Somehow I managed to combine work and parenthood and she grew into a sweet toddler. I was lulled into a false sense of security. Parenting was easy, I thought.

So we had another.

My son, Christian, was born with the umbilical cord around his neck and that was the first of the struggles he encountered with the world. After he stopped being blue he was gorgeous and, drama over, we were happy with our growing family. So happy we went on and had another one, Sam.

By the time number three came into the world I was accomplished at giving birth but what came after the birth was beginning to be more taxing. Babyhood was fine, even the six o'clock screams of colic were manageable, but after that some of my children's encounters with the world were more trying.

Christian, in particular, tested all my parenting abilities – and they were found wanting. Parenting Christian provided the crisis that set me off on the adventure during which I discovered the skills, strategies and insights set out here, often by seeing what didn't work. He was rough and mean with his brother, he irritated his sister, he got into scrapes at playgroup, he broke things and didn't do as he was told. He was like a whirlwind, getting into everything, especially anything sharp or dangerous. He got lost in busy places as he wandered off, and anything forbidden was like a magnet. He did the opposite of what he was asked to do. Not all the time, but enough for me to not always like being with him much, which made me feel sad and guilty. His early childhood was characterised by him doing one thing or another that got him into trouble, both at home and at school.

Parents were invited to visit his nursery school and when it was my day I was down one end of the room doing an activity with him when up the other end of the room something went wrong. I can't remember what happened but I do remember that several of the children said that Christian had done it. I knew that wasn't true as he had been right next to me. But it made me realise how often he must have been the cause of upsets for them to assume that he was behind this one.

Once he started big school my husband and I spent quite a bit of time in the head's office. We were sat on the sofa and made to feel like we had a uniquely awful child – we thought we were uniquely deficient parents. I wasn't used to being told off as I'd been a compliant child and this felt *really* uncomfortable.

Many's the time I was reduced to tears at my inability to find the secret to keeping the lovely Christian front and centre. I can remember wondering what I'd done to deserve this. My instinct was to be loving, which I could be. But then he'd do something awful and I'd think – *he needs to be punished.* So I'd do that. That didn't work either and the behaviour continued. We tried all the things that parents were 'supposed to do'. When he was little we'd tried ignoring and distracting only to be met with greater persistence. We sent him to his room, we withdrew privileges – sometimes quite big treats that we'd all been looking forward to for a long time (such as a trip to Warwick castle to see the knights jousting – Christian stayed in the car with an adult) – and he got told off, lectured and scolded. A few times, when my buttons had really been pushed, I smacked. I certainly tried cajoling, pleading and bribing too. None of it worked. We felt powerless.

When Christian was told off for something he'd cry or he'd make excuses, lie or blame someone else. He thought it was terribly unfair. Often he just stayed silent and wouldn't look at us. (Why would he want to look at me when I was yelling at him?) He'd do anything to avoid taking responsibility. Now I understand why but then I just thought it was a character flaw, one that would end with him behind bars.

Here is one story from the family annals, now infamous as a particularly terrible example of the behaviour at the time.

We had gone on holiday to Australia and were with my family on the Gold Coast in Queensland, staying in high-rise apartments. We were

living in the UK at the time and it was a special treat for all my Australian family to be together for a beach holiday. Expectations were high. The apartments had balconies on which were planters with pebbles in them. Christian, by now aged 7, and his younger cousin decided it would be fun to drop the pebbles off the balcony. I'm sure they thought this was a great game (there may have been a quite scientific analysis of the trajectory of the missile) and maybe they didn't stop to think of the consequences, but several of the pebbles had landed on a car parked below before one of the adults twigged what was going on and put a stop to it. The car was of course damaged and the parents had to pay for repairs.

Christian had been suspended from his primary school twice and I'd been a parent for nearly ten years before we found the help we needed. My husband and I took a parenting course at The New Learning Centre in north London and our lives turned a corner. What we were seeking was peace in our family, an end to the shouting, scolding, punishing and tears. We weren't just looking for cooperation – we wanted happiness. It's not overstating it to say that when we crossed that threshold we stepped into a new world.

Before I had children I was a solicitor. I had studied for years and had two degrees. I was well educated and I think reasonably intelligent. I was competent at my job. I was analytical and had good attention to detail. But none of the skills or knowledge I'd acquired equipped me to parent this boy. What John and I learnt initially from Noël Janis-Norton and then from many other writers and educators completely transformed our family.

I now know that Christian wasn't uniquely awful – in fact many parents have told me stories of similar behaviour, some just as bad as the pebble-throwing incident. And I know that my husband and I weren't awful parents either. We were doing the best we could with the resources that we had and actually getting quite a bit right – especially with our other two, who were easier at that time. We just didn't have the tools we needed or a real understanding of what made him tick. Later we learnt that Christian had dyslexia and that much of his behaviour at school served as a distraction from his difficulties in the classroom. Other behaviours were attributable to his then low self-esteem and to our inconsistent approaches. I wish I had understood sooner his temperament and how to work with it to get cooperation and kinder behaviour. Christian was intense, persistent, highly distractible, impulsive and energetic and he is also an introvert, so being with others for protracted periods exhausted him. It took me some years to discover the tools that helped me understand him, appreciate him and redirect his behaviour. Now as an adult those qualities serve him very well as he is tenacious, creative, perceptive and very loving, and while he's socially adept he still likes just being alone with his wife to recharge.

Thank goodness we found the skills we needed before our children hit adolescence, which was comparatively plain sailing! It wasn't a quick turn-around, although I began to feel more confident very quickly. I can remember learning about Descriptive Praise on day one and thinking it was a wonderful idea in principle but I couldn't see how to use it with *my* son. After all, I *would* praise him if he ever did anything remotely praise-worthy! Crucially we found tools to help us understand what our children were going through in different developmental stages and to appreciate each of their temperaments. We learnt strategies for building self-esteem, which was really vital for Christian. We learnt how to teach him better and he learnt to take responsibility. We were able to show him and to teach him empathy and to control his impulsivity. He coped with secondary school and excelled at university and is now working hard in an industry he loves. He is able to admit when he's wrong and to put it right. He has very good emotional intelligence and I'm confident that his future doesn't involve any time in jail! Had I had a more straightforward child I would never have learnt as much as I did. I remember once reading that you are sent the child you need to learn the lessons you need to know in life. Certainly our children are our teachers. The transformation in my own family was so profound that I wanted to share it with others. I did my parenting facilitation training at The New Learning Centre where I worked for six years and also took a post-graduate certificate in Systemic Therapy for Families and Couples at the Institute of Family Therapy. In 2004, together with Camilla McGill, I founded The Parent Practice. I have found sharing these ideas with families and coaching them to have happier family lives and bring out the best in their children is so much more rewarding than anything I had done before. When I was a solicitor no one told me how the agreement I'd drafted for them had changed their lives, whereas that is our daily experience at The Parent Practice! Camilla left The Parent Practice in 2009 and I was joined at the helm by Elaine Halligan.

Elaine's story

Let me tell you Elaine's story. Elaine has two children, Sam and Issy. When we first met them Elaine and Tony's son Sam was 7 and they were struggling with him. He had already had a tough life up until that point. He is very dyslexic and had been diagnosed with Oppositional Defiance Disorder as well as Attention Deficit Disorder and possible placement on the Autistic Spectrum. He felt very different and most inadequate. He believed he was a bad person. Indeed he was a very angry young boy. The first time I met him he brought his fist down really hard on his mother's foot, which she'd injured. He was generally quite aggressive and definitely oppositional. His parents were at their wits' end, having received much conflicting advice and having tried most opportunities available for a child with his set of difficulties. Travelling on public transport was a complete nightmare as he was all over the place and wouldn't listen to anything anyone told him to do – it was sometimes dangerous and always embarrassing. He had been to three schools including one special needs school and been excluded from all of them. One school had been so unable to manage his behaviour that they shut him in a room and told him to calm down! Luckily his parents did not give up on him. Parents don't generally give up on their children but sometimes they do accept that there are limits to what can be achieved. Elaine and Tony took our positive parenting courses and trained hard to help him. They discovered the strategies they needed and practised using them. They knew he was a good and capable person. Elaine says, "We had a rock covered in mud, but over time, peeling back layers, we discovered a diamond underneath."

They found schools that could support him and it finally became possible for him to attend school again because of all the work they put in at home. In all the years I've known him I've always been amazed at the way Sam progressed. He has always had drive and a self-belief that I think comes, not in small part, from his parents' belief in him. Literacy is still a struggle for him but this young man will not be stopped by that. He has great resilience and a maturity well beyond his years. His social skills are very acute and he has insights about people rare in someone his age. He earned the respect of his peers and teachers and was made head boy for his final year of school, which speaks volumes about his leadership abilities. In his gap year he took on a challenging car rally from London to Mongolia, which says a lot about his confidence. (The anxiety nearly killed his mother!) He coped with all kinds of difficulties en route. At the time of writing he has just started university. Who would have thought that was possible 11 years ago?

What about you?

Your children may not have any of the difficulties that Sam was landed with. They may not be exhibiting the same behaviours that Christian showed when he was young. The challenges you face with your children may be different but some of those stories may have resonated with you. Some of you will have the intense children that Mary Sheedy Kurcinka calls 'spirited'[1] and will therefore have much greater calls on your parenting skills. You will need to drill down to understand your children better and find reserves within yourselves. It's important to realise that this is where we do our most important parenting. The easy bits are easy, although of course they do count. The tough bits are where we really do the very best possible...

Over my 18 years of working with parents I have encountered many different issues that families grapple with. In a recent survey of our clients the top issues that currently concerned them were:

☐ finding ways to discipline calmly and positively, without shouting, threatening and scolding

☐ encouraging harmony and managing conflict between siblings

☐ cooperation; getting kids to listen to parents

☐ building confidence and resilience

☐ getting kids to communicate more

☐ helping children deal with emotions

☐ encouraging respect for others

☐ homework; getting children to do it to a satisfactory standard, helping them to be focused and organised

---

[1] *Raising Your Spirited Child*, 2009

- ☐ helping children deal with exam pressure
- ☐ friendship difficulties
- ☐ fostering a united front between partners and with other child carers
- ☐ finding a balance between keeping children safe and encouraging independence

Whatever the issues that you are facing in your family, you don't need to face them alone. When I was struggling I felt really alone. I felt embarrassed around parents of Christian's peers, sensing their judgment; my family were on the other side of the world and I was floundering. I felt as if I should know how to do this. By this time I'd left my job as a solicitor – my family was my job now. I thought parenting was supposed to be instinctive.

I do think parents should trust their instincts but sometimes what we think are instincts about how to bring up children are in fact deep conditioning, legacies of the way we were brought up ourselves or conventions around parenting that we've heard so often we believe them to be truths. It occurred to me that I think of driving as 'instinctive' in that I do it largely without thinking (and I don't run into things) but of course it's not instinctive, it's just that I've been doing it for so long that I no longer have to think about it. So it is with beliefs that have been around a long time. Let's just check to make sure that we're not confusing learned behaviours, what 'everyone else is doing', with *our* values, what feels right to us. When Christian was behaving badly I followed the accepted belief that punishment would teach him how to behave. Not only did it not change the behaviour but it damaged his self-esteem and made it harder for me to connect with him. His behaviour grew worse.

> "Believe nothing, no matter where you read it or who has said it, not even if I have said it, unless it agrees with your own reason and your own common sense."
>
> – Buddha.

Running is an instinctive behaviour but the science around how the body works gives athletes a greater understanding of how to achieve maximum performance and it takes a good coach to make an exceptional athlete.

"Parents need a special way of relating and talking with their children. How would any of us feel if a surgeon came into the operating room and before the anaesthesiologist put us under, said 'I really don't have much training in surgery but I love my patients and use common sense'? We would probably panic and run for our lives. But it's not that easy for children whose parents believe that love and common sense are enough. Like surgeons, parents, too, need to learn special skills to become competent in coping with the daily demands of children. Like a trained surgeon who is careful where he cuts, parents, too, need to become skilled in the use of words. Because words are like knives. They can inflict, if not physical, many painful emotional wounds." – Dr Haim Ginott

There is much knowledge that has accumulated around child development and neuroscience which greatly enhances our understanding of how our children grow. Such understanding allows us to be compassionate, strategic and effective in our parenting. But as well as theory we want to know what works in practice in busy families.

The masters of parenting

A few years ago I came across the remarkable work of Drs John and Julie Gottman. They have researched and worked with couples and families for many, many years. I did their Bringing Baby Home training (about the transition from a couple to a family) in Australia in 2011 and then took their couples relationship training in Iceland in 2012. They have studied what makes a successful couple relationship and have analysed the elements that make these relationships work. They call these successful couples the 'masters of relationship'. I realised that in the work we do at The Parent Practice we also have a unique opportunity to observe masters at work. In our face-to-face work with parents, in courses, workshops and consultations at our centres in London, New York and Sydney we have learnt much from our clients. We hear about the issues they have faced and the solutions they have devised. We have incorporated into our trainings many of the ideas generated by these masters of parenting. They would hasten to deny that they are masters but we are not talking about attaining any kind of perfection, just continuing to improve all the time, getting to know our children better and devising solutions that work in our own families.

Many parents when they hear about these skills feel guilty that they have not been parenting this way up until now. Well of course they haven't. They were doing the best they could with the resources they had at the time. And they may have been doing a perfectly good job too. If you're reading this book it means you're open to new ideas so ditch the guilt and add some more really effective tools to your existing tool basket and recognise the good things you've been doing as we celebrate the masters of parenting. As Ellen Williams and Erin Dynowski say, "if you're worried about being a good parent then you already are one."[2]

Guilt and anxiety are common feelings for parents today. Now as Ericka Christakis put it, "we live in the information

---

[2] Sisterhood of The Sensible Moms bloggers, speaking as part of the Happy Families Summit in June 2015,

age and that causes huge stress for families... because now we're aware of what crummy parents we are."[3] Christakis was speaking on The Purpose of Parenting at the Aspen Festival of Ideas in 2012 and she referred to a 'crisis of information'. The proliferation of information about what is healthy and unhealthy and the culture of judgment of parents in the media has certainly contributed to parents' anxiety. My aim is to allay some of that anxiety by pointing to examples from perfectly ordinary families who have become the masters of parenting with the help of the skills herein.

One such master sent us this note from her husband (she was away visiting family at the time).

At bedtime, Lucas was quite chatty, and explained to me why he preferred you to cuddle him than me! "No offence, dad" he said "but..." He mentioned three reasons:

1. *You're softer/cuddlier (I know you'll think fat, but get rid of such a negative thought – we like to cuddle you!)*
2. *When he does half of what he was supposed to do, you praise the bit he has done and then remind/explain about the bit he hasn't.*
3. *You understand him... You understand him when he doesn't explain anything.*

You may be familiar with a progression of learning characterised by different stages:
1. **neophyte** – this is a state of blissful ignorance where we don't know what we don't know. We are unconscious of our incompetence.
2. **beginner** – at this uncomfortable stage we have enough learning to be aware of what we don't know or can't do – we are consciously incompetent.
3. **competent** – by this stage we have developed skills

[3] http://www.aspenideas.org/session/what-goal-parenting

and strategies but it takes effort to implement them – we are consciously competent, at least some of the time, in some areas

4. **mastery** – by now there are some areas where we use our skills without too much effort, maybe even without thinking about it – we have achieved unconscious competence.

Once we have taken on the initial learning we will oscillate between stages 3 and 4 and our mood, hormones, sleep levels and general wellbeing will affect our competence on a daily basis. As parents we have the power to impact our children's development in a profound way. Our responses to our children's behaviour will be governed by these variable factors and also by more deep-seated factors such as how we were parented ourselves – what are the habitual learned behaviours for us? – and our temperament or how we tend to respond to the world generally. Awareness can help us alter these ingrained factors too. When we're busy and stressed of course we will default to 'automatic parenting', when we revert to our less-considered responses, the parenting habits that are in our subconscious. It will take time to make the new ways of doing things the habit that takes over. The more we practise the more we create new neural pathways.

At The Parent Practice our work is based on sound, well-researched psychological theories and the latest research in child development and brain science but it is also tested at the coal face with busy families in everyday life. We draw on the experiences of our own team of facilitators but also on those of the parents we work with – the masters. Here we offer you the accumulated wisdom of the masters of parenting as you help your child navigate their world en route to adulthood.

How to get the best out of this book

So welcome to *Real Parenting for Real Kids*. I'm Melissa and I'll be your guide through 7 essential skills that every parent needs to understand their children and bring out the best in them. Then we'll explore 7 spheres in which those skills can be applied. *Real Parenting for Real Kids* is written primarily with parents of primary school-aged children in mind but the skills have applications for children from the age of 2 right through adolescence and beyond so if your child is older, say 14 or 44, then don't think it's too late for you.

I recommend you read the 7 skills chapters first and then go on to dip in and out of the chapters in the second part, which look at how these skills apply to everyday challenges in your child's world. There will be lots of stories generously shared by our team and by the parents we've been privileged to work with. And in accordance with our practical philosophy I invite you to get into action with your own family and do the exercises throughout each chapter. You can get PDFs of these exercises and many additional resources from our website here: www.theparentpractice.com/book-resources. Where there are references to our website it will be to the appropriate chapter on this page; so for example if you are reading chapter 8 and there is a reference to a problem-solving discussion for siblings, go to the chapter 8 section on the web page to find it.

On a note of authorship you will see that to avoid cumbersome references to 'he or she' throughout I have referred alternately to he/him or she/her. It doesn't imply any gender bias. Many of the stories I've used have been sent in or told to us by mums but we know of plenty of dads who have also changed their parenting approach with phenomenal results. In fact one dad also reported using some of the skills on his sales team at work with a great effect on the bottom line.

I have also referred to children as 'kids' sometimes. I know some adults don't like this so I want to reassure you that I am not comparing your offspring to baby goats but sometimes some variety in expression and a more informal tone is a good thing, I think. I apologise if this offends anyone.

Keep developing your own parenting practice and watch those areas of mastery grow.

Part One

*7 essential skills for bringing out the
best in your children*

1

Skill 1: Knowing your child

Parenting isn't a one-size-fits-all science. You need to have a real understanding of the real child in front of you at the stage he is at *now* to know how to apply the techniques and strategies that follow. Bespoke parenting, tailored to the needs of the individual child, means that the strategies you use will really fit. Without this understanding the skills may not work as well.

An understanding of what is taking place in your child's brain and what he is capable of at each stage of development as well as his temperament and any special needs he may have will help you to adjust your expectations of him and adapt your approach so you can provide the right kind of support and environment, encouragement and discipline for your child.

Ages and stages of development

"A 3 year old is not half a 6 year old."

– Ken Robinson

When Sue was driving with Nick aged 12 and she said "I wish that blue car would hurry up," he just said "It's not blue." "What do you mean it's not blue?" They then started one of those surreal conversations until she realised he just had to disagree with her whatever she said – because he was approaching adolescence and arguing is something they have to do – so she dropped it.

One of my LPMs (low parenting moments) involved me stamping my foot and yelling at my boys (then aged 7 and 5) in a very immature manner (before I learnt better skills), *"Why are you being so childish?"* An understanding of how behaviour fits with what's happening in our children's brains at the time makes it more likely that we can be compassionate and effective in our approaches (and less childish ourselves).

Children go through genetically determined distinct phases of development as they progress through childhood to adolescence and adulthood but they develop at their own pace so any information about stages of development should be seen only as a guide, not as prescriptive. It's not that 'my child SHOULD' be over tantrums by 4 years old, just about understanding that with language development, in the normal course, children can use words to express themselves better around the age of 4. We all know children much older than that (and indeed some adults) who have tantrums if they haven't yet learnt better strategies. Children can revert to behaviour characteristic of an earlier stage if they are stressed or distressed. Older children often engage in babyish behaviours when a new baby comes along.

William's father was a bit concerned when, a few years ago, William, aged 12, decided to take up colouring again in a smart restaurant. His mum realised that as William was about to start secondary school and embark on adolescence it was a last opportunity to engage in some childish activities. At the time of writing adult colouring has actually become a popular craze.

So, when we learn about developmental stages it is not to establish standards for our children to live up to but general indicators to guide adult understanding, empathy and teaching.

Our brains have evolved into three sections governing different functions. The rational or higher brain, in the frontal lobes, deals with reasoning, logic and problem-solving.

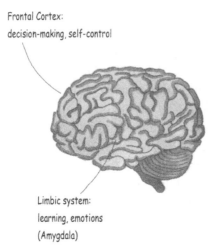

Frontal Cortex:
decision-making, self-control

Limbic system:
learning, emotions
(Amygdala)

Psychologist and author Walter Mischel[4] calls this reflective part the cool brain. The mammalian or emotional brain, in the limbic system, deals with emotions and impulses. Mischel calls this reflexive part the hot brain. There is also the ancient or reptilian brain which controls essential bodily functions. We are concerned with the first two parts of the brain and how they interact with each other. The cool brain can regulate the impulses of the hot brain but its success depends on age, parental input and the child's exposure to stress. The frontal lobes won't be fully developed until the early 20s!

Babies, toddlers and pre-schoolers (Newborn to 4 years)

The human baby is born in a very immature state. Enormous growth and development in the body and brain happens in the first four years after birth. This age group is not the focus of this book so we mention it here only to summarise what's gone before and to distinguish what the school-aged child is now capable of.

When your child was a toddler he was developing a growing awareness of himself that started as a baby. This stage of development is egocentric, in the sense that a child in this age group is only beginning to develop awareness of others and their feelings. It does not mean your child is selfish if they want what they want and they want it now.

---

[4] Walter Mischel, The Marshmallow Test

The frontal lobes are immature at this stage. Young children are governed by the emotional centres of their brains and so respond to their own feelings and are sensitive to atmosphere. Their ability to communicate in words is limited (but growing incredibly rapidly) so their capacity to express their needs is variable. This can lead to much frustration and tantrums.

This age group is active, curious, learning, impulsive, emotional and messy, with raisins in their nappies and sweetcorn up their noses. They operate at a different pace from adults and they have different agendas. They want and need a lot of loving attention. A huge amount of learning happens through play.

They need to be learning about their environment so it is entirely right that they should want to stop and examine the ladybirds and the leaves and count the cracks in the pavement as you walk along, but you may need to get to the post office before it closes!

Primary school-aged children (4–7)

In the UK children start formal learning from the age of four whereas in other countries it is generally not till five or six. Since four seems to be a significant marker in terms of brain development we will characterise this stage as starting at four even if your child hasn't started 'big' school yet. We will look at the stages that children progress through in terms of their emotional, intellectual, social and moral development.

The massive growth in brain matter that occurred in the first four years of life (appropriately called 'exuberance') has now slowed down but if you're the parent of a four year old you'll know that doesn't mean the child has! Boys get a surge of testosterone about this time that often makes for heightened activity and sometimes aggression. It can be like living with a tornado.

Emotionally

During this period children:

☺ Have some understanding that others have a mind of their own with different emotions, desires and beliefs, not necessarily the same as their own, but your five year old may still offer you her teddy if she thinks you're upset.

☺ Can be empathetic, especially if they are not involved in someone else's upset. They are still sensitive to atmosphere and may feel stressed if the adults are in conflict. The capacity to think about another person's feelings develops slowly and depends on many examples of you showing concern for them.

☺ Will be developing awareness of their own feelings and a vocabulary for them. They will (depending on parental input) be increasing their ability to regulate their emotions. They can express their emotions more in words and with stronger communication skills their problem-solving ability increases. They will generally not be able to answer questions like "How are you feeling?" or tell you about the emotional root of their behaviour when you ask "Why did you do that?"

☺ May still have tantrums when it will be ~~difficult~~ impossible to reason with them. Don't try to explain that she's already got lots of toys at home when making a stance about not buying something in the toy shop.

☺ Have very little experience, so it can be hard to realise that the feelings they've got right now won't last. That can make it difficult to put the pain of losing a game into perspective and prompts a tantrum.

☺ Are still somewhat egocentric and so will not be able to distinguish between themselves and their behaviour when a parent describes it as 'naughty'. They may think of themselves as 'bad' when told off.

☺ Will believe the labels adults apply to them, so beware of calling your child naughty, shy, lazy, mean or disorganised.

☺ Will at some point explore issues of mortality, perhaps with some attendant uncertainty and worry.

When Mark was starting school and didn't want to go in, Sue would say, "Well, just don't say goodbye to me," and of course, being 4, he said "Goodbye". So she said, "Well, at least don't say it with a smile," and he'd say, "Goodbye Mummy" with this huge smile and turn on his heel and go in.

Intellectually

During this period children:

☺ Are becoming more independent, creative, analytical and less self-centred.

☺ Are developing (so are not yet very good at) impulse control and understanding.

☺ Have limited perspective or ability to look into the future. A four year old still lives in the moment so finds it hard to wait, and delaying gratification is difficult.

☺ Are acquiring information about the world, including their own bodies and gender. They can be quite stereotypical at first in their views about gender roles.

☺ Are still very curious and their logic is developing – they ask *lots* of questions. They are learning, not trying to irritate or test us.

☺ Can only focus on one or two aspects of a task at a time – so they may forget what we've asked them to do or get distracted. The capacity of short-term memory develops over time.

☺ Will not be able to concentrate for long and may get bored when engaged in more adult activities like waiting for the meal in a restaurant, shopping in the supermarket or travelling in cars or on public transport. Having nothing to do is stressful for a young child. A child in this age group has a high need for stimulation and if it's not provided via entertaining activities she will find her own entertainment such as playing with things or exploring where she shouldn't.

☺ Think in concrete, not abstract, ways. They may be quite literal and inflexible, very black and white, which can make it difficult to explain things like social 'white' lies. They have a heightened sense of fairness, especially in relation to themselves.

☺ Are learning mostly by doing, and by copying us – no pressure then!

☺ Understand the difference between reality and pretence and still engage in a lot of imaginary play.

Socially and morally

During this period children:

☺ Are developing their social skills, but may not be very advanced – the child is learning empathy, sharing/turn-taking, following rules, to not be bossy or aggressive, to make eye contact and say hello, conflict resolution and saying sorry. It can be hard for adults to understand the feelings of invasion a young child has when someone takes her toy.

☺ First become aware that they can manipulate another's emotions and beliefs together with the possibility of deceptive behaviour. Lying and stealing are not uncommon, especially around age 7. Don't catastrophise – it's a stage.

☺ Are learning the principles of right and wrong – there will be some testing of the boundaries still, and more so if these are not consistent. They are learning the consequences of their actions – it depends how parents administer discipline whether a child accepts responsibility. They follow rules to avoid punishment.

☺ Will still be saying no, not following rules, shouting, screeching and sometimes tantruming, but less often.

☺ Tend to play with children of the same sex. Girls tend to play in small groups and boys' play is generally more physical and in larger groups. Boys and girls enjoy rough and tumble play, constructive activities like Lego or craft and dramatic or imaginary play as well as electronic toys.

☺ May be developing a sense of humour – you may have to endure many knock-knock jokes. They make up their own jokes which may begin to make sense soon.

We had been to a Star Wars exhibition with my sons, aged 6 and 5. The boys had an amazing time, and my younger son had even met Darth Vader and been allowed to wave a light saber at him. We left County Hall and knew we needed to get something to eat and drink urgently as we could see both boys were flagging. But Fred would not come into the restaurant. He stood in the doorway, with tears in his eyes, even though I knew pizza was his favourite and I could literally hear his tummy rumbling. I was a bit tired by then and not feeling that sympathetic at what looked like rude and ungrateful behaviour. But, despite battling Darth Vader a few minutes before, I also knew that he was 5 years and just one day old. And things are often much more complicated than we think for young children. They often see and understand things very differently. So I simply said "How confusing for you, I know you like pizza and I can hear that tummy rumbling, and yet you don't look like you want to come in," and he looked up at me and said "I can't come in because I can't read curly menu writing yet, and so I might get the wrong pizza," and then burst into tears. I was so glad I had remembered to think about the situation from his 5-year-old perspective before I had got cross. We agreed that I would read the curly writing and then he could order his pizza himself, just like a grown-up.

Jill, mum of two boys.

Primary school-aged children (7–12)

Emotionally

During this period children:

- ☺ Can feel anxious or unsuccessful and need lots of attention and approval. These feelings can lead to shyness, withdrawal or clinginess or to aggression, excessive competitiveness, bragging, putting others down, sibling fighting or lack of cooperation.

- ☺ Can reason more about their wants and needs so emotional outbursts may occur less often.

Intellectually

During this period children:

- ☺ Are better able to think logically and be more organised, however some may have problems with organisation well into their teens.

☺ Are learning many skills and can learn from their mistakes if failure is tolerated in their environment.

☺ Can retain more than one piece of information at a time with the increase in working memory capacity and greater proficiency at encoding material (such as by rehearsal) and retrieval (subject to any learning difficulties).

☺ Can solve concrete problems but cannot yet think abstractly.

☺ Test ideas and values.

Socially and morally

During this period children:

☺ Begin to internalise values, i.e. may follow some rules because it is the 'right thing to do'.

☺ They can distinguish between moral rules (to do with fairness, harm and rights) and social conventions.

☺ Understand about rules and consequences. This doesn't mean they will always follow the rules. They will be learning to take responsibility but may still blame others, lie or make excuses.

☺ Begin to understand the subtleties of white lies and diplomacy.

☺ Are now playing games with quite complex rules.

☺ May have a single friend or small groups. Bullying or teasing (ranging from name calling or excluding to physical or verbal taunting) may happen at school, which would have an impact at home. Falling out and making up with friends is an important part of social development in this phase. The peer group is becoming quite important by the end of this period. They are learning to respect others' space, opinions and confidences.

☺ Can be quite competitive, depending on their environment. This may show up as bragging, showing off, needing to be first or not wanting to try in case of failure.

Turning off the computer had been a big issue for us; my 9 year old and I had had huge rows in the past.

Then I thought about what it was like to be 9 and about how much my son loved his games. He got so involved and found it really hard to turn off. His ability to delay gratification and his impulse control aren't highly developed yet. He always 'just' wants to complete the next level. With that in mind I took the time to get down to his level on the sofa and empathised that it would be hard to turn the computer off before he wanted to, before it felt 'finished'. I explained that I appreciated his helpfulness and understanding and asked if he thought he could return to his game the following day. He looked at me strangely. And smiled. And turned it off. This was sheer genius – I much prefer it to my previous strategy of criticisms and threats!

Libby, mum of two

Getting into action:

When our expectations for our children are unrealistic, we create stress – not only in us, but also in the children. (More about expectations in chapter 7.)

For example:

A more reasonable expectation:

I expect my children to be calm in the car on the way home from a full day at school. I expect them to keep their seat belts on and keep silent or entertain themselves quietly, so I can concentrate on driving through the rush-hour traffic, regardless of what happened during their day or how long the journey takes.

I expect that my children may be fractious depending on how their day has been. They need to keep their seat belts on and my goal is to get them to talk about their feelings, perhaps before we get in the car, rather than taking them out on their siblings. I will brainstorm with them about how to occupy themselves while I'm driving.

Your turn

Some of the statements below contain explicit expectations – change these to more reasonable ones given what you know about children's stages of development. Some of these complaints contain implied expectations. See if you can make these explicit and make them more reasonable for a child of that age:

My expectation is that my 9-year-old son should always turn the TV off whenever I ask him, with good grace, regardless of whether he is in the middle of a programme or not, without arguing or complaining.

....

....

....

I want my 5-year-old daughter to listen and do what I ask her. I tell her to get out of the bath and dry herself, get into her pjs and choose a story and then I go to put her brother to bed. When I come back she hasn't done anything!

....

....

....

My 10-year-old son should be more modest and not brag and show off to his friends.

....

....

....

My 6-year-old son should have self-control. It's wrong for him to hit others.

....

....

....

My 4 year old is so destructive. He pulled the head off his brother's Ben Ten action figure and squeezed all the toothpaste out of the tube!

....

....

....

Temperament

"We do not have control over our child's basic temperament, but we can choose to alter our response to him."

— **Mary Sheedy Kurcinka**

When my youngest child was a little boy I can remember thinking I could be a really good parent to a slightly different child and if only he would change we would get on famously. He was a somewhat glass-half-empty sort of person and I worried that this outlook on life wasn't going to serve him well, that he'd have no friends and that he wouldn't be able to overcome obstacles in his life. We used to refer to him as Eeyore or Puddleglum, not realising the devastating effect that labels, even those applied affectionately, can have. Not only was I wrong about his future (at 24 he has friends and a most effective problem-solving approach with great tenacity) but my efforts to change him into someone with a more positive disposition stopped me from seeing the good in him and made him feel wrong. It got in the way of connection. Now I can appreciate his serious and analytical nature and I certainly appreciated his cautious side when he was in his teens and not taking part in the risk-taking activities that were worrying the parents of his friends.

While I'm no gardener even I can appreciate that in order to get the most out of your plants you have to understand what conditions work best for them, what they need in order to thrive. If we don't understand our children, don't accommodate their temperaments, their stages of development, understand their agendas, their likes, their upsets and their emotions, and we just wish that they were different, it's a bit like wishing we were growing a rose instead of a hibiscus. They're both beautiful flowers but they need different conditions in which to thrive. If we're going to be able to truly nourish our children we need to understand what will make them grow. When you adapt to your child's temperament it's not pandering or coddling them, it's giving them what they need to help them thrive.

How your child relates to the world around him depends in part on his genetic make-up. When he's not behaving in the ways that you would like and expect it's never because he's trying to wind you up but because of the combination of his temperament, his stage of development, his experience and his training. And also temporary things like tiredness, hunger and what's happened to him that day. Bonnie Harris puts it best when she says, "Your child is having a problem, not being a problem."[5]

His temperament determines his in-built instinctive  response to his environment. But this doesn't mean that his reactions are permanently fixed. It's a genetic predisposition, not his destiny. Our actions as parents work with the neuroplasticity of our children's brains. While we can't choose our children's temperaments, if we understand them (and our own) we can help our

---

[5] *When Your Kids Push Your Buttons: And what you can do about it* (Piatkus Books, 2005)

children understand (and respect) themselves and develop coping strategies and in doing so new neural pathways in the brain are created. Their brains are changed by their experiences. Fortunately I learned how to encourage my son to look at the world more positively while not denying his personality.

There are different ways of defining temperament but I'm going to use the model suggested by Dr Stella Chase and Dr Alexander Thomas that was developed in the 1950s. They refer to nine personality traits as set out below. Each of us falls somewhere on a continuum from mild to strong reactions for each trait. I'm going to give some examples of behaviours that reflect these personality traits and then I suggest you complete the table at the end of this section to build a temperamental portrait of your child. Each of these traits can be perceived as problematic or as beneficial. In her wonderful book *Raising Your Spirited Child*,[6] Mary Sheedy Kurcinka points out positive ways of looking at each trait. Some of the qualities you're seeing in your children you will really appreciate in them as adults, even though you may be finding them difficult to live with right now.

Intensity	Some children have relatively mild reactions, others are explosive. The intense child feels things strongly and swings between emotions rapidly.

---

[6] *Raising Your Spirited Child*, 2009

Intense children feel anger, frustration, unfairness, humiliation and excitement to a greater degree than others and need help to express those emotions with appropriate words rather than actions. Parents of intense children need to be emotion coaches (see chapter 3). This child needs to learn to soothe himself and initially parents can help with this – sometimes a bath will help or massage. He will need lots of sleep. It's good if you can catch an intense child before he blows by taking him away from the intense situation for short periods to chill.

Josh, aged 10, felt everything quite intensely so when he went to visit a prospective school with his parents he was very anxious. When he saw all the boys who looked like adults running around in a boisterous way he couldn't possibly imagine himself at that school and was completely overwhelmed by the size of the place. His parents wanted him to be on his best behaviour to make a good impression and had pulled a few strings to arrange a meeting with an admissions tutor friend but Josh didn't speak, wouldn't make eye contact and shovelled food into his mouth in a way that appalled his mother. Josh was overwhelmed by his feelings – he wasn't trying to let his parents down. But this intense child could have been prepared for such a visit, he could have coped and he could have seen that he had coping strategies. It depends on the parents really knowing their child.

Think of intensity as zest, passion and enthusiasm, rather than being overreactive.

Persistence   Some children are willing to let things go, others lock in and never give up. Persistent children are very determined, independent and assertive and don't take 'no' easily. Parents of a persistent child need to find solutions that respect both parent and child. Acknowledging your child's agenda is an essential first step towards finding solutions. *"You really, really want to stay up to see Uncle Tom, don't you? You wish you could be the one to say when bedtime is. It's really important to you because you love Uncle Tom don't you? You love it when he tells you stories from when he was in South Africa..."*

Tools used will be listening with the purpose of finding solutions, allowing reasonable independence, having rules, brainstorming and consensus finding.

Think of persistence as assertiveness, determination, perseverance and independence, rather than stubbornness.

Sensitivity   Some children are not particularly affected by noise, smells, lights, touch; others are highly aware and feel every wrinkle in their clothes or bedding, hate crowds, need absolute quiet to sleep and may be very fussy about food.

Ned (12) said it was hard for him to concentrate during his exams because his socks were irritating him. Sherry (8) found excuses to go to the library at break times because the playground was so overwhelming. Sam (10) can last about 30 minutes in a shopping mall before he starts to get grumpy.

This can be exhausting for them so parents need to monitor and regulate the level of stimulation they're getting (this means having rules about the use of electronics and ensuring they're getting enough sleep) and gradually teach children to do it for themselves. If children don't understand their own experience and don't have the words to say it feels scratchy, smelly, loud, tight, lonely, scary, hot or irritable then parents will see tears or disruptive or defiant behaviour.

The sensitive child will pick up on the mood of others around her. She forms deep attachments and can be very nurturing but can also be hurt easily.

Think of sensitivity as tender-heartedness, heightened awareness and creativity, rather than being difficult.

Distractibility/ perceptiveness

Some children hardly notice things around them; others are very perceptive and pick up details. The distractible child needs help to prioritise information and to focus. He often appears to not be listening but he's not meaning to be disrespectful. Teach him to say *I need a minute*. The parent of a distractible child learns to be an expert communicator, using a variety of methods including touch and other non-verbal forms of communication (see chapter 2). This parent learns to give clear, positive instructions in an intentional way.

Josh is highly distractible and his mother has learnt not to give him too many instructions at once. She now says, "Take your bowl over to the dishwasher and put it in," rather than, "Clear your breakfast things, go upstairs, brush your teeth and bring down your library book." She used to do that and would go upstairs 20 minutes later and find him sitting on the stairs 'thinking'.

Think of this quality as perceptiveness, awareness, openness to ideas and stimuli and creativity, rather than lack of focus.

Adaptability Some children find changes to their routine or environment easy to handle, others find it hard and are reluctant or get upset – they favour consistency and need stability. The slow-to-adapt child doesn't like transitions (from one place, action, topic, mood or person to another) and so may need extra support to stop doing what they're enjoying and do something the parent wants them to do. He will feel strong disappointment.

Harry's mother was taken aback when she came to pick him up from school with the good news that his best friend Ben would be coming to play that afternoon because Harry was surly and unpleasant with Ben. It turned out that Harry had a plan in his mind to play with the new gerbils and it took him a while to see how Ben could fit into that plan.

These children don't like surprises, even good ones. This is the child who finds it difficult to leave a play date or go into a room full of people at a party or settle at school in the morning. This child will have a hard time with beginnings or endings and may take a while to adjust to holiday routines or visits to grandparents. These children flourish on routines and planning and they need time. They love schedules and benefit from time warnings. Parents of slow-to-adapt children recognise when their kids have had too many transitions and accommodate as necessary.

Paola could see her 4-year-old son didn't want to stop having 'adventures' in the park and so said that she had forgotten the way home and needed him to guide her. He proudly showed his mum the way home.

These parents use emotion coaching (chapter 3) to help their child deal with disappointment. They help them feel in control and to become problem-solvers.

Think of this as organisation, stability and reliability, rather than inflexibility.

Regularity

Some children are hungry and tired at regular times; others are not. Unpredictable kids aren't trying to be contrary – their bodies just don't have regular rhythms. These children need more support and time to adapt to schedules, and some may never fit in with a normal your desired timetable perfectly. They take longer to be toilet trained and want to eat at odd hours. They're not tired at bed time.

Think of the irregular child as flexible, rather than contrary.

Reactivity   Some children are willing to jump in
and try things and they learn by doing,
others prefer to hang back and watch
first. The cautious child will be upset in
unfamiliar situations so he may refuse
to take part in swimming lessons,
musical or sporting activities or social
situations at first, rejecting new people,
tastes or experiences. She may seem
ungrateful if she doesn't appear to
appreciate an outing you've planned or
an outfit you've bought for her.

*My sister was furious with her daughter when we took the
extended family on holiday to the Great Barrier Reef in
Australia and my 12-year-old niece didn't want to snorkel
but sat on the boat being grumpy. Of course her mother didn't
want her to miss out on this special opportunity and worried
that she would always miss out with this attitude.*

She needs encouragement, not pushing,
to help her cope with newness. Parents
of cautious kids can teach them coping
strategies for unfamiliar situations
like arriving early at social events and
observing before joining in with new
activities. Shaming them, trying to
persuade with logic or being cross never
works. Often these strategies prevent
a child from changing their mind and
joining in later.

Think of the cautious child as someone who thinks before they act, rather than lacking courage.

Energy   Some children never stop moving, they wriggle and fidget, they need to move constantly and are kinaesthetic learners; others can hold themselves quietly and find it easy to be still. High-energy kids express themselves with their whole bodies and discomfort may come out in racing around the room, jumping on furniture, taking things apart or hitting. Their general need to move must be planned for.

I wasted a lot of time and energy and lost connections with my two sons by nagging them incessantly about their moving around, chasing imaginary pencil sharpeners round the floor, jumping up, fiddling with anything within reach, when we were trying to get homework done. I didn't understand then that they needed to move to be able to do their work. As they got older we learnt to release that movement in positive ways with aids like squeezing 'stress balls' and going to the park before homework.

If the burst of activity is expressing an emotional need then the underlying need must be addressed. Parents of high-energy kids will use gentle touch as well as words to help direct these children.

Think about how high energy can be great when properly channelled, especially in a fast-paced society.

| **Mood/ outlook** | Some children are naturally positive, and see opportunities; others are negative, and see potential problems. This disposition appears to be wired into our brains. Serious analytical kids need help expressing their concerns in ways that aren't too extreme or don't offend others – they may need extra training in diplomacy or saying thank you for gifts. Parents of these kids can encourage them to see what is working and the things they enjoy. Practices like keeping a 'gratitude' book in which they write down a set number of things they've enjoyed or are grateful for each day (even if they're only small things or parts of bigger things) can form new patterns. Parents may need to remember that when this child points out the things that he doesn't like he isn't necessarily unhappy. |
| | Think of the glass-half-empty child as serious and analytical, someone with a critical eye and good attention to detail who considers all the possibilities, rather than gloomy. |

Added to this list is a tenth factor which governs where your child fits on the continuum between extrovert and introvert. This has nothing to do with shyness or sociability but more about from whence your child draws their energy. If an extrovert needs to recharge they will seek out the company of others, be very chatty and share ideas. They need and may demand lots of feedback. An introvert will need time to be by themselves and their own space; they will be quiet and thoughtful and will not share ideas or experiences until they have been thought through. This may not be until bedtime and then parents often think it is procrastination.

An extrovert child will be happy to be physically close to others and work well in groups while an introvert child may be uncomfortable being close to others and work best on their own. Each will need to recharge in their own way. *My daughter is right on the extrovert end of the spectrum whereas my boys are more introverted, which caused clashes between them. She needed help to understand that her youngest brother was not being rude when he secreted himself away in his room when she had friends over.*

William was always reluctant to go to school at the start of each term, even after the half-term break. It didn't make any sense to me, and I would end up pushing him through the door with tears in his eyes. Until we talked. And he told me that he didn't like the newness of the fresh classroom. He didn't know where he would be sitting, he didn't know what lessons were coming up, he didn't know what the new lunch menu would be like. And when I saw it from his point of view, and took into account his temperament of finding change difficult, and being a very regular child, I was able to make the shift from him being a problem to having a problem.

We brainstormed how he could walk in, even when he wouldn't be able to know what he wanted. We practised things for him to say, something to take in to show someone, just to get him through the door. That, in conjunction with accepting how he felt about the start of each term, was enough. He went in with a little smile and a big breath, and hasn't looked back.

Juliet, mum of two

You may already have a good idea where your child fits in the personality spectrum – you are the expert on your child. But have you thought about your own temperament and how it fits with your child? If you have a similar disposition to your child it may mean that you can understand them and their difficulties, or does it mean you clash as you struggle to meet the same needs? If you are the sort of parent who jumps in to activities wholeheartedly it may be hard to understand the child who hangs back and assesses first. You may worry about them and be irritated by them. If you have a highly sensitive child but you are not so disposed it may be hard to appreciate that they really are being driven mad by that itchy label and that this brand of yoghurt tastes very different from the one you had yesterday, the one he likes better. If you find yourself digging your heels in and arguing with your five year old who insists that the red block is black it may be that you are just as persistent as she is.

Being aware of our own temperaments, being kind to ourselves and giving ourselves what we need is good topping up of our emotional bank account so that we can be calmer with our children (more on this in chapter 7) but it's also good modelling for them – they can see what they need to do to manage themselves.

On a scale of 1 to 5, circle where your child falls in each continuum. Remember, wherever they fall on each spectrum has its pluses, and its minuses. Once you have done that, go back and put a square around where YOU fall on each spectrum. (This form is available as a downloadable PDF in the www.theparentpractice.com/book-resources#chapter-1 section of our website.)

Name: ....

	1	2	3	4	5
Intensity	1	2	3	4	5
	Mild reaction				Intense reaction
Persistence	1	2	3	4	5
	Easily lets go				Locks in, doesn't let go
Sensitivity	1	2	3	4	5
	Usually not sensitive				Highly sensitive
Distractibility	1	2	3	4	5
	Hardly ever notices				Notices everything
Adaptability	1	2	3	4	5
	Adapts quickly				Slow to adapt
Regularity	1	2	3	4	5
	Regular				Irregular
Energy	1	2	3	4	5
	Quiet, still				Always moving
Reactivity	1	2	3	4	5
	Jumps right in				Rejects first
Outlook/ mood	1	2	3	4	5
	Usually positive				Often negative
Extrovert/ introvert	1	2	3	4	5
	Needs quiet time, solitude				Needs people

What surprised you about your child? What about your own temperament? How do the two fit (or not fit) together?

....

....

....

Special needs

It is beyond the scope of this book to explore special educational needs in any detail but it should be clear that for parents to really understand their children and to accommodate their particular needs in order to bring out the best in them they will need to understand as much as they can about the permutations of their child's special needs. What does it mean to have sensory processing disorders or ADHD or to be on the autistic spectrum? How does your child experience learning with dyslexia or dyspraxia? How does that difficulty affect their self-esteem? How does it show up in behaviour? What does it mean to have diagnosis of conduct disorder or oppositional defiance disorder? (See the www.theparentpractice.com/ book-resources#chapter-1 section of our website for more resources to help you understand these conditions.)

How to get to know your child even better

When you really know your child you can anticipate difficulties and prepare for them, you can understand how your child is feeling and why he is behaving the way he is, you can be more compassionate and more effective, help him resolve problems, teach him how to interact successfully with the world, and you see so much more in him to appreciate.

You already know your child pretty well. Nobody knows better than you what they like and don't like and how they are likely to react in different situations. Maybe now you also know a bit more about their temperament and have a bit more understanding of the stage of development they are in.

Special time

To make really deep connections with your child you obviously need to spend time with her. When you spend one-to-one time with her she feels cherished, she knows she has your attention for that period and you discover what makes her tick. Conversations need time. Many parents of boys find that conversations flow better when they are doing an activity alongside their sons. Steve Biddulph calls this 'sideways talk'. Some of my best conversations with my boys have happened when we've been walking together.

Special time needs to be scheduled or it won't happen. It doesn't need to be lengthy but does need to be regular. Let your child choose the activity – it might be cuddling, reading, pillow fighting, doing puzzles, drawing, cooking, cycling, gardening etc etc. Homework doesn't count!

Sometimes special time can be created out of nowhere.

Candice took her children to a museum with another mum. The other mum took the two boys and Candice found that she had 20 minutes on her own with her daughter while they completed the museum quiz. Other parents have turned waiting in a queue at the fishmonger into some impromptu special time.

When you're with your children it may take some practice to be really with them, to be fully present. Switch off or leave behind your digital distractions and focus on being with your child without trying to improve them or teach them anything! Often making eye contact makes for good connections but we all know some good conversations happen without eye contact too, such as when you're in the car – when hopefully your eyes are on the road! Take some deep breaths to allow yourself to slow down and tune in to them. It will help to build rapport and bring yourself into harmony with your child if you match your body language and breathing to theirs, i.e. exhale when they breathe out and inhale when they breathe in. This is the NLP technique of mirroring.

Ask open-ended questions[7]

Parents often make statements or give instructions to their children more than asking questions. But when you ask a question it invites a response and requires the questioner to pay attention to the other. Asking questions helps you to discover more about your child's internal world, to find out their preferences, desires, likes and dislikes, their stresses and worries, their values and goals and their feelings. Using questions continually enables you to stay updated on what's going on in your child's world.

Questions need to be open-ended to elicit deeper responses than just 'yes' or 'no' or 'fine'. *How was your day? Fine. Did you go to football practice? Yes/no. How was ballet? Fine.* Open-ended questions like *what do you love to do best on a sunny/rainy day?* Or *who is your favourite friend and what do you like about him/her?* result in conversation. When someone asks an open-ended question it means they are really interested in knowing about you.

Try asking your child these questions or similar ones (you'll find a downloadable PDF in the www.theparentpractice. com/book-resources#chapter-1 section of our website):

---

[7] Adapted from ideas in the Bringing Baby Home training by Drs John and Julie Gottman

- [ ] What do you love to do best on a sunny/rainy day?
- [ ] What is your favourite game/sport/activity?
- [ ] What do you like to do with mummy/daddy best?
- [ ] What do you like to do with grandma/grandpa/uncle/aunt/cousin?
- [ ] What makes you laugh?
- [ ] Where do you like/not like to be tickled/stroked?
- [ ] What makes you feel sad?
- [ ] What makes you mad?
- [ ] What do you like to do all by yourself?
- [ ] What do you like to do best with one friend/ lots of friends?
- [ ] What is your favourite food?
- [ ] What is your favourite colour?
- [ ] What is your favourite book at the moment?
- [ ] Who is your favourite character from a film or TV show? What do you like about them?
- [ ] What makes you worried?
- [ ] Who is your favourite friend and what do you like about him/her?
- [ ] What would be your ideal holiday?
- [ ] Where is your favourite place to be when you want to be by yourself?
- [ ] Of the adults you know who would you like to be like when you're grown up? What qualities of theirs do you admire?
- [ ] What do you want to do when you grow up?
- [ ] What would you like to change in our family?

There are also some commercial products available designed to stimulate conversations in families such as cards like Table Topics which can be fun to try at out at family meals.

Build a culture of appreciation[8]

Develop a habit of appreciation of your children by focusing on the positive things they do. Catch them doing good and comment favourably on it. When we make this a priority we can discern the good that was always there and really get to know the positive qualities of our children. More on this in the next chapter.

Your turn

What practices are you going to set up in your family to get to know each other better?

....

....

....

When are you going to make time for this?

....

....

....

How are you going to ensure this happens regularly?

....

---

[8] Adapted from ideas in the Bringing Baby Home training by Drs John and Julie Gottman

....

....

Mark is an introvert. I am extroverted. Mark is hypersensitive to physical stimuli and I am not. Once I realised these two enormous things for him it was the beginning of our recovery. We'd prepare more for weekend events. If he didn't want to go to a birthday party I understood and offered for him to come but sit on the side. Sometimes he'd say yes, sometimes no, and over time he started saying yes more often and then started joining in. When his sensitivity really hit his eating we dialled way back on the variety of food – but didn't just go for pasta and biscuits. By NOT pressuring him and by NOT making him wrong he now chooses THE most unusual thing on menus and his favourite food when we were in Istanbul was... fried sheep's intestines. He came to a varied palate MUCH sooner than his mother who felt wrong about being so hypersensitive herself.

Sue, mum of three

Knowing your child in a nutshell

Ages and stages:

☺ Children go through genetically determined distinct phases of development as they progress through childhood.

☺ These are guidelines only as children progress at their own pace but they can help parents understand why their children are behaving in particular ways.

Before he's achieved that stage of development the child is unable to behave with more maturity than he's got.

☺ Changes in brain development mean that as they get older the rational frontal lobes gain more control over the emotional limbic system and children get better at impulse control, delayed gratification and regulating emotion. They become able to solve problems more logically and memory retention develops.

☺ With improvement in language children are also better able to express themselves in words and don't need to communicate solely through behaviour.

☺ With the right parental input children develop empathy and learn to resolve conflict.

☺ It is part of normal development for children to develop notions of morality, to learn right from wrong and fairness. They also develop ideas about gender.

Temperament:

Your child is genetically predisposed to relate to the world in particular ways because of temperament, but this is not fixed. Parents can teach children to understand and appreciate their temperament and can actually fashion new neural pathways as a result of their actions.

Parents need to accommodate temperament in order to help their children thrive.

Your child, and you, will be anywhere on a continuum for the following traits and each of these traits has pluses and minuses. Help your child to see the positive aspects of her character:

☺ Intensity

☺ Persistence

☺ Sensitivity

☺ Distractibility

☺ Adaptability

☺ Regularity

☺ Energy

☺ Reactivity

☺ Outlook/mood

☺ Extrovert/introvert

Getting to know you...

☺ Schedule special one to one time with each child and allow them to choose the activity

☺ Ask open-ended questions to really create dialogue

☺ Build a culture of appreciation by using Descriptive Praise and practices like the pasta jar and golden book... see next chapter.

Further reading

Mary Sheedy Kurcinka, *Raising Your Spirited Child*, 2009

Margot Sunderland, *The Science of Parenting*, 2008

John Gottman, *The Seven Principles for Making Marriage Work*, 2011

2

Skill 2: Encouraging cooperation and confidence with Descriptive Praise

---

"People will forget what you said, people will forget what you did, but people will never forget how you made them feel."

– Maya Angelou

A little girl was standing next to her mother in the queue in a department store. The mum was preoccupied with her phone and her daughter was just standing next to her. The lady at the front of the queue had a complicated query and it was taking a while. The little girl got bored and started blowing raspberries – pprrttttwlhhhh. (I am informed by a reliable source – Mumsnet – that this is how it is spelt.) Her mum didn't like this and told her to stop. The little girl did stop. The mum went back to her phone. The little girl was still bored and started blowing raspberries again – pprrttttwlhhhh. Her mum got cross and said, "I told you not to do that. Stop it at once." The little girl did stop but the mum turned her attention back to her phone and a minute later the raspberries started again – pprrttttwlhhhh. The child was doing exactly what her mum didn't want her to do.

Cooperation

Before writing this book we surveyed our clients and asked them what their current goals were with their children. The majority said that they wanted more cooperation. Probably you too want your children to do what you ask, not just so you can have an easier life but because it's your job to train your children into good habits for life. And for that you need some cooperation.

You may wish your child was more polite or would eat his greens or go to bed and stay in bed or focus more on his school work or try harder at swimming or would try again when he failed or do more around the house or get off his Xbox when you ask him to or get dressed promptly in the morning. You may wish your child would show more consideration for others or take responsibility when she does something wrong or wouldn't flare up and bite your head off when she is upset about something. You may want her to do her eye exercises or stop sucking her thumb or to put her clothes in the laundry basket or to look people in the eye when they talk to her. To teach your child good habits and attitudes you'll need them to cooperate with you.

That doesn't mean your child can't have an opinion or feelings about what they've been asked to do. I usually suggest that we don't want to be breeding mindless automatons, but some of the parents in my classes admit they would settle for some blind compliance! If you'd like your child to listen to you more this is the chapter for you. Nothing opens the ears of a child (of any age) more than the skill we're exploring here – Descriptive Praise. This is magic.

At the beginning of our courses we ask our clients to 'begin with the end in mind', as author Steven Covey advocates, and think about the kind of adult they'd like their child to grow up to be. One of the qualities invariably suggested is confidence. Every parent wants their child to have a good sense of self-worth and with good reason, as there is much research that proves its importance.

Let's start by thinking of the destination at the end of our parenting journey. Your children are now adults. What kind of people are they? Are they the kind of people you'd like to spend time with? What characteristics would that kind of person have? Take a moment to jot down words that describe the traits you admire and would want your children to have.

Some parents have suggested humour, self-control, patience, confidence, tolerance, flexibility, consideration, helpfulness, politeness, positivity, organisation, assertiveness, creativity, kindness, integrity, openness, humility, focus, honesty, courage, willingness to take risks, responsibility, resourcefulness, resilience, gratitude, appreciativeness....

....

....

....

Keep coming back to this list as it will provide goals for your child-training.

Confidence

"There is no value judgment more important to man, no factor more decisive in his psychological development and motivation – than the estimate he passes on himself...
The nature of his self-evaluation has profound effects on a man's thinking processes, emotions, desires, values and goals. It is the single most significant key to his behaviour."

– Nathaniel Branden, The Psychology of Self Esteem

The way a person feels about himself determines how he behaves and the meaning he ascribes to the behaviour of others towards him. A child with low self-esteem may think: *I'm the naughty one. I can't get attention by being good but I can get a lot of attention by being bad.* When his dad tells him off he doesn't hear it as care for him, he hears that his dad thinks he's hopeless.

When a child has a healthy self-esteem he is:

MORE likely to:

☺ behave well, in appropriate and considerate ways

☺ take responsibility for his own actions because he feels basically OK about himself and feels that mainly he gets things right (he is less likely to deny, make excuses, cheat, blame others)

☺ try new things, put up her hand in class even if she may make a mistake, take reasonable risks and to persevere

☺ value others; i.e. he doesn't need to put others down in order to build himself up

☺ accept positive and negative feedback and learn from her mistakes

☺ form loving relationships

☺ stand up for herself and put herself forward when opportunities arise

☺ expect (and require) that others will treat her with respect

☺ weather life's knocks better

LESS likely to:

☺ be dependent on others for approval

☺ be hyper-sensitive to criticism, to construe others' actions as critical of herself

☺ seek to make up for feelings of inadequacy by bragging, putting others down, using physical or verbal violence to assert himself or by bullying others

☺ demonstrate the sort of learned helplessness that comes from not trusting oneself to do anything alone, not believing in one's own abilities. (If she seeks help for everything she lessens the risk of failing.)

☺ be vulnerable to (can say no to):
- peer pressure (he is able to trust his own judgment)
- bullying
- when older, smoking, drinking and drugs and inappropriate sexual relationships (equating sex with love)
- self-harm, including eating disorders

In recent years there has been a debate that questions the value of good self-esteem. You may hear it argued that a child has *too much* self-esteem, looks down on others, is inconsiderate or intolerant of others, has a sense of entitlement and an inflated idea of their abilities and therefore doesn't take steps to improve. This is a myth which depends on a misunderstanding about the meaning of self-esteem and it confuses bravado with real self-confidence. When a person gets on a TV 'reality' show such as The Apprentice and announces that "I am a miracle" when they're about to be booted off the show, that's not self-esteem, that's denial, or bravado. Someone who is parading his abilities is looking for external affirmation of his value so is not really certain of his own worth. He is deeply insecure that he isn't good enough, so he must constantly measure himself against others and win. People with good self-esteem are secure about their value so they don't need to compare themselves to others or inflate their abilities.

A dad jokingly said that there was nothing wrong with his 4-year-old daughter's self-esteem when she said to her mum: *"Mummy, you really love me don't you? When I grow up I want a little girl just like me."* That speaks volumes about the relationship between that mother and daughter and that's real self-esteem.

The term self-esteem comes from the same root as the word 'estimate' – the evaluation of one's self or self-awareness; it involves knowing one's good points and flaws and it includes being willing to improve. Psychologist Dorothy Rowe says: *"[Vanity] is where we over-value our strengths and ignore our weaknesses... With self-confidence we recognise our strengths and weaknesses without feeling ashamed or guilty."*[9] Self-esteem is made up of the thoughts, feelings and opinions we have about ourselves and so is subject to fluctuation over time.

A healthy self-esteem comes from a child having many experiences which demonstrate that he is a worthwhile and capable person and that his opinion and feelings have validity.

To build strong self-esteem in children parents can:

☺ AFFIRM, APPROVE and ACKNOWLEDGE our children by praising them specifically and sincerely. They learn through their parents' approval that they are important and significant to, and cherished by, them.

☺ ACCEPT our children by listening to their feelings, ideas and opinions

☺ ENCOURAGE the development of skills and competencies – help them to feel capable and trusted, including helping them deal constructively with their mistakes

☺ MODEL confident behaviour, avoid putting ourselves down and handle failures constructively

---

9 'How do you build self-confidence?' in *Psychologies Magazine*, June 2006

Descriptive Praise is the tool that encourages children to cooperate and builds self-confidence.

How to get cooperation

The key to encouraging behaviour of any kind is motivation and giving attention appropriately. You *can* use the stick approach to get children to behave but it won't encourage self-discipline, and such cooperation comes at the cost of the relationship with your child and of their self-esteem. And they will learn to wield sticks themselves.

The motivation circle

There is a circular relationship between a child's behaviour, how a parent responds to that behaviour, the child's future motivation (how she feels) and how she behaves. (See diagram below.) If a child behaves well and adults respond positively the child is motivated to behave in that way again. But if she behaves in a way the adults don't like and they respond negatively the child feels badly about herself and that leads to a cycle of poor behaviour and negative responses. It's up to the adults to change the cycle by not reacting to poor behaviour with drama and punishment but taking steps calmly to deal with it without making the child feel like a bad person. We'll look at how to respond to poor behaviour in chapter 6.

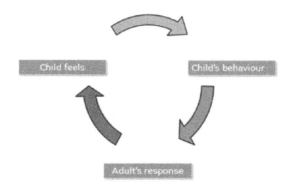

How to motivate

How do we motivate children? Well here's an example of how *not* to motivate your children. Don't cringe when you read it – chances some of these words may have come out of your own mouth. The purpose of this exercise is not to make you feel bad but for you to put yourself in the shoes of these children and see how motivated you feel. Ask yourself:

- ☐ How did you feel about yourself?
- ☐ How did you feel about your parent?
- ☐ What were your levels of motivation?

Come on you two what are you doing? I leave the room for two minutes and you immediately mess around. Why can't you just do as you're told? It is not time for playing with the Minions now. How many times do I have to tell you? You're so slow. We're going to be late now. It'll be your own fault if we don't have time for a proper breakfast.

Jamie, will you get your shirt on! No I will not do your buttons up for you. You must be capable of doing them by now. Sarah can do them and she's younger than you. You're just lazy.

Sarah, if you touch that doll again I'm going to put it in the bin.

(Voice rising) Get dressed! You two are giving me grey hair. It's not nice to start the day off like this with you both being so unhelpful and making me upset.

Oh for goodness sake Jamie you've done your buttons up all wrong. I'll have to do it for you! And now you've pulled the button off your trousers! Right that's it – there's no swimming on Saturday now!

(Exasperated and begging tone) Sarah, leave Jamie alone. You're so mean – how would you like it if I poked you? (poking Sarah). Oh don't make such a fuss, it couldn't have hurt.

Jamie, have you got your library book? You didn't leave it at after-school care again? You're always forgetting something. I think you'd forget your head if it weren't attached to your body.

Please, please will you just get your shoes on Sarah? If you put them on by yourself and come downstairs quickly I'll let you have a chocolate croissant for breakfast. No, you can't watch TV... Oh alright, alright..., but only for ten minutes while I'm getting breakfast.

So how did you feel as the child in this scenario? Did you find yourself tuning out your parent after a while? Did you feel keen to get on? What did you think about yourself?

What did this poor beleaguered parent do in her attempt to get cooperation?

She nagged	*Come on you two what are you doing? I leave the room for two minutes and you immediately mess around.*
She criticised	*Jamie you've done your buttons up all wrong. And now you've pulled the button off your trousers!*
She labelled	*You're just lazy. You're so mean. You're always forgetting something. I think you'd forget your head if it weren't attached to your body.*

She threatened	*Sarah, if you touch that doll again I'm going to put it in the bin.*
She punished	*Right that's it – there's no swimming on Saturday now!*
She shouted	*(Voice rising) Get dressed!*
She played the martyr	*You two are giving me grey hairs. It's not nice to start the day off like this with you both being so unhelpful and making me upset.*
She made comparisons	*Sarah can do them and she's younger than you.*
She begged	*Please, please will you just get your shoes on Sarah?*
She bribed	*If you put them on by yourself and come downstairs quickly I'll let you have a chocolate croissant for breakfast.*
And, she gave in	*No, you can't watch TV… Oh alright, alright.*

This scene is familiar to many of us. We're in a rush, trying to get everyone out of the house washed, dressed and fed with all necessary kit by a certain time, and no one under the age of ~~18~~ 25 cares! We feel like we play the same broken record every morning and are sick of the sound of our own voices, especially when what comes out of our mouths reminds us of our mothers – and we swore we'd never talk to our kids like that. Nobody takes their baby home from the hospital, looks down into the swaddled bundle in their arms and says, *"I'm going to nag you and criticise you and scold you and label you and ridicule you...*" But many of us fall into those habits unwittingly.

How does that happen?

In case you're not convinced have a look at the sentence below. What do you notice about it?

The cat sat on the matt.

Most people notice the mistake – 'mat' is spelt incorrectly.

Criticism

Why is that the first thing that comes to mind? Why do we point out their mistakes to our children (criticise them)? Does becoming a parent turn us into nasty people? No. It's not because we're trying to make our children feel bad. When we criticise we do so with good intentions. We feel we have to teach our children and we are conditioned to think that if we point out what they've done wrong they will alter their ways. If that were true we'd only to have to say it once, surely?

In fact when we keep telling children what they're doing wrong they stop listening.

Human beings have evolved to pay attention to the negatives as that's what kept us and our children safe in our ancient past. But it's important we keep this instinct in balance as criticism can also be de-motivating.

Parental criticism hurts children in profound ways because young children believe what their parents say to them. Critical words can have the effect of a self-fulfilling prophecy. Criticism discourages; it makes it less likely children will try something new. It doesn't give them any reason to want to do the right thing. If they get a lot of criticism children may withdraw and give up. It damages their sense of self-worth to get many messages of disapproval and children who feel badly about themselves don't behave well. They may feel angry and unloved. Negative self-definitions acquired in childhood can still exist deep within the subconscious minds of adults as the foundation of their thoughts, choices, reactions and behaviours. As adults they may still be seeking approval and be driven but never satisfied, or they may be unable to accept compliments that don't fit with their self-image. Conversely they may become hyper-sensitive to criticism, perceiving it where it is not. They may not be able to accept feedback and so deflect it. Dr John Gottman, therapist and relationships expert, asserts that there is no such thing as 'constructive criticism'.[10]

The magic ratio

Professor Gottman is a psychologist and researcher who has worked with both couples and families. He found that criticism was one of the factors which damaged relationships. He discovered that there are a number of negative interactions compared to positive interactions beyond which a relationship suffers, and that number is 1:5. This is The Magic Ratio. If it takes five positives for every negative comment to keep an adult relationship intact then with vulnerable young children, so dependent on the positive regard of their parents, the ratio must be at least 1:10.

The chances are we grew up with criticism ourselves so it's a deeply ingrained habit and will take time, attention and effort to shift. Luckily there are much more effective ways to teach children.

"In studies in schools, research has showed that when teachers withdraw praise off-task behaviour increases threefold and when criticism increases the off-task behaviour goes up to four times as much as previously. The conclusion of this research was that children needed to hear 5 positives to every negative

---

[10] John Gottman, Bringing Baby Home training manual

comment to be happy, produce accurate and sufficient work, stay on-task and show positive behaviours."[11]

It's all about attention

Children are programmed to seek their parents' attention – it is an evolutionary thing. Having your parent's attention is what kept you alive when a predator was likely to eat you. When parents pay attention to behaviour they get more of that behaviour. Yet we often unwittingly give attention to exactly the behaviour we don't want as in the example at the beginning of this chapter. It seems curious to a parent that a child would want negative attention but any attention is better than nothing and children often find it easier to get our attention through negative behaviour.

What happens if your children are sitting at the dinner table and they are sitting with their bottoms on their chairs with all four chair legs on the floor, eating their food with their mouths closed, using their knives and forks and not aggravating their siblings? Mostly parents breathe a sigh of relief and get on with whatever they have to do. However, if a child starts flicking peas across the room the parent jumps on that behaviour and generally scolds and maybe punishes the child. The child learns that negative behaviour wins attention.

Noticing what our children do right and commenting on it is a much more effective way of giving attention

The reticular activating system

"The physical architecture of the brain changes according to where we direct our attention and what we practice doing."

– Daniel Siegel and Tina Bryson[12]

---

[11] Chris Borgmeier, PhD Portland State University cborgmei@pdx.edu www.pbisclassroomsystems.pbworks.com

[12] *The Whole Brain Child:12 Proven Strategies to Nurture Your Child's Developing Mind*, 2012

There is an area of our brain called the reticular activating system (RAS) which acts as a portal through which all information enters the brain. Since the brain can only focus on so many things at once it constantly searches for what's important, and filters out what it perceives to be unimportant to us. Your RAS determines what is important by reference to what you focus on most. This is why when you are thinking about buying a new car and you've decided on a Volkswagen Golf, you suddenly see lots of Golfs around! The number of Golfs on the road hasn't increased but you are noticing them more.

However, when we're paying attention to one thing we may miss other things of importance.

To illustrate this have a look at the Selective Attention Test video on YouTube: https://www.youtube.com/watch?v=vJG698U2Mvo. (This link is also on the www.theparentpractice.com/book-resources#chapter-2 page of our website.)

When we're looking for something we can see it, but if we're not focused on it we may miss it. This is true of our children's good behaviour. It's amazing how well we find they're behaving once we start looking!

Praise

"Praise needs to be a central part of raising children, not a luxury that we can leave off if we prefer."

– Elizabeth Hartley Brewer

Using effective praise is one of the most fundamental skills of positive parenting and can produce dramatic and very positive results in children's behaviour and attitudes.

But most of the praise parents use isn't effective.
When parents use praise effectively:

☐ the child develops a healthy self-esteem – a positive and realistic sense of self-worth

☐ parents see more of the behaviour and values they want to encourage and less inappropriate or undesirable behaviour

☐ a positive relationship is nurtured between parent and child and communication flourishes.

There has been a lot of focus on praising children since the 1960s with the development of a more child-centred focus to parenting but recently there has been a bit of a backlash because that praise has been mostly evaluative, with some poor results. Some children have developed over-inflated opinions of themselves, have not learned how to handle failure and have not learnt to try their best. As a result all praise has been discredited.

At The Parent Practice we would say these problems are not a result of too much praise but too much of *the wrong kind of praise,* as well as adults stepping in and doing too much for children and shielding them inappropriately from failure.

Many parents try to praise their children. When we ask parents why they use praise they say they want to reinforce good behaviours, build self-esteem and foster a positive relationship with their children.

They use words such as *well done, good girl, clever boy, you look so pretty, marvellous darling, super, awesome, wonderful, brilliant.* We call this type of praise evaluative praise.

Evaluative praise is the wrong kind of praise.
Most adults will have received this kind of praise themselves as children and it is familiar to us so it is not surprising that we should use it with our own children. Unfortunately this

kind of evaluative praise, while extremely well intentioned, doesn't achieve parents' goals. It certainly doesn't have the effect of building strong self-esteem or leading to better behaviour. Why not?

Evaluative praise doesn't work because:

Children don't really believe it

Children don't really believe that they are 'amazing', 'awesome' or 'brilliant'. Children compare themselves to other children. They will always find evidence of someone who does something better than them. They can think of someone who runs faster, climbs higher, draws better or does sums more adeptly than they. They don't believe the praise and they may doubt the judgment of the person giving it. They may think *well that's nice of Dad but he's supposed to praise me – it's his job.* It doesn't seem to be much more effective when they hear it from teachers either. Some children report feeling that *the teacher must think I'm a real loser as she's giving me so much praise.*

Superlative language loses value and credibility – it can be 'over the top'

Once children hear meritless praise they discount sincere praise as well. Research has shown that 'inflated praise' actually damages self-esteem and children find it very pressurising.[13]

It isn't specific enough

When we say 'clever girl' it doesn't give the child enough information to repeat the behaviour.

It doesn't show real interest

It's too easy to toss 'good boy' over your shoulder without really thinking.

---

[13] Eddie Brummelman, Brad Bushman, Ohio State University 2013

It focuses more on the result than the effort or particular skill employed by the child

This makes the child feel that approval is dependent on their achievements, which might, especially for a child who is struggling, feel unattainable. If achieving is so important it can make it impossible for the child to countenance failure. Children need to be accepted as unique individuals, appreciated for who they are and not who we'd like them to be or for what they achieve. (For more on the dangers of this kind of praise see chapter 9.)

Children learn that whatever parents pay attention to is important. So when your child plays in a match, if you ask him first if he won he will understand that winning is important. If you ask him *did you enjoy the game, did you pass the ball well, did you do your best, did you try out those tips from the coach?* he will get the message that those things are important.

If you comment mainly on your daughter's appearance, she will learn that how she looks is an important part of her identity.

> *"If you focus on results, you will never change.*
> *If you focus on change, you will get results"*
>
> *– Jack Dixon*

Descriptive Praise

Descriptive Praise is credible. Children can't argue with it because it is simply a description of the facts – there is no evaluation involved. We want our children to take responsibility for their own behaviour and evaluate what they do for themselves, rather than rely on what other people think.

It is obvious from Descriptive Praise that the parent is really paying attention. The effect of using such specific praise is that our children feel uniquely appreciated as individuals. They see that we care enough to notice what they are doing right. The language is measured, not excessive. When praise is descriptive it gives children the precise information they need to repeat the behaviour.

With its focus on process rather than outcomes, Descriptive Praise encourages children to try hard and persevere.

How to do it

FOCUS on what they're getting RIGHT, rather than on what's going wrong

"You hung up your hat, so you've already done one of the three things you need to do when you come home." "I appreciate the way you let Glen join in your game. I know he's a bit little to understand all its subtleties but he loves doing what his big brother does." "You remembered to bring home your violin today." "I noticed you looked at Miss Norton when she was talking to you then." "You got on your bike again even though you fell off just now – you're persevering." "You're thinking ahead about what you might need to take on the school trip tomorrow." "I'm glad to hear you're willing to voice a different opinion and that you expressed it politely." It's more effective to focus on your child using an alternative strategy than the absence of a behaviour. So instead of "You're not sucking your thumb" notice that she's sitting on her hands while in the car.

NOTICE and mention tiny steps in the right direction

Descriptive Praise is very specific and therefore takes more effort than the 'well done, good girl, clever boy' kind of praise or simply not commenting at all. There will always be something to praise if you are looking at tiny detail even if not all behaviour is good.

When I first learnt about Descriptive Praise I thought it was great, in principle. But I also thought *You haven't met my son. I would praise him if he were doing anything remotely*

praiseworthy! It took some time for me to be able to notice the small things he was doing right. At first you may need a magnifying glass! But if you wait for something significant to happen you may be waiting a while and you'll lose the motivating effect of the praise.

"Sophie, you've taken your pyjamas off so you're beginning to get dressed." "You're sitting at the table at the right time and you've got your worksheet out. You look like you're getting ready to start your homework." *"You put your pillow on your bed." "You've put all four legs of your chair back on the floor." "You've picked up some of the books that were on the floor. I can see carpet now! I'd forgotten it was green!" "You've brought your attention back to your work."*

At Sam's school they had a House point system where points were given generously with descriptions. Sam was given a point for settling in well on his first day of school. He was very encouraged. At Christian's school they had a merit and demerit system. Demerits were given very freely but merits were only given for significant behaviours. Christian had no incentive to behave well – he thought he couldn't earn merits.

IDENTIFY the quality shown by the behaviour

"You felt shy but you still went and asked the waitress for the menu – that was brave." "You stood up for yourself when Ethan

pushed you – you used your words and you said 'Don't push me.'" "You are being a really good friend Sam. You told Tom *what the homework was and you even offered to help him with it." "You showed a lot of self-control when you didn't hit your brother for snatching your toy." "You're brushing your teeth without me having to remind you – what great initiative!" "You went to get the nappy for the baby when I asked you to – that was co-operative."*

ACKNOWLEDGE effort, attitude, improvement and strategies

"I love the way you got up and tried again when you fell off the bike." "You came up with a good idea for sorting out the sharing of the toys with Jack." "I noticed that when the first approach you tried didn't work you tried another tactic. How's it going?" "You had a smile on your face at the start of hockey practice and you were really putting effort into your running. That shows a great attitude." "You're really slowing down your writing so you can get it neat – look at all these letters on the line!" "You've been practising getting dressed quickly and I'm sure you're much faster than you were at the beginning of term. That must be helpful when you're getting changed for sport."

FOCUS on the individual

Descriptive Praise needs to be tailored for the individual child at their age and with their personality, strengths and challenges. You're not going to praise your 12 year old in the same way you do your 4 year old. He will feel patronised if you use the effusive tone more appropriate for a younger child and if you praise him for something he has been doing for some time, like tying his shoe laces, he will look at you like you've sprouted another head! Descriptively Praise children for things that are a bit of a stretch.

Make sure your praise is non-comparative. This is important if the child is not to think he is better than others.

Being the best (coming first) is not the same as doing your best. We want our children to feel uniquely appreciated, not just considered in relation to others. Comparative praise undermines intrinsic motivation – it takes away the pleasure of doing something for its own sake, and substitutes doing it because it makes you 'better' than someone else. It encourages children to view others as rivals, rather than collaborators.

"That's a great test result. It reflects all the hard work and commitment that you put into your revision." As opposed to, *"Well done. You came top of the class." "You ran your hardest in that race. I'm sure that's faster than I've seen you run before."* As opposed to, *"You're the winner!"*

VARY your delivery

Use different methods of communicating your approval and choose the modality that works best for your child. So if he's a kinaesthetic person you will need to accompany your words with smiles, hugs or pats. If she's an auditory person she'll be happy with the words but may also like song! If he's visual he may like notes or pictures. If you're not sure which style suits your child, try them all!

Descriptive Praise is catching

One holiday I arrived at our destination with my four kids at 3am and had the nightmare of waking them up on the plane and trawling through the airport in their sleepy state. We then got into a taxi and my 5 year old, obviously imitating how I use DP, turned to her older siblings and said, "I am so impressed that none of you argued about where you were sitting and got straight into the taxi without making any fuss."

Rachel, Mum of four

How not to do it

☺ Don't use Descriptive Praise just when you want something done – children will work this out and its association with instructions will contaminate it. They will feel manipulated.

☺ Don't use Descriptive Praise to control – only to support unconditionally.

☺ Don't say *"I'm so proud of you"* – although it is not the worst thing we can say, it runs the risk of making the child dependent on your approval and can be pressurising. Instead, encourage them to be proud of themselves – ask them what they did well, and why it was good. *"You got 10/10 in your spelling test. I hope you're proud of yourself – that result is a reflection of the hard work that you put in."*

What are you worried about?

To begin with parents say Descriptive Praise takes a long time and that it feels a bit false.

In fact it doesn't actually take more time than criticising and dealing with uncooperative children but it feels like it takes longer because it doesn't come naturally to us at first. Sadly, nobody ever complains that it takes too long or that it feels unnatural to criticise or nag their children! Those words roll off our tongues without any effort. With practice Descriptive Praise won't seem so unnatural.

How do you think your child will react?

Sometimes kids don't like praise at first, even Descriptive Praise. This is because they have built up a negative self-image over time that doesn't allow them to believe it. They may be afraid of trusting this new view of themselves. They might be afraid that this new approval is only temporary so don't want to get used to it. Over time they will see that they can trust in what you're saying and build up a new, more positive picture of themselves.

Do check that you're not being patronising. It can help to acknowledge that you won't be very good at this new language to begin with and that maybe they can help you to get it right for them.

My children told me not to speak to them in 'that New Learning Centre voice' when I first tried it out. It probably didn't help that I dropped into the American accent of my mentor until I found my own voice. When I explained that I was just trying to notice the good things they were doing instead of focusing on what was going wrong they were quite keen on the idea. Do tell your kids what you're up to!

Are you worried that your children may become dependent on praise?

People with low self-esteem are dependent on others to feel good. Using evaluative praise means that the child is dependent on the other person's evaluation of him. We want to develop our children's self-esteem by using Descriptive Praise so that they believe they are valuable people without constant reference to others. Using Descriptive Praise trains our children to see for themselves what's good about them.

In the real world they will have to deal with criticism

True – in the real world our children will receive criticism. A child with low self-esteem can easily be crushed and defeated by criticism. We can help them weather this and accept it as useful feedback by giving them a strong sense of self-worth and resilience. Exposure to constant criticism at home does not prepare them for the real world.

You might think that there are some things children should just be doing without getting praised

To begin with if you praise pretty much all the good stuff you notice it will get you and the children used to it. As you get more familiar with it you can become a bit more selective. For some habits that are already well established (such as brushing teeth for some 10 year olds) your child may find it condescending or unbelievable if you offer Descriptive Praise. It is more effective if you think about the behaviours that you want to improve and find opportunities to notice when your child gets those right.

Most parents stop praising too soon, before the behaviour has really become a habit. You'll still need to occasionally reinforce the behaviours you want to see. It will take time to form new habits of looking for and commenting on the positives so we have some strategies to help.

You might think your child doesn't *deserve* to be praised because they have done something you really don't like

This is the kind of thinking that may take time for us to shift. Descriptive Praise is a wonderful tool but it is not the only one we have in our tool baskets. We do need strategies for dealing with the behaviour that needs to alter (read on). But if we are to turn around the inappropriate behaviour we have to train ourselves to notice the small things that are good, because that is the way to motivate kids to do better.

Pasta jar

Keeping a pasta jar handy is a great way to remind yourself to descriptively praise the children. When children are doing the right thing acknowledge it with Descriptive Praise – make it physical and visible with a pasta jar (or your equivalent).

The beauty of the pasta jar is that it's easy (and cheap!) to acquire. And it's also easy to manage. You can even carry it around with you. We have heard remarkable stories of how effective it can be – even with older children. The effectiveness lies in the fact that it is so visual and uncomplicated.

Top Tips for the Pasta Jar

☺ Small jar, big pasta

☺ One jar for the whole family – make it motivating, not competitive

☺ Fill it up fast – make it as easy as possible to get a piece

☺ Be generous and be detailed

☺ Once it's in, it stays in!

The key with pasta jars or sticker or tick charts is to be really generous – an empty jar is not motivating.

Parents often ask what to do when the jar is full. Well you don't have to do anything – the full jar is achievement in itself. If you want to reward further can you think what your child would like to do? They often suggest playing a game rather than buying them a thing (more on this in chapter 5).

Golden book

Another way to develop a ritual around Descriptive Praise is by keeping a 'Golden book'. Choose a nice book that you'll want to write in and maybe get the kids to decorate it. Capture and commemorate all the little things – and the funny things as well. Creating a Golden book will be a highly treasured memory of moments you won't want to forget.

Top Tips for the Golden book

☺ Set a target of how many DPs to write each day – we recommend at least three

☺ Set aside a time each day to do it – maybe write notes during the day, and read it through with your child at bedtime

☺ Use different coloured pens and stickers to make it lively and fun to look at

☺ If you're out and about or away from home, send a postcard or write a note that your child can stick into the book later

☺ Involve your child – ask them to tell you what you should record. This is not us being lazy, but it is to help them self-evaluate.

Sinus spray

4-year-old Hans lay down cooperatively to receive his nasal spray of salt water for sinus problems (YEUCH!) and he lay ever so still, had the spray and then said, "Mummy, are you going to put that in my 'Praise' book – I was being brave..." And his Mum was so proud of her little boy for saying that, and so grateful he was being cooperative.

Leave a Thank-You note

Leave a DP thank-you note for your children to find on their bedside table after they've gone to sleep or in their lunch box, or hand them out at the end of the day. Try a text message for older children who have a mobile. Writing down what we appreciate about our children lends it extra gravitas.

When we were attending our parenting course years ago we'd have to leave the kids with a babysitter (sometimes quite a trying experience – we got through a few babysitters) and when I got home I would ask the sitter how things had gone. Anything positive I put into a note for the children or if there wasn't anything then I'd find something from the rest of the day. Sam couldn't read yet and he'd come running up to me the next morning wanting to know what his note said. Months later I found that Christian had collected up all his notes and put them in an envelope marked 'Mummy's notes to me'.

How to remember

The rituals of the pasta jar and the Golden book help parents to remember to descriptively praise. Other aids include old-fashioned post-it notes (Sue had them on her dashboard to help her remember to have a positive greeting for her children at the end of their school day) or a more technologically advanced alert on your phone. One mum had a 5pm DP alarm as that was their most challenging time of day. The kids knew what it meant and would say "DP, mum!" If your partner is involved that makes it easier and if you're feeling stressed you can hand over to them to take up the DP baton.

Your turn

Write down 5 qualities you appreciate about your child (repeat for each child, and for yourself)
☺
☺
☺
☺
☺

Select an area where your children are showing improvement. Describe it in detail – focus on the progress, not the result.

For example: *Ethan is improving in organisation. This week, he remembered to ask me to sign his homework diary three times. He keeps it by the front door. He's beginning to plan ahead and think of solutions.*

....

....

Choose an area of difficulty in your family (such as homework, mornings, car journeys, tidying up etc). Identify 5 things you CAN praise them for already in this area, rather than focus on what isn't working.

For example: "You asked me in a polite voice – you're not whingeing."

....

....

See if you can turn the following evaluative praises into Descriptive Praises:

When Sally takes her plate over to the dishwasher, instead of "Oh, good girl...."

....

When Ahmed does well in his maths test, instead of "Great result, clever boy..."

....

When your 5 year old shows you his Lego construction, instead of "Well done, darling..."

....

And lastly
When your 9 year old finishes her homework, what will you say?

....

....

Looking at his bed

Sam (aged 5) was using every delaying tactic in the book to avoid going to bed. There really wasn't much going right, but I had nothing to lose so I tried some DP, as an alternative to scolding him. As he paused briefly in his attempts to wrap himself up in a curtain, I said quickly "Sam, that's great, you're facing the right way towards your bed." He was so stunned at this change in attitude, that he stopped still and then, tentatively, took a step towards his bed. And I piled in with the Descriptive Praise then! It's not been all plain sailing this week, but it's definitely getting better.

Hillary, mum of two

Forgetful boy

I waited for my 'chronically forgetful' son from the bus. He got off, and the first thing I noticed was that he wasn't wearing his glasses, again.... And he only had his kit bag with him, no homework bag for the weekend. "When will he EVER learn!" I thought, exasperated. By the time he reached me, I had realised that that statement was not going to help or motivate him, so I simply said "Hi, Nick, happy weekend – glad you have your kit bag with you!" to which he replied with a smile "Yeah, and I was able to fit my homework bag inside so I could be more organised and when the guys on the bus were really getting out of hand with their rough-housing, I took my glasses off and put them in my pocket so they wouldn't get broken!"

I was so relieved I hadn't launched at him, but had looked for something positive.

Sue, mum of three

Descriptive Praise in a nutshell

Descriptive Praise is the tool that will help you encourage cooperation and build confidence in your children.

☺ Children want their parents' attention and approval and will do more of what gets them attention even if that attention is negative.

☺ Nagging and criticism make kids tune out and can damage self-esteem.

☺ Conventional praise is less effective at encouraging good behaviours or building strong self-esteem because it lacks credibility and specificity.

☺ Descriptive Praise is a great motivator as the adult
  o focuses on the positives
  o comments, specifically, on the small things the child is doing right
  o notices the child's effort, improvements and strategies, rather than results
  o describes the quality shown by the behaviour
  o sometimes appreciates the absence of negative behaviour

☺ Descriptive praise is never comparative.

Use rituals and tools like the pasta jar and the Golden book to get you in the habit.

Further reading:

Adele Faber and Elaine Mazlish, *How to Talk so Kids Will Listen and Listen so Kids Will Talk*, 2013

3

Skill 3: Listening and connecting

"The most basic of all human needs is the need to understand and be understood. The best way to understand people is to listen to them."

– Ralph Nichols

"Listening is noting what, when and how something is being said. Listening is distinguishing what is not being said from what is silence. Listening is not acting like you're in a hurry, even if you are. Listening is eye contact, a hand placed gently upon an arm... Listening involves suspension of judgment. It is neither analysing nor racking your brain for labels, diagnoses, or remedies. Listening creates a safe space where whatever needs to happen or be said can come."

– Allison Para-Bastien

My daughter, being an extrovert, used to come home from school talking nineteen to the dozen about what had happened that day. *"Sophie told Hannah that she wasn't going to be her friend anymore and Hannah won't invite her to her party and... I want to be friends with both Hannah and Sophie but if I go to Hannah's party Sophie won't be my friend anymore...!"* etc. I was very tempted to jump in with my pearls of wisdom that I 'knew' would solve the problem and teach my daughter some valuable life skills. Luckily something stopped me and I looked at her and just nodded and said "hmmm" occasionally. I discovered that if I bit my tongue and just listened my daughter would talk her way round to her own solutions. She needed opportunities to vent, she needed me to be her sounding board and, having off-loaded, she felt heard and understood.

My daughter has always been a talker but my older boy was not, particularly as a teenager. While Gemma's feelings were all out in the open for anyone to hear, Christian buried his deep inside. We became aware of them not through his direct words, but through body language and through his actions, and sometimes in reading between the lines when he did speak. On one occasion I recall talking to him when he hadn't been ~~very~~ at all kind to his brother. He had used his words then… to put his younger sibling down. He teased him and called him names and belittled him. He made an 'L' shape out of his fingers and mouthed the word 'loser' whenever he passed him. Lurking behind these hurtful words was a big painful feeling. I talked to Christian first about how *he* was feeling, not about how he had made his brother feel – that would come later. Christian struggled at school and had exams coming up so I knew he was probably feeling stressed – although he would have said he didn't care about the exams. I didn't ask him what he was feeling as I had learnt that would have drawn a blank. I just sat with him and stroked his back and reflected back to him what I thought he was feeling. *"Maybe you're feeling a bit stressed about these exams. You might be worried that they'll be hard and you won't do well. You might think that Mum and Dad will be disappointed if that happens… You might be comparing yourself with Gemma and thinking she always does well in tests. Perhaps you feel it's not fair that she finds school work easy and for you it's more of an effort…"* etc. Christian didn't say much but his shoulders dropped from where they'd been up around his ears and his breathing slowed. He stopped clenching and unclenching his fists and jaw. Afterwards I heard him playing with his brother. He was being kind and teaching him how to play a new game of his own devising. This is also 'listening'. It's enabled me to connect with my son and him to connect with his own feelings and understand that they were driving his behaviour.

"Children want to be successful... Children's behaviour is symptomatic of their internal emotional, physical or neurological state. To affect their behaviour, their internal state must first be understood, then accepted, then addressed."

– Bonnie Harris

We have all experienced behaviour driven by feelings, even if we didn't recognise it at the time. You may have witnessed meltdowns in the toy shop when your child can't have the new super duper Lego helicarrier (you only went in to buy some playing cards) or an unreasonable flare up at breakfast when you've run out of Shreddies or complete defiance and rudeness when you ~~suggest~~ insist the Xbox is turned off. You may have seen nastiness between siblings or withdrawn behaviour and an upset face when you pick your child up from school. You may have been embarrassed by your child's unsportsmanlike upsetting of the game board when he's lost a game. You may have despaired over your child refusing to get into the pool for swimming lessons or behaving in an ungrateful way when you've taken them on a treat outing. You may have berated yourself for failing to pass on your values to your children if they make unkind remarks about other children's achievements. You may also have seen a super-charged excited child racing around the house or jumping on the sofa. These are all behaviours driven by feelings (and sometimes sugar).

When parents react to the behaviours only without considering the feelings causing them it's a bit like pulling

up a weed without getting the roots. The poor behaviour will materialise again.

Our children's behaviour is akin to that part of an iceberg which sits above the water while their feelings are the part below the water. In other words, what we see on the surface is only a fraction of the whole.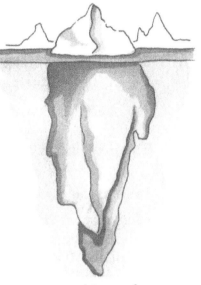

You may know adults who still don't handle feelings well. If children aren't taught how to manage emotions they grow up to be people whose actions are fuelled by stress, anger, disappointment, feelings of inadequacy and fear. These adults may be depressed, angry, violent, permanently dissatisfied or unable to connect emotionally. They may not be able to handle the anxiety associated with taking on new things; they may not put themselves forward for opportunities. In their relationships they may not be able to communicate or be available in loving ways. They may not have learnt how to be compassionate and generous and demonstrate caring.

"The ability of a human being to manage his or her emotions in a healthy way will determine the quality of his life in a much more fundamental way than his IQ. In fact, psychologists have come to call this ability EQ, or Emotional Intelligence Quotient."

– Dr Laura Markham.[14]

---

[14] Aha Parenting http://www.ahaparenting.com/Blog

Understanding and connection come from real listening and acceptance – this is at the heart of positive parenting.

Parents are personal trainers for kids. They need to be emotion coaches to help their children understand their emotions and to:

☺ build emotional intelligence and self-esteem,

☺ foster deep connections with them, encouraging them to talk and solve problems and

☺ help them learn to regulate their behaviour.

Emotion coaching

Back to the brain

What happens in your child's environment brings about changes in his adaptable brain structure and chemical systems. So if a child lives with bullying he can develop heightened aggression or fear reactions and hypervigilance with heightened attack and defence responses.

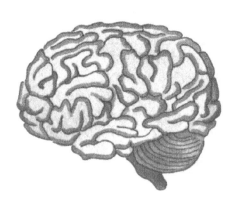

Your young child, with his immature frontal lobes, is very much driven by his emotional brain but you can help his logical brain develop with emotionally responsive parenting. When parents are emotion coaches the child's brain is shaped and connections made between the higher (cool) brain and the lower (hot) brain. When parents help children deal with their feelings connections are formed that help control and quieten the primitive impulses of rage, fear or distress that can overwhelm them. You can help your child think about and rationalise her feelings rather than just act on them such as by hitting out or running away. Emotion coaching allows neural connections to form that last into adulthood to enable him to cope with stress, form loving relationships, handle anger, disappointment, frustration and other upsets, have ambitions and the motivation to pursue them and be compassionate.

Emotion coaching – what is it?

Emotion coaching is about recognising, respecting and responding constructively to a child's emotions. It involves modelling how to handle feelings and coaching children in what to do with their feelings.

Emotion coaching is not permissiveness – acknowledging the emotional background to a behaviour doesn't mean the behaviour goes unchecked; sometimes further action is needed. (Have a look at this video on YouTube of Haim Ginott talking about the difference between permissive and strict parenting: https://www.youtube.com/watch?v=sMo80A_AAEw. (Also on our website – www.theparentpractice.com/book-resources#chapter-3 page.)

It's also not entering into the feeling with the child or agreeing with them. So if your child says, *"I hate it how I never get any headmaster's commendations, I will never get a triangle on my blazer, it's just not fair!"* Instead of saying *"Yes, I agree the system isn't fair"* maybe say something like *"You really, really want a triangle on your blazer don't you? You feel like you've worked really hard and that you've earned a commendation. It feels unfair that your efforts haven't been recognised."*

When we are emotion coaches:

☺ our children feel accepted and validated and their self-esteem grows. If a child grows up in an environment where her feelings are respected she will expect others to treat her with respect. She will be able to assert herself without hurting others.

☺ they learn to be compassionate. If the culture at home is to consider others' feelings then that is what they will do in the wider world.

☺ children develop resilience; they can work through feelings and pick themselves up after set-backs.

☺ children can free up their rational brains to focus on other things like school work; if emotions are occupying them they will not be able to concentrate on other things. Professor John Gottman found that academic results improved when children developed emotional intelligence.[15]

☺ children develop a vocabulary for feelings that makes them better able to express themselves in words. They do not need to resort to actions to let us know how they're feeling. Behaviour improves.

☺ children learn to regulate their feelings. They develop self-control and turn to problem-solving.

☺ we are listening without judgment so our children are more likely to confide in us when they have problems. Do establish good communication before your child becomes a teenager and enters the grunting phase! We are closer to our kids when they talk to us about school, friends, their hopes and plans, their worries and disappointments. We are able to offer support but we also enjoy them more as people. Communication

---

[15] John Gottman and Joan DeClaire, *Raising an Emotionally Intelligent Child,* 1998

builds closeness and love and we can repair rifts in relationships.

☺ we are considering our children's perspective more and understand them better – this often avoids battles and allows us to be more targeted with our strategies to support our children. When children's thoughts and opinions are considered they resist less.

"A friend's son was in the first grade of school, and his teacher asked the class, 'What is the colour of apples?' Most of the children answered red. A few said green. Kevin, my friend's son, raised his hand and said white. The teacher tried to explain that apples could be red or green or sometimes golden, but never white. Kevin was quite insistent and finally said, 'Look inside.'

Perception without mindfulness keeps us on the surface of things and we often miss other levels of reality."

– Joseph Goldstein.

If we disregard our children's feelings (and we don't mean to):

☺ we teach them that (their) feelings don't matter. The child may think that *she* doesn't matter.

☺ the child will feel misunderstood and communication will falter.

☺ unexpressed feelings don't go away and if repressed can sometimes come out in physical symptoms such as stomach aches, headaches or eczema.

☺ repressed feelings can resurface another day in another way, sometimes explosively, and it can be difficult for us to identify the source of the behaviour. Repressed feelings can also come out later in life as mental health issues.

☺ we condition our children into thinking that they need to keep problems to themselves and that makes it difficult for them to seek help when they need it. Men generally have a poor track record when it comes to seeking help such as going to a doctor, or even asking for directions!

☺ children don't develop a vocabulary for feelings and they are placed at a disadvantage in describing their experiences. They can't understand what they are experiencing and can't manage their feelings. The connections between higher and lower brain have not been made.

☺ the child may resort to the primitive impulses of hitting out or running away if she doesn't have constructive ways of dealing with feelings.

When we say things like "*You don't hate your sister. You love her really.*" the child gets the message that he is mistaken about his feelings, which is confusing, or that he is wrong to have them. This doesn't stop him from having them but adds to the child's difficulties by making him feel guilty.

Children's feelings need to be acknowledged before they can change their behaviour.

So, even though we do it with good intentions, it just doesn't work to say: "*just get on with it and stop moaning, you know you have to have a bath/do your homework*" or "*there's nothing to be frightened of, don't make such a fuss, you'll be fine*" or "*we can't always have what we want in life*" or "*just ignore those silly children calling you names and go and play with someone else.*" I know; I've tried it. In my experience this just makes kids dig their heels in or bottle up their feelings.

Boys

We need to consider boys separately here for a moment because there are some natural differences between the sexes and boys and girls are often treated differently, in Western society at least, when it comes to the expression of feelings.

First, the biology. Boys generally develop language a bit later than girls and tend to express themselves more physically. This can mean that when they have uncomfortable feelings they choose actions over words unless they're helped to connect their rational brain with their emotions.

Carol's son Felix was behaving badly at a family gathering. His mum was surprised as she thought he would have enjoyed being with his many cousins. She hadn't really understood his slow to warm up and introverted personality. She was embarrassed by his aggressive behaviour towards the younger children. Turned out he felt overwhelmed; he knew he was disappointing his mother and he didn't know what to do with those feelings, so he hit out.

There was a dad in one of my workshops once who said, "*if my son was talking about his feelings all the time I'd question his masculinity.*" It's a great sadness that Western society tends to regard being a man as synonymous with bottling up feelings. The worst thing you can say to a boy is "be a man", if what you imply by that is "stop expressing your feelings". Probably what this father wanted for his son was for him to fit in and for him to be strong and to have strategies within himself that help him to cope with problems. Of course. But that doesn't mean the boy shouldn't seek to understand his feelings himself or share his problems with others when appropriate. Sometimes it is appropriate not to show your feelings, such as when you're being teased in the playground. Have a look at this YouTube video https://www.youtube.com/watch?v=hc45-ptHMxo which talks about the impact on boys of this attitude and how it contributes to the high rate of suicide amongst young men. (The link is also on our website – www.theparentpractice.com/book-resources#chapter-3 page.)

Understanding their inner lives empowers men, rather than making them weak. We need to provide our sons with the skills they need to connect with their feelings and channel their anger into productive alternatives. It is not difficult to see how boys, without these skills and vocabulary, turn to violence as a means of expressing themselves and proving their competence.

Understanding feelings is an important first step toward managing them and moving on to solutions. Sometimes it will be appropriate for him to talk about how he feels and sometimes he'll use other strategies but a boy will need emotional intelligence to be resilient. We want our men to be able to empathise even if they have different styles of communication from women. This is really important if your son is to be able to form loving relationships.

Bill, aged 9, was waiting with his older cousins at the top of a 20-foot near-vertical drop of red plastic. From the bottom, Jean could see he was very anxious, and although his cousins threw themselves down the slide, Bill froze on the ledge. Family members were shouting encouragement – "come on, it's not bad, you can do it, close your eyes and push" – but Jean climbed up the back and whispered in his ear that he could respect his instincts and come back later. And they climbed down the ladder, very much against the flow. It wasn't a comfortable few moments as no-one really knew what to say to Bill or to Jean for what looked like giving up – "never mind, don't worry", they suggested. During the day at the adventure park, Bill told his mum how frightened he had felt, and what thoughts had been going through his head. And she just listened. As they were leaving, he said "I want to do it now" and within a few minutes he climbed the ladder, sat on the ledge in his sack, took a huge breath, pushed off and arrived in a heap at the bottom of the slide. He was engulfed in a huge family hug!

How we discourage communication (bit uncomfortable this bit)

We don't pay attention	*Yes, that's nice dear,* while looking at our phones.
We dismiss the feeling	*Don't worry. You'll love it when you get there.*
We deny the feeling	*You shouldn't be upset about that. That's just silly.*
We contradict the feeling	*Of course you don't hate maths. You're really good at it.*
We minimise their experience	*Oh don't go on so. What possible difference could it make if you sit next to Jemma or Claire just for the bus ride?*
We interrogate the child	*Well what did you do to upset Jimmy? Were you being mean to him? What did you say to him?*
We take the other's point of view	*Well Miss Smith is very busy and can't always be expected to notice your hand up.*

We lecture or jump in with advice	*You know what you should do…*
We judge, blame or criticise the child	*I'm sure you must have done something to make Mr Patel get so cross. You were probably not paying attention again. There was a lot of that in your report.*
We shame, ridicule or make them feel foolish	*Aww. Little baby, crying over a little falling out. Man up boy. Big boys don't cry.* *I knew you were too young for that film – it's the last time I take you anywhere nice.*
We punish them for expressing 'bad' feelings	*How dare you speak about granny like that – go to your room.*

Let's see what this is like in practice

Imagine you are at the doctor's surgery with your toddler who hasn't been well for a few days but there's been so much going on that this is the first opportunity you've had to get to the doctor. Your older child was doing well at school but then suddenly hit another child and you had to go and see the principal. You also had to take your mother to visit her old friend Beryl who was visiting from Glasgow and there was no food in the house so you had to get to the supermarket. The car insurance still needs to be renewed and you got a parking ticket while collecting Beryl from the station.

The doctor examines the child and prescribes some medicine and then walks out to the waiting room with you where there are many people you know from the neighbourhood including a teacher from the school. He says in an audible voice that it was irresponsible of you to let it go so long before bringing the child to the doctor. You feel very embarrassed. Your neighbours and friends in the waiting room pretend not to have heard and you get out of there as quickly as possible.

Later on you meet a friend. You're still so upset that you find yourself telling him/her what took place. Your friend tries to help you in several different ways. As you read each response notice what your gut reaction is. **How do you feel about yourself? How do you feel about your friend? How ready do you feel to move on?** Make a note of your reaction – there is no correct response. You may not think the responses of the friend are what any of your friends would say – the point is to try to see what it's like for our children when we respond in equivalent ways.

1. There's no reason to be so upset. You're blowing it all out of proportion. It can't be as bad as all that. Once Toby's had the medicine I'm sure it will be fine. Don't worry about the silly doctor. **Denial of feelings**
2. Look, life's like that. Things don't always turn out the way we want. You have to take things in your stride. In this world nothing's perfect. **Philosophical response**
3. You know what I think you should do? Have a look at your schedule and cut out some things so that you've got time to concentrate on the baby. Maybe Ella could go with someone else to ballet and does Jack really need to do karate as well as football? Surely your mum doesn't really need you to ferry her around? You do need to make Toby's health a priority – the last thing you need is for him to get really sick. **Advice**

4. What happened that made you delay going to the doctor? What were those things you had to do that made you neglect something as important as Toby's health? Didn't you realise he was that sick? What were the symptoms? Why didn't you go after the doctor and explain to him? Don't you think it's important to stand up for yourself? **Interrogation**

5. Well the doctor's just trying to help – it *is* important to pay attention to Toby's health and at least you've got the medicine now so that's alright. He probably didn't mean anyone else to hear what he was saying. **Defence of the other person**

6. Oh you *poor* thing. That's just *terrible*. I feel so sorry for you. **Pity**

7. Boy that sounds rough. To be subjected to a humiliating lecture like that in front of others, especially when you'd been trying to take care of so many needs, must have been pretty hard to take. **Empathetic response**

Did you find that you were encouraged by your friend's attempts to help you in each of these scenarios? No?

While there are different reactions when we put similar situations to parents in our classes most agree that the empathy expressed in response number 7 was the one that was most supportive.

> 1 and 2. Most people say that the dismissal of feelings in responses 1 and 2 left them feeling unheard and misunderstood.

> 3. Some people think that advice in general is ok, even if they didn't like this particular advice. But to be able to accept advice as something helpful one has to be able to access one's rational brain. Generally when we're very upset we're operating out of our hot emotional brains. In the case of adults, time passing may help us to cool down and to be able to reflect on

what happened logically. So if the timing is right we can hear advice. Since a child's immature cool brain will be taking a back seat when he's upset, for advice to work we need to be able to switch on his frontal lobes. More on this below.

4. It may be that when the friend was asking lots of questions you felt interrogated and overwhelmed – now answering these questions is one more thing you have to deal with. (Quite apart from the criticism implied in the questions.)

5. Most people say that when the friend took the point of view of the other they felt betrayed. When we do this to our children we are trying to encourage them to look at other people's perspectives but we are more likely to kindle compassion in our children by considering their own feelings first. The capacity for caring about another person's emotions develops over time and depends on the child having had many experiences of parents showing concern for them.

6. Some people say they felt understood but worried that pity made them pitiable and a bit of a victim. If our children feel like victims this is unlikely to spur them on to positive action.

Why do we do this?

Like the friend, we mean well.

We don't want our children to have painful feelings so we contradict them if they express fear, sadness or disappointment or if they're feeling inadequate.
It's not our job to shield our children from uncomfortable feelings. Our role is to equip them to deal with such feelings and teach constructive ways of responding to pain or distress.

When we see our children in pain of course we want to fix it but **our children are not broken, just human.**

We don't understand

Since our frontal lobes are mature, our understanding and sense of perspective greater and we have much better impulse control it can be hard to identify with the strength of the feeling our children experience. Why does it matter if they have the Maisie plate or the Peppa Pig plate? Our priorities are different.

We regard some feelings as 'bad' feelings and we try to discourage them.

All feelings are valid and can be accepted. It's the actions that may need to be modified. Many feelings regarded as bad can have a positive outcome. One should be angry about injustices. Anger can fuel action – look at Nelson Mandela. Jealousy can spur one on to improve.

We might think that paying so much attention to our children's feelings is 'soft' and pandering to them and children just need to 'suck it up' and get on with life.

Hopefully the material on brain science above has gone some way to dispelling this view. We can help our children to be strong by giving them the mechanisms for dealing with feelings. Ignoring feelings doesn't make them go away, it just reduces our ability to handle them effectively.

Many of us were brought up without any acknowledgment of our feelings and we don't ourselves have an awareness of or a vocabulary for our own emotions.

Our children are sent to teach us! Luckily emotion coaching is a skill that can be learnt.

Tiredness, stress and our own self-doubt may lead us to be dismissive of our children's feelings.

We can't access any of our positive parenting skills easily when we're tired and stressed. This is why it is so important to take steps to care for ourselves. (See chapter 4.)

We think that if we talk about our children's fears or upsets we'll make it worse

Acknowledging an existing fear doesn't make it worse but helps the child control it. Bombarding a frightened child with logic rarely works as they are not operating out of their logical brain in that moment. Naming a child's feelings helps them engage their higher brain.

Sometimes we don't want to acknowledge their feelings because we know our actions have caused the feeling and we feel guilty

Sometimes we will need to apologise for our actions. Sometimes our actions were appropriate or unavoidable. Either way we can acknowledge how our child feels as a result. We mustn't let our feelings get in the way.

How to listen reflectively

"While we are not free to choose the emotions that arise in us, we are free to choose how and when to express them... While we can find our child's behaviour to be unacceptable at times, his or her feelings should never be."

– Haim Ginott

"You've got to let the bad feelings out before there's room for the good ones."

– Andrew, 9[16]

---

[16] Quoted in Jan Parker and Jan Stimpson, *Sibling Rivalry, Sibling Love: What Every Brother and Sister Needs their Parents to Know*, 2002

LISTEN

STOP what you are doing and convey with your body language that you are listening. Really think about what this looks like.

SHOW your child you are interested. You actually need to make time for this kind of conversation to become possible. Use your Special Time (chapter 1) to make connections with your child. You might sit close to him, cuddling him, maybe making eye contact if it is appropriate. Eye contact is not always essential – some children find it easier to talk when they're doing an activity alongside you. Psychologist and author Steve Biddulph[17] recommends this for boys – he calls it 'sideways talk'. Some of the best conversations I've had with my sons have been while we've been doing the washing up or going for a walk. Motion seems to activate their talking muscles!

USE empathetic noises, such as 'umm' or 'I see' or 'tell me more' but don't offer an opinion or any suggestions at this stage.

IMAGINE what your child is feeling

PUT yourself in her shoes. Can you understand the personal attachment your child has to a toy and the deep pleasure she gets from playing with it? Can you imagine how it feels to have a favourite toy taken by a sibling and perhaps

---

[17] Steve Biddulph, *Raising Boys: Why Boys are Different – and How to Help Them Become Happy and Well-Balanced Men*, 2015

damaged? Can you delve deeper? Does that toy represent her territory which has already been invaded by the very existence of the interloper sibling? Is it not so much about the toy but about the relationship between the two children and each one's experience of having some control?

It's harder to identify when the favourite 'toy' is a cardboard box but we need to focus on what it means to your child. When you see the problem from your child's perspective you are being a truly empathetic parent.

REFLECT back what you think your child is feeling in words – NAME IT TO TAME IT

LOOK for the feeling behind your child's actions or words.

"You look sad/ cross/ frustrated..." "It sounds like you are really upset about that." "Maybe you felt humiliated then." "I guess you found that very difficult." "I imagine that you felt jealous when Sarah moved up to level 3." "Perhaps you felt left out when the others wouldn't let you play with them." "When you get stuck on a sum I think you sometimes feel a bit stupid and maybe it feels like you can't do what everybody else seems to be able to do. That could make you feel a bit alone." "It takes courage to try something if you're worried you might not get it right. Maybe you think you will look silly if you make a mistake." "Maybe it feels like people are telling you what to do all day long and you wish you could be the one to say what happens."

DESCRIBE how they feel

"I bet you wish you didn't have to go to school today" "I'm guessing you don't want to have a bath right now as you are really enjoying that game." "It can be hard to get started on something if you feel you're not going to do well at it/you're

not going to win." (Parents need to model getting enjoyment out of activities without winning or excelling at them.) "*I know you think tidying is boring*" "*You don't feel like doing your homework right now as you'd rather be playing. You're finding the new sums very challenging*" "*In the mornings when it's time to get ready you really want to play with your Sylvanian families and Mummy keeps asking you to get dressed or have breakfast or make your bed or brush your hair. I'll bet you wish you could just be left alone to play as long as you like.*"

Emotion coaching doesn't mean that you have to give children what they want; it actually helps lower their resistance when they see that you understand.

GIVE wishes in fantasy

Giving your child her wishes in fantasy provides understanding and humour without trivialising or making light of the situation.

Example: if your child complains that you always 'boss her around' you might say: "*I bet you wish you could be the queen and have lots of servants to order around. Maybe you'd have them bring you breakfast in bed and bow to you and do your homework for you. I bet you wish you could watch television all day and eat as much ice cream as you like...*" etc, etc.

When your child joins in and the fantasies get even more elaborate it becomes fun and the mood lightens but there is no suggestion that the fantasy will come true.

When your child says: "*I hate my new school. I wish I didn't have to go to school at all.*" You say: "*I'll bet right now you're wishing you could have stayed at primary school where everything was familiar. You were at the top of the school there and now you're the youngest again. You were used to the teachers and it was small so it was easy to find your way around. And you didn't have to wear a tie! I'll bet you wish you didn't have any uniform at all. Maybe you'd like to wear your pyjamas all day and not go into school at all but lie about on the sofa watching TV and eating popcorn and playing on your Playstation and..." etc.*

Kick the but...

'But...' has the effect of negating your empathy. What comes after the word 'but' is seen as the important part of the sentence, which makes their feelings the less important part.

It's usually not necessary to repeat your rule or say again what the child has to do. They already know that – it's their feelings that are getting in the way of them doing what they have to do.

If you have to add something further use the word 'and'.

"I can see you're having so much fun on the computer and it's really hard to draw yourself away. And your homework also needs to be done. How are you going to sort this out?"

Some Descriptive Praise will also help motivate them!

Calm is catching

We need to stay calm if we are to help our children deal with their emotions and not be overwhelmed by them. Your mature brain and body help regulate your child's immature systems. Your calmness will influence her state. Using touch (hugs, stroking, holding) triggers the release of oxytocin, the calming chemical, in her brain. Of course the reverse is true too so if we're not calm then we can't expect our children to be! (See chapter 7.)

Powerful feelings can be scary for a child. If we seem

afraid of their feelings then children feel overwhelmed. We need to show that we understand these emotions and we know what to do with them. Very often we don't ask our children to do something because we are afraid of the reaction they will have. This gives them the message that feelings are scary and that they can wield power with them. Sometimes to help our children we need to remain a little detached – you can't help someone out of a hole if you are down in the hole with them. Don't get down into the pit of emotion with your child – you can help them out better from above.

When we acknowledge their feelings and our children feel connected to us their upset feelings may come to the surface. It might feel as if our emotion coaching has been 'rewarded' with a tantrum! In a way it has. Although a tantrum is inconvenient and may feel uncomfortable it is a sign that your child feels safe and is processing their feelings. When it subsides you could say (to a younger child) *"There! That's better isn't it?"*

Modelling

Much of parenting is done through modelling. This means we need to be really conscious of how we deal with our own feelings in front of our children. It's not just what we say, we also need to be conscious of what we're thinking, because kids are very susceptible to atmosphere. You may be saying everything is alright but if underneath you are feeling distressed your child will pick up on it. This means you need your own emotion coach – someone who can listen to *your* feelings. Many partners can fulfil this role (with the right training) and failing that a parent or friend may be able to listen to you with empathy. Have a look at this very funny YouTube video on the difference in styles of communication between men and women: https://www.youtube.com/ watch?v=-4EDhdAHrOg (Also on our website, www. theparentpractice.com/book-resources#chapter-3 page.)

We need to show our children what to do with feelings. What constructive tools do you use (not including a glass of wine) when you feel sad, disappointed, anxious, overwhelmed or angry? You may already be modelling good ways of dealing with uncomfortable feelings. If you feel angry with your kids and you tell them you're feeling so mad that you need some time alone to cool down, so that you don't do or say something you'd later regret – that's great modelling. You may choose to go for a run at moments like that. If you're sad you may use music to lift your mood. If you're feeling anxious or inadequate you may remind yourself of previous occasions when you've been resourceful or you may watch comedy videos to distract you or cheer you up. If you're feeling overwhelmed you may choose to write down everything you have to do on a list or sort out something (even if it's just your sock drawer) so that you feel more in control. When you feel frustrated or annoyed you may take deep breaths to bring calming chemicals into your brain. **Anything you do to change your physical state will also have an impact on your emotional state** so getting outside and breathing deeply or splashing water on face and hands can work to 'break state' and literally lower the temperature.

When you do these good things let your kids know what you're doing so that they can use similar strategies – they can use many of the same mechanisms we do to calm ourselves down or happy ourselves up.

Coaching

As well as overtly demonstrating what to do with your feelings you will need to teach your kids what they can do with theirs. If your child is susceptible to hitting when he's mad or sulking or lashing out verbally when she's feeling disappointed, hurt or jealous then you will need to teach them alternative strategies. Practise when they're calm. Some families use a punching bag or a pillow to release anger or you may prefer some other vigorous activity like running up and down stairs or ripping up paper. My sons got rid of a lot of big feelings on our trampoline! Others do drawing to help themselves express feelings. It can also help to coach your child to use visualisation strategies, e.g. *imagine your anger is a balloon. Maybe a red balloon. Imagine it getting bigger and bigger in your mind. Now what do you want to do with that balloon, pop it, or let it go and watch it float away?*

You can teach your children to recognise the physical cues that tell them they're getting wound up like feeling hot or butterflies in their tummies or breathing faster or clenching fists. If we describe these things to our children when these symptoms are still small and manageable they can more easily employ strategies to calm down.

Remember that children won't be able to use words satisfactorily or consistently for some time. They will move towards that in small steps. You can practise good words to use even if your child has already used an inappropriate non-verbal strategy. So if your son has just hit his sister because 'she was being annoying' help him find the right words to tell his sister how he is feeling. He needs to use the words once he is calm and emotion coaching is what helps him to be calm. We call this doing a 'take two', of which more in chapter 6.

A child who is reacting very angrily and getting upset over little things may be responding to a big problem in his life. This may be with friends or it may be that he is feeling unsuccessful at school. He may have a learning or a physical difficulty. He may feel the subject of much criticism at home or teasing at school. If this is developing into a pattern can you look carefully at his life and see what steps you can take to help him feel happier and more successful?

Children are individuals and will respond differently to bereavement, family break-up or other emotional turmoil and we need to recognise how each child feels. One child may be very angry while another may be very sad. Many will feel powerless and that may show up in defiant behaviour. They need to know that there is someone who will listen, answer questions honestly and accept whatever feelings they are experiencing.

Creating a culture of empathy

How often do conversations about feelings come up in your family? Do you find it is only when you are caught up in them? Making feelings a more general topic of conversation allows us to develop emotional awareness in the family in an unpressured way. That means also talking about how *we* feel. When we do this, we can use "I" statements. So, instead of saying "*you make me so mad*" we say "*I feel really cross when I see this mess in the kitchen. It seems like you are leaving it for me to clean up and I feel taken for granted.*" This way you're taking ownership of your own feelings, rather than blaming the children for them.

And remember, we can also talk about positive feelings! For example: "*I felt so relieved and excited when I heard the news about Grandpa, I couldn't stop smiling!*"

Discuss how others around them feel too – friends, neighbours, characters in books or on TV. Without interrupting their enjoyment of their favourite programme or story, ask your child how he thinks the characters are feeling and what they might do next.

Beyond words – building rapport non-verbally

Over 80% of our communication is non-verbal so let's use it consciously to reinforce the message our words convey. You are probably making connections with your children through:

- ☐ **Touching.** Touch is an obvious way to increase connection. We use touch to calm an upset child. You can synchronise your touch with his breathing for a greater sense of rapport. If you're stroking your child you can increase the pressure of your touch as he exhales and decrease as he inhales.

- ☐ **Mirroring your child's body language** to increase the sense of rapport.

- ☐ **Matching energy levels.** When your child is upset it will be discordant if you seem very calm initially. Match his level of energy by increasing the speed and volume of your voice at first and then slowing and lowering the volume to help him calm.

- ☐ **Matching breathing** – watch her head and shoulders to see when she is exhaling – exhale and inhale when your child does.

Match loneliness

Nick (10) had a rugby tournament on Saturday morning. We had a really busy weekend planned so Paul dropped him off and I'd arranged to get him. I told him I would try to get to the match before the end. I got there about 15 minutes before it was due to end. I was rather disappointed to see that it had already ended so I ran in and he came up to me apparently quite happy saying that his team had won and he'd done a good tackle.

We got in the car and he asked in a slightly wobbly voice why I hadn't been there. Instead of making excuses I turned round and observed his face. I could see that his mouth was puckered a bit and his eyes were looking down. I said 'Nick you look sad; I think you must have been really disappointed that no one was there to watch you.' At that point he nodded, grabbed a jumper and buried his face in it and started to cry. I felt so awful myself but wanted to focus on his feelings rather than mine. I just said 'It is so much nicer when you are playing and you have mummy or daddy watching on the side. You can look up and see us rooting for you. It must have been hard to play the whole game wondering if we were going to come and feeling a bit lonely without anyone there for you.' He nodded and snuffled into his jumper and continued to quietly sob. I did say after that that I wished I could wind the clock back and how sorry I was not to have been there. Shortly afterwards he moved on but it was from releasing the feeling rather than sweeping it away and he looked visibly lighter.

Emma, mother of two boys and two girls

Swimming strop

I had taken my 5 year old to his swimming lesson. Normally I'd be at work when he had his lesson so another mum took him but today I went. I was catching up on some work emails while he was in his lesson when suddenly he came storming over to me! "Mummy, you're supposed to be watching me!" I got the message – he was feeling less important than whatever was on my phone – and I put my phone away. Afterwards I realised how good it was that he had let me know how he felt and that I had paid attention. If I hadn't he still would have had the feelings but they may have come out in an attention-seeking way and if I hadn't realised what it was about I could have been quite brusque with him.

Clarissa, mum of three

Your turn

Here are some examples of things children say and do. How do you think they might be feeling? Try not to get distracted by their behaviour! This can be REALLY hard to do sometimes but we can deal more effectively with their behaviour AFTER we've acknowledged how they feel. The first one is an example from a parent in one of our classes. There is also a short glossary of feelings words below and a much more comprehensive one on our website (www.theparentpractice.com/book-resources#chapter-3).

Your child's words or actions	What is s/he feeling?	What can you say?
Stewart aged 5 had a massive tantrum, screaming and shouting for 20 minutes of his 30-minute swimming lesson	Fear Lack of control	His mum felt really cross with him and on the way home said (rather frostily) *"You seemed really angry,"* and then, relenting, she asked *"were you frightened?"* He said yes, because in the previous lesson the instructor had asked him to swim without goggles. Although she was thinking that didn't excuse the tantrum mum delved deeper and found that Stewart was also nervous about having to converse with new people, especially adults, so he couldn't tell the instructor about his fears. She realised she had been criticising him for his behaviour without understanding how it was for him. With a little descriptive praise he was able to apologise to the instructor at the next lesson and ask to keep his goggles on for a bit longer.

Your child's words or actions	What is s/he feeling?	What can you say?
Charlie (4) is building a Lego castle as you are bouncing his baby sister on your knee. Suddenly he howls "*I hate Melanie, and I wish she'd never been born!*"		
Olivia (6) is watching you get ready for a rare evening out with friends. She's very quiet and suddenly says "*I don't want you to go out tonight, it's not fair!*"		

Your child's words or actions	What is s/he feeling?	What can you say?
Davit (8) is refusing to go to his tennis lesson, the one for which he clamoured for weeks. He says *"I'm not going to tennis, there's no point, I never win."*		
Anastasia (9) is just settling down to sleep when she says *"Today in English, Mariam and Jessie were whispering together and writing notes about me. They told Emily that I can't play their skipping game anymore."*		

Your child's words or actions	What is s/he feeling?	What can you say?
Daniel (10) is refusing to come and do his maths homework. It's a subject he struggles with and his marks this term have been poor.		
Ivan (12) has been very sulky and unkind to his brother recently. You and your partner have been discussing his brother's forthcoming birthday outing to the laser range.		

angry	confident	happy	pressured
annoyed	confused	hopeless	proud
anxious	determined	insignificant	put down
ashamed	disappointed	judged	relaxed
belittled	excited	lonely	reluctant
betrayed	foolish	loving	sad
burdened	frightened	mischievous	vulnerable
calm	guilty	overwhelmed	unlovable

Emotion coaching in a nutshell

☺ Emotionally intelligent children have greater self-esteem, resilience and compassion for others and become good problem-solvers and communicators.

☺ Parents can help children develop emotional intelligence and build key connections between their rational and emotional brains by being emotion coaches.

☺ The listening and connecting involved in emotion coaching makes for closeness and understanding between parents and children. Battles are avoided and behaviour improves.

☺ Being an emotion coach means recognising, respecting and reflecting back to the child what he is feeling. This doesn't mean accepting the behaviour arising out of the feeling.

☺ Children learn constructive ways of handling feelings through parental modelling and coaching.

☺ When your child shows through words or actions that they are in the grips of an emotion:

- ○ Listen, without offering advice
- ○ Imagine how he is feeling
- ○ Describe that feeling to him
- ○ Give wishes in fantasy
- ☺ Don't try to take her feelings away
- ☺ Don't say 'but'

Further reading:

John Gottman and Joan DeClaire, *Raising an Emotionally Intelligent Child*, 1998

Adele Faber and Elaine Mazlish, *How to Talk so Kids Will Listen and Listen so Kids Will Talk*, 2013

4

Skill 4: Setting up for success

'If you fail to plan, you are planning to fail!'

– Benjamin Franklin

Without preparation things can go pear shaped.

Emily was expecting her mother-in-law from New Zealand. They hadn't seen her for two years, when she visited last. Emily had made up the guest room with flowers. She'd scrubbed the bathroom within an inch of its life and put out fresh towels and new soap. She'd cleaned the kitchen and planned the menu for the first few days and done the supermarket shop. She'd planned some excursions that she thought her fussy particular mother-in-law would enjoy. She'd persuaded her husband to take a couple of days off work and he'd gone to the airport to collect his mother. She'd put the boys in smart clothes, despite their protests. When the car turned into the driveway she was satisfied she'd done everything she could to prepare for the state visit. Glancing around she saw with satisfaction that both boys were engrossed in activities; Toby was quietly colouring and Ben was building something out of Lego. Having greeted the great dame herself Emily turned to the boys to get them to come and give their grandmother a kiss hello. Toby, 8, glanced up from his colouring and said hello but Ben, aged 6 wouldn't even look up. Emily went over and hissed in his ear "come and say hello to your grandmother!" Granny, being magnanimous, came over to him and said "hello, Ben" in an expectant way.

Emily still wanted Ben to stop what he was doing and give the expected hug but when pushed Ben just shouted, "No, she smells and I don't know why you're making such a fuss – even you didn't want her to come!"

Parents are great planners. We make menus, do shopping and cook meals, we organise children's extra-curricular activities including pick-ups and deliveries, we organise clean clothing, when we go on outings we pack bags full of necessities, we provide great storage solutions. But sometimes what we don't prepare is our children. We don't always think about what they need to be successful in a particular situation or longer term. While there is definitely a role for experiencing failure (which we explore more in chapter 9), children need to be successful so that they feel happier, more confident, are more cooperative, more willing to take on new challenges and more resilient.

Nobody feels inclined to try if they think there is no possibility of success. This is true whether we're talking about academic or sporting prowess or skills in the social arena or regarding behaviours or attitudes. A child who thinks there is no chance of pleasing his parent is not motivated to try. If he feels he can be more successful at being naughty then he may well choose notoriety.

*Sam, looking at his Spanish homework **covered** in red corrections, said "There's no point in trying any more. Nothing I do is right."*

Positive parenting is not just about responding to behaviour we like or don't like but about actively teaching our children our values and training them in good habits to last a lifetime, both for their sakes and ours. In this chapter we are going to look at some really effective training tools.

A proactive rather than a reactive approach involves changing the question *"what do I do when my child interrupts me when I'm talking to others?"* to *"how can I teach my child to wait until I'm free to talk?"* While it takes time to plan, it is an investment recouped many times over when things go smoothly. Being successful, and getting acknowledged for it, makes a child feel proud of himself and motivated.

Setting up for success

The main points to remember are:

☺ BE REALISTIC. If we ask a child to do something too difficult for him he is likely to fail. Feeling a failure does not motivate anyone to try. Don't expect a young child with a volatile temperament to be calm when things don't go as expected. Don't expect a child who's very sensitive to sounds to enjoy or be well behaved at big, loud gatherings without a lot of coaching. Don't expect a child having difficulty with reading to want to do reading practice until he can see that he is making some small headway. Don't expect a child under 6 to be able to retain and follow an instruction with more than one or two components.

☺ BE PREPARED. Children, like all of us, find it easier to succeed when well prepared, especially if what we're asking them to do is different or a challenge.

☺ BE CLEAR. Have clearly thought out and expressed rules and give instructions in a way that makes it more likely that children will do what we've asked. *How?* you ask. Read on….

Skills covered so far

In the last three chapters we have looked at skills which are essential for setting up for success. When we take time to really understand our children's temperament and the stage they're in we can more effectively develop strategies to support them. When we use Descriptive Praise we determine the mood; we help our children see themselves as good, kind, helpful, considerate, cooperative, problem-solving people and to behave accordingly. We give them the attention they need in positive ways. When we are emotion coaches we build self-esteem and resilience and help our children regulate their feelings, which leads to better behaviour. In the next chapter we will look at values and how we pass these on to our children with rules and the judicious use of rewards.

In this chapter we will look at a number of micro-skills which together make up a tool basket of really practical strategies for bringing out the best in children.

Your turn

This chapter will work best if you have in mind an area that you'd like to address. It may be an area where there are already some difficulties, one of the 'hot spots' of family life, or it may be something that you anticipate your child may need support with in the near future. Think about this area as we go through the various skills and consider how that skill could work for you.

....

....

How to set up for success

Have realistic expectations

If we ask a child to do something that is beyond his capacities he is likely to fail. What is your child capable of, given his developmental stage and his temperament? Does he need more instruction or more training before he can do a task or develop a habit? What have you taught him about struggle and failure? (See Chapter 9.) Have you ever felt yourself get angry or disappointed when your child doesn't act like an adult?

It is unrealistic to expect most boys under 10 to sit still and do a cognitive task like homework for very long unless they are particularly motivated. Even if he is engaged don't expect him not to fidget or wriggle. Don't be surprised if your 11-year-old daughter doesn't speak to you politely when you're pointing out the deficiencies in her friends when saying no to a proposed pouting.

Accommodate temperament

If your child is an introvert allow them enough time to reflect and to re-charge on their own. If they are an extrovert make sure they get time with friends and with you and give them lots of positive feedback.

Teach your intense child to be aware of her cues of building intensity by gently pointing out to her when she's becoming more hyperactive or clingy, more agitated or louder, testing the rules or fussing, and to take remedial action such as some cool down time. "*I notice you're getting really bothered about this – this could be a great chance to try that breathing we practised at the weekend.*" Make sure the intense child gets enough sleep and exercise and don't forget humour to reduce tension and change the mood.

Persistent children need rules and they need them to be consistently upheld but they also need to have some personal power. Get their input when solving problems.

If you have a sensitive child you'll need to be very aware of the amount of stimulation he's getting and teach him to recognise it too. Give him words to express his emotions and sensations and let him see that using words works, i.e. that you respond sympathetically to what he says. Make sure your sensitive child isn't getting too much screen time and he is getting enough sleep.

The distractible/perceptive child will need greater input when giving instructions. She needs eye contact, touch and lots of descriptive praise. Instructions need to be simple, clear and positive. (See below.) Teach her to say *"I just need a minute"* rather than blocking people out when she feels overwhelmed.

Slow to adapt children thrive on routines and need more time to make transitions from projects, people and places. Give lots of forewarnings and use schedules. Help them to deal with disappointment using emotion coaching.

Irregular children will need help and time to adapt to routines. They will need consistency and empathy.

The high energy child will need lots of outlets for his exuberance. He needs his high energy to be directed in positive ways. Encourage involvement in sports and don't expect him to be still during homework and mealtimes. Use gentle touch to calm as well as emotion coaching. You'll need to ensure your own resources get replenished to give the attention this child needs! Consider whether high energy is also related to over-stimulation or even fatigue.

If your child's first reaction is to reject new situations, sensations, tastes and people she will need to be encouraged, not pushed. Forewarn her of new things and allow time for her to assess before being expected to participate. Identify and accept her fears (don't try to reason her out of them) while giving strategies for dealing with them. Point out past successful strategies and break down the new situation into manageable chunks (see below). Allow time for this.

Children with a negative outlook may need help to see the positives. Keeping a 'Good things' journal as part of a bedtime routine could help. Help your child identify small things that worked (or parts of things) that happened during the day and record them. Teach him to express himself diplomatically when there are (aspects of) things he doesn't like.

Plan

Think about what habits or qualities you'd like to encourage in your children and ask what are the ways you can do this? Go back to the list of qualities you created in chapter 2. If you want to see more consideration in your child then maybe make that the value or quality of the week and put it up on the fridge. Look out for signs of consideration in your children, and others, and mention it. Put pasta in the jar for it. Be particularly aware of modelling that quality yourself.

If you want to make sure your family is getting a balanced healthy diet what are some ways of going about that? Will it help to make a menu for the week and then shop only from that list to reduce waste and provide variety?

If you have trouble remembering to descriptively praise can you put post it notes with 'DP' or smiley faces on them around the house to remind you or use alerts on your phone? I have a brain like a sieve so I write everything down. Also it can be really helpful to prepare some Descriptive Praises in advance if you get tongue tied in the moment.

If you think your child could benefit from some social skills training how and when will you go about that? Do you need to enlist help from someone else? See some ideas below under role play.

Studies show that families who eat together are more likely to develop language, do well at school, enjoy better mental health and eat more nutritious food; they are also less likely to engage in underage sex or use drugs and alcohol.[18]

Time

Have you allowed enough time and is this the right time? Avoid asking your child to do something new and difficult

---

[18] Professor Snow, Harvard 1996, National Merit Scholarship Corporation 20-year study

if he is tired or hungry or emotional – or you are! If it has to happen this way, take this into account. Arrange for rewards to follow tasks. For example: watch TV after homework, story after teeth are brushed etc. (See chapter 5.) Is it better for *this* child to do homework in the morning rather than the evening? Should clothes be laid out the night before?

Be a time realist, not a time optimist. Things take longer than you think. Juliet asks her class how long it takes to boil an egg and when they say either 3 minutes or 5 she claims it takes 23. And it does… once you take into account the fact that you have to get out the saucepan and fill it with water and meantime your son asks you to cut his toast into squares and you have a debate about the need for that at his age and you need to help your daughter brush her hair and it gets in a tangle and the cat is sick on the rug…

Don't rush your child, and don't pressurise yourself to do things within a fixed time. Instead allow him the time it takes him, while training him to do things efficiently.

"Rushing is the enemy of love."

– Steve Biddulph

I've never met a parent who has greeted this next idea with any enthusiasm – yet many have agreed it's the best investment of time they can make for the day ahead… Get up 15-20 minutes earlier and let the benefit of that ~~sacrifice~~ investment pay off for you throughout the day in terms of peace of mind and harmonious relationships. That bit of time to yourself allows you to have your shower and get dressed so that you're then free to focus on the kids in a positive way. Alternatively/additionally can you engage your partner to help at this time of day?

Spending time with your children doing fun things is a great investment in them and builds positive connections which make cooperation more likely.

"It may be that the long-term investments that we make in children, like spending time with them, showing that we love them and listening to them, have a more powerful positive effect on behaviour than any form of discipline."

– Andrew Grogan-Kaylor

Break tasks down

There is no elevator to success. You have to take the stairs.

– Author unknown

Break a task into smaller manageable chunks. Tidying up the bedroom is easier when broken down into specific tasks, such as putting the books on the shelf and the clothes in the washing basket. Doing a maths problem is easier if the basic skills involved have been mastered such as knowing how to add, carry numbers, arrange the figures in columns etc. When parents descriptively praise the smaller components children are encouraged.

When training a child to occupy themselves independently you would start by choosing a particularly fun activity, engaging with the child at first and then gradually withdrawing. Explain what you are doing and that you are going to be nearby. Pop back in after a short time to descriptively praise him for his willingness and for playing quietly by himself, mentioning that he is showing self-reliance and resourcefulness. Look out for and mention signs of self-reliance and resourcefulness elsewhere in his life. Don't make the first session of playing alone last too long. Don't have high expectations of extroverts here.

Prepare the physical environment

Look about you and see what can be done to make things happen. Parents often tell us about practical measures they've taken to help things work better – such as putting coat hooks or having cups and plates where the children can reach them or having toothbrushes or hairbrushes downstairs so the children don't disappear at the crucial moment or having storage containers for children's possessions.

Homework will go more smoothly if you can eliminate or minimise distractions – such as putting phones on silent, using timers and having pens, rubbers, paper, rulers, calculators and other equipment at hand and setting up homework in a clutter- and distraction-free environment. Get the children to leave toys elsewhere. Have a drop off/re-charging zone for electronics so that kids don't take electronic gadgets to the table or into bedrooms, which really disrupts sleep. Keep computers in common areas. (More in chapter 11.)

Chat Throughs

You will know that one of the best ways to set up for success is by talking through situations, events and changes in advance. This is so much better than hijacking children at the last minute with a situation that they don't like, such as having a babysitter when you go out or a trip to the dentist! We do this to try to avoid anticipated aggro but it usually backfires as we get a lot more resistance, and we lose trust.

Chat Throughs can be used for everyday situations such as what needs to happen when you get home after school or a muddy trip to the park or during homework. Or they can be used for bigger scenarios such as the birth of a new baby or moving house or family illness or separation.

This is so helpful for a child who doesn't react well to change. Although he may not like it in the first chat-through, you revisit the conversation frequently before the event, and every time the reaction will be less, until by the time the event itself comes round he will be more used to the idea.

For example: *if you're instituting a change like having to earn sweets where the child is used to just getting them, or having to do eye exercises, tell the child the new system will start, for example, next Monday and between now and then refer to it often and acknowledge how he might feel.*

How to do it

It is crucial that the child does much of the talking. The best way to encourage your child to start talking is to begin with some Descriptive Praise. If we say we need to talk to them about something children usually expect us to tell them off – disarm them with something positive.

Start by setting the scene. Then ask them questions to find out what they know about

☐ what needs to happen,

☐ what challenges might arise and

☐ how they can overcome these.

This is so much better than simply telling them what is going to happen. It's not about sharing what *you* know! When the child is engaged and they feel like they have some input you will get more cooperation.

Example: *Hamish is coming over to play this afternoon. You two have a really good time together don't you? You built a brilliant den in the garden out of those cardboard boxes last time – that was really creative. And then you made up a game of your own – what was it? It seemed to involve lots of warriors... Last time Hamish came over Liam wanted to join in didn't he? You didn't really want him involved because he's a bit little to play the games that you and Hamish like. What will you need to do if he wants to play with you big boys?... That's right, we discussed playing a game that he could join in with for 15 minutes or so and then I'd take him off to do something with me. What game would work for Liam as well?... Yes, UNO is a good idea. You both like that. Good thinking. When Hamish arrives you might feel like going straight into your own games. You might feel frustrated at having to include Liam. Do you think that might happen?... What can you do if you feel that way?... Where's the best place for you big boys to set yourselves up? Do you remember our rule about time on electronics when you have a friend over?... Thank you for telling me even though you might have wished I'd give you even longer today. That's really responsible of you.*

As you can see the chat through is peppered with descriptive praise and emotion coaching and it engages the child in thinking of solutions. It works best when parents ask the child 'what can we do to make it easier for you to do what's required?' (Just like your manager at work should be supporting you to do the best job you can.) Ask them for solutions and strategies and be prepared to try them! They often have better ideas than us and it gives a great boost to self-esteem and makes for greater commitment to the strategy. It also helps them to see themselves as solution-seekers. Don't worry, you can offer your own ideas too, e.g. to help a reluctant child leave a playdate give a five-minute warning or have a favourite toy waiting in the car.

One five-year-old child who was waking up in the night came up with idea that, as his cuddly toys slept all through the day, he could give them a hug and take some of their stored sleep to help him sleep. This worked a treat because it was his idea.

It really works to use children's ideas because they are creative and because it shows respect for their thinking.

Role plays

A chat through is a wonderful way to engage your child's brain but the most effective tool is doing, rather than talking.

Tell me and I forget. Teach me and I remember.
Involve me and I learn.

– Benjamin Franklin

Use role plays to help your child rehearse tricky situations, such as what to say to someone teasing them or when another child is snatching or not sharing or being annoying (more in chapter 8) – or other situations that make them feel uncomfortable, such as making phone calls, or looking someone in the eye or saying thank you at the end of a play-date – or for practical everyday situations such as packing school bags, or getting in and out of games kit quickly. Families tell us they have used role plays successfully to prepare for long distance travel or visits to granny.

Role play can be very useful for improving a child's social skills.
Practice **how to join a group of children** – help your child find ways to say hello and ask to join in. *Hi my name's... what's yours? I like your Inside Out notebook. Do you like Joy?* Don't worry about taking it too seriously – children

learn more when they are enjoying themselves. You can laugh about funny ways to say hello in the process of finding a way that works for your child.

Be realistic, and look for a small improvement first rather than the finished product. Training in small steps can mean **practising in non-threatening areas first**. For example, eye contact can be really hard for some children, so rather than insist on holding the gaze of a grown-up, first start with catching their eye or practice with dolls or teddy bears to begin with and build up from there. You could pretend that different family members are strangers and say hello to each one in different ways. Practice also what to say if the child says "no you can't play".

Role play is also a good way to teach children to **read social cues** from words and body language. We can teach our children to recognise how another is feeling and to gauge their impact on others and adjust accordingly, including the amount of space a person needs.

A fun way to practice skills at reading **body language and facial expressions** is to watch video without the sound and try to work out what the characters are thinking or feeling, and what they are going to do next. Or get your child to read your face and say what you're feeling. Ask what you're likely to do next if you're feeling that way. Have fun with it!

We can also teach them to **hold conversations**, getting the balance right between talking and listening and keeping to the topic. We do this just by having conversations with them.

You can also use role plays to help your child work out how look after their needs and **state their feelings without hurting anyone else**. Practice saying something like *"I don't like it when you take my things. Stop that!"* *"I* *want to play with you but I don't like this chasing game – it hurts when you get slapped.*" If your child tends to dominate group play, insisting on doing an activity or game in a particular way, you can also use role plays with dolls or teddies to work out how it feels to be told what you have to do all the time, compared to being asked what you would like. Doing it in role play makes it easier to avoid it becoming a lecture or being critical. Help your child to see that **playing is more fun when there is input from everyone**. You can also acknowledge that she likes to run things and know what is happening, that maybe it helps her to feel more in control. In fact uncertainty may be what's driving the bossiness.

Role plays can be great fun – many young children love it but even older ones will find it useful. Many parents tell us how much they enjoyed spending this time with their child. Others hate the idea! Even if you don't join in it's an advanced learning tool for the kids. Experiential learning is the most effective – children can visualise and remember themselves doing it right.

Actually doing what's required creates 'muscle memory', like when you practise a tennis serve or a golf swing. You're told how to do it, you watch Federer, and then you have to do it for yourself, and repeat it sufficiently so that when in the line of fire or heat of the moment you can pull it off.

Girls' shoes

Noah, aged 5, came home from school upset because his friend Fred had said his shoes were 'girls' shoes'. Noah's mother was furious with Fred and thought maybe she should have a word with his mother or maybe she should buy Noah different shoes but decided instead to help him deal with the teasing himself through role play. They took turns being Noah or Fred and discovered that if Noah said something provocative back to Fred things got worse. They practised using a form of words that didn't give Fred the satisfaction of getting Noah upset, eventually settling on "Oh, do you think so?" said in a nonchalant manner. Noah went back to school better equipped to deal with the inevitable recurrence of teasing than if he'd just been told to ignore Fred.

The toy shop

I have a very large family and found that I was spending many weekends in shops with my son trying to buy presents for relatives while being badgered by my son to buy something for him. I thought about it and realised that I wanted him to learn to delay gratification and to learn the value of his pocket money and to budget so I told him that we would not be buying a present for him the next time we went shopping and we needed to practise this. We set the living room up as a toy shop using all the children's toys and my wife was roped in as the shopkeeper. We practised choosing something for someone else. Then I asked my son to act out being disappointed that we could not get a toy for him that day. He rose to the challenge. But then he said "Never mind, seeing that Lego set there reminds me that I haven't built anything out of Lego for ages. I'm going to do that when I get home." I was amazed and gave him lots of descriptive praise for using a good strategy to help him handle his disappointment well and I really enjoyed playing Lego with him for a while.

Omar, father of four

Fun

Your kids probably respond well when you're being silly. Wherever possible use humour or any way of making tasks more palatable such as music, company, racing against the clock (not against siblings), doing things with funny voices/hats etc, etc. You won't always be able to make things fun so don't beat yourself up for not being a creative parent – sometimes they just have to brush their teeth! *Example: put a bit of doggerel on the towel rail to remind the child to hang up the towel "Please remember, don't forget, hang me up or I'll stay wet!"* Play upbeat music or an audio recording of a story for tidying up time or teeth brushing.

> **Pups**
>
> **Chris has just started big school and was feeling a bit wobbly. His teacher has a puppet called 'Pups' who sits on her shoulder and whispers in her ear. Pups tells her about the boys who are sitting down. Injecting a bit of fun with the puppet has a magic effect on the others.**
>
> **Justine, mum of two**

Giving instructions

Ideally we should be trying to reduce the number of instructions we give so that our children don't hear it as nagging. (We call it reminding.) We can do this by having more routines and checklists and we can *ask* the children what they need to do and brainstorm with them more often rather than issuing commands. But sometimes we will need to tell the children what they need to do.

Give clear, simple instructions so that children are more likely to do what we've asked. Consider the timing of the instruction – don't ask children to do something challenging or new when they're tired, hungry, emotional, or in front of a screen. Below is the three-stage approach, a magic formula for maximising cooperation. If you anticipate cooperation you need not use all 3 steps but it is very useful if you think there will be resistance and should be used to encourage children into habits of cooperating.

The 3-Stage Approach

1. PREPARE

STOP – what you're doing and go to your child, rather than flinging an instruction over your shoulder while you're making dinner or shouting up the stairs!

ENGAGE – enter into your child's world and descriptively praise him. When he looks at you, descriptively praise him for doing so. *"Thank you for looking at me. That's really polite. I can tell you're listening to me now."*

2. INSTRUCT

CLEAR AND SIMPLE – children find it hard to remember multiple instructions.

ONLY ONCE – otherwise children get used to parents repeating and learn not to pay attention until they've been asked several times and our voice has reached that particular pitch!

One boy, when asked why he hadn't done what his mum asked him to do, replied that she didn't mean it until she shouted!

ASK your child to repeat to you what it is that they have to do. This way you ensure that they have heard and they are more likely to do it if it has come out of their mouths.

3. FOLLOW THROUGH

WAIT – rather than walk away, stay in your child's space until the instruction is carried out to your satisfaction. Make sure your body language and facial expressions are positive and authoritative, i.e. standing in a symmetrical stance with your head level and hands by your side or at your waist. Smile.

DESCRIPTIVELY PRAISE tiny steps in the right direction and/or **EMPATHISE** that he doesn't want to do what he has to do.

What happens next? In real life, you may have to leave to attend to something else. Nothing else the child wants to do happens until he has done what he has to. You may have to come back to it later.

The power of words

The language we use when we ask our children to do something is crucial in determining whether they listen and cooperate. We often couch our instructions in too-soft language in the mistaken belief that we're being polite. We can still be polite, and smile, while using the authoritative language of requirement. Unless it really IS optional, avoid requests such as *"Would you like to set the table?"* or *"Shall we have a bath now?"* or *"Do you mind making your bed?"* Instead, be intentional:

☺ *You need to do....*

☺ *It is time to do....*

☺ *What do you need to do now?*

☺ *What is the rule here?*

We can say "*Please would you...*" if our child is feeling cooperative and generally does as he's asked, but beware the clever answer to "*I would like you to...*" which is "*You might like me to but...*" Say thank you at the end of the instruction – it's polite and it conveys an assumption that the task will be done.

The power of body language

Consider how your body language can help convey authority too.

Rather than towering over your child with hands on hips and crossed arms or wagging your finger, which appears intimidating, stand close to your child with your arms loosely by your side or at your waist, with shoulders back and square on to your child. Or crouch down next to your child. Keep your head still and level.

If you use your hands, keep your palms down – palms up indicate questioning or inviting input – now is not the time for that. Speak slowly and in a low voice – you can still smile!

The power of eye contact

Research has found that when we make eye contact with someone, the brain sends messages to the middle ear that allow it to open up and focus on the human voice, rather than trying to pay attention to potentially threatening background noises as we have evolved to do. So eye contact really does help hearing!

However, for this to happen we need to feel very safe.

Children find it hard to cut themselves off from all the sights and sounds around them, particularly if they are strongly perceptive and find it hard to filter anything out, or if the subject is intimate or they feel guilty or threatened, so we need to make it as easy as possible for them to feel safe and want to focus on us and what we have to say.

Descriptive Praise will help get them in the habit of looking at us, and listening to us – because they will want to hear what we have to say.

But sometimes if what we're saying is negative, emotional or difficult it may be easier for our children to hear what we have to say if we are not looking them directly in the eye but are still close to them and indicating our love and support through other body language signals.

Solution Time

As far as possible, all the adults dealing with the children need to be in agreement about how to pass shared values on to the children. A consistent approach will help the children learn faster.

Set aside regular Solution Time to identify and discuss solutions for any current or forthcoming issues with everyone involved in caring for your children – partner, nanny, childminder, grandparents, etc – rather than waiting to have an emergency crisis meeting.

Of course, it's not always possible to have one single approach and children can cope with the idea that different behaviours are appropriate in different places. For example: they get to watch more TV at Granny and Grandpa's house than they do at home. However, they may continue to nag, whine or pester in the hope that they will be able to get more TV at home and parents will need to be particularly consistent at home. (We can empathise that they enjoy watching TV at their grandparents' house.)

What to do in solution time....

☺ **IDENTIFY** the issue – *the children are not making their beds/packing their school bags so I end up nagging them and doing it myself. I want them to be self-reliant and learn how to do these things for themselves.*

☺ **AVOID** blame and criticism. It's easy to fall into the trap of looking for who is/was at fault when things aren't going right. Not only is this a waste of time, it will probably alienate the partner or child being blamed.

☺ **KEEP** a notebook to help you remember what was agreed.

☺ **CONSIDER** what skills will help – typically it will be Descriptive Praise, Emotion Coaching and Rules. Use the same techniques you use on the children with your partner, nanny or grandparent – that is, notice and mention anything they're doing that is a step in the right direction and empathise that it can be difficult to be a parent or child carer. Don't patronise though!

☺ **REWARD** yourself with dinner or a movie (or a glass of wine) afterwards.

☺ **ACT** – take the first step!

United Front

"A happy home is one in which each spouse grants the possibility that the other may be right, though neither believes it."

– Don Fraser

It often happens that one parent is more skilled than the other either because only one parent is attending parenting classes or reading this book or because the other partner is less committed to the techniques for some other reason. You can help your partner be more positive, firm and consistent by your example with the skills. Model the ways you connect with the children and tell your partner about your experiences of using a positive approach. This worked for me with teachers too. I didn't want to tell them how to do their job (well, I did but…) so I would say *"what's working at home is…."*

☺ Parents in our classes came up with the following ideas for promoting a united front: REFLECT BACK your partner's point of view to him/her, *especially* where this is different from yours. For example: *You don't see why they can't be online whenever they want to. You see computer skills as essential for modern life.*

☺ COMPROMISE where there is disagreement – consistency is more important than the actual rule

☺ DON't CRITICISE when there is conflict between you, but make requests and state your needs. Example: *I need more help with the children. Please can you take them to swimming on Saturdays?* Be honest and question whether your style of involving your partner in the past has largely been to nag and criticise them. Use 'I' statements, rather than 'you' statements. Example: *I find it hard to manage what they are seeing and doing online without having rules about when and where they can do it. I feel worried about this.*

☺ CONFINE yourself to the matter under discussion, and don't bring up the past or use the words 'always' or 'never'. Example: *With the new term about to start,*

> *it is a great opportunity to get an evening routine that works for us all.*

☺ TAKE SOME RESPONSIBILITY for problems and avoid defensiveness. Example: *I guess I can be a bit bossy about how things go in the home; I really want to do such a good job and I don't always take time to listen to your side of things.*

☺ ACKNOWLEDGE each other's strengths. *My husband and I used to keep a little book by our bedside in which we wrote one thing each day that we appreciated about each other, in relation to parenting or otherwise. A real atmosphere of trust developed and we also felt more confident about our parenting.*

☺ SAY POSITIVE THINGS to and about your partner in front of the children.

☺ DON't UNDERMINE or criticise or argue with your partner in front of the children.

☺ CONFER with your partner before promising something to the children. If your child comes to you when you suspect they've already asked their other parent, ask them *"What did mummy/daddy say?"* and go along with their decision. If you can't, don't say anything to the child until you've spoken to the other parent.

Get your partner involved by asking for his/her ideas about the rules even if s/he has not been following through on them. When it comes to setting rules, you may need to compromise in order to achieve consistency. This may be because of a difference in values or because one parent thinks that requiring the child to do what you want will be too difficult. (See next chapter.)

Karate lessons

Dylan badly wanted to take karate lessons with his friend Kyle and badgered his parents until they agreed. Now, half way through the term, he has gone off the idea. Dad feels it is important that Dylan learns to honour commitments and doesn't want to waste the money already expended in fees. Mum is the one who has to get the reluctant boy to lessons and is inclined to let him give up. She doesn't see any point in forcing him to do a non-essential activity when it is causing so much aggravation.

Mum says she shares Dad's value about seeing things through but explains her concern about making it work. Dad concedes that it will be mum in the firing line of Dylan's upset and resolves to support her. They agree that Dylan will continue until the end of term and if he doesn't want to continue next term he doesn't need to, and they work together to come up with some emotion coaching words they could use to reflect back to Dylan how he feels when he has to go. They talk to him together in a non-judgmental way to explain why this matters to them.

Looking after yourself

You are an important resource for your family – your family needs you and you need to be well taken care of. When you're short on sleep, exercise and appreciation and your to-do list is enormous... how do you behave? Will you say and do effective things? Are positive results likely?

When we're rested, getting some exercise, eating healthy food, our self-esteem is being nourished as well as our brains and our souls. When we get a little time for ourselves, we are making deposits in our resourcefulness bank account so that there is something there to withdraw when we need it. Only then can we access the parenting skills we already have, and the ones we're learning and developing.

"When we truly care for ourselves, it becomes possible to care far more profoundly about other people. The more alert and sensitive we are to our own needs, the more loving and generous we can be toward others."

– Eda LeShan

We explore this topic in more detail in chapter 7.

Getting your child's input

All of the above ideas are ways that parents can plan for success but we will really be missing a trick if we don't get input from our kids.

Family Meetings are a great opportunity to engage the children in finding ideas and answers to difficult issues, and planning how to put them in place. Set the rules for the meeting beforehand (e.g. everyone gets a turn to talk and no bad-mouthing anyone else) and keep the focus on problem-solving. (See chapter 8 for some ideas on using a talking stick.) For example: rather than *"That was appalling behaviour in the back of the car this afternoon – what on earth was going on? It must never happen again"* We start with *"Next time we're in the car, we need to find a way to be quieter so I can concentrate on the driving and keep us all safe. How do you think we could do this?"*

Having made a plan, we need to determine a first step and decide when it will be taken. Then take action.

For a fun and enticing invitation to family meetings see our website (www.theparentpractice.com/book-resources#chapter-4).

A good way to encourage problem-solving and planning is to ask kids questions of the 'What if' variety, e.g. *What if the bus doesn't come on time?* Or, *What will we do if they don't have Granny Smith apples at the supermarket?* Or, *What can you do if you don't understand a word in your German homework?*

Car share

My older two kids used to argue on the school run over who was allowed to sit in the front seat. I could never remember from one day to the next who had sat where. My 6 year old then came up with a simple suggestion. "Mummy, let me give you my little notebook to leave in the front of the car. Just write down the date and the name of who sat in the front so you don't forget and they can take it in turns." They never argued about that issue again.

Ruth, mother of four

Preparation of School Sports Kit

We decided that Jack (7) could learn to take responsibility for preparing his own sports kit. He is very motivated by sports and we thought this would encourage him to develop good organisational habits.

We started with a chat-through about his weekly timetable and what sports happen when and what kit he needs. I asked him "When is the best time to prepare your kit?" and I reminded him how hectic school mornings can be – we even did a quick role-play of trying to leave the house and pretended that Grace slowed the process down with an urgent nappy change! Jack decided that getting his bag ready the night before was going to be the best idea.

We then made a rule that "Each night after tea we prepare the kit for the next day" and then we started training in small steps.

First, we put the sports kit where he could reach it. We also wrote up a timetable and stuck it on the cupboard door where it could have maximum impact. Week 1 I prompted him with "let's get the kit ready" and I used lots of DP and lots of pasta in the pot. I even got parts of his kit that he forgot.

Week 2 I asked him what he needed to do after tea. I also encouraged him to check he had got everything on the list, but I didn't put things in that he had forgotten...

One day he forgot his trainers. He realised when we were almost at school and I was really tempted to go back and get them. Instead I explained I would be late for 'my school' if I did that because of the traffic and I asked him what normally happens if boys forget their trainers. He seemed to realise that maybe it wasn't that bad and he would just have to do PE in his shoes. After school I did some emotion coaching and we also did a role play where I was one of his friends saying "Why is Jack playing football in school shoes?" and then Jack was another child saying "Oh, he's just forgotten his trainers" and then I said "Well, he's running really fast in his shoes!" and Jack loves anything to do with speed so he was quite happy! I gave him lots of DP for handling the situation well and he's not forgotten his trainers since!

Amanda, mum of 2

Your turn

STEP 1: Go back to that area you chose where you would like things to go better for you and your child(ren) and say **how you would like it to work**:

....

....

....

STEP 2: **Break the task down** into smaller components and choose one small part to tackle first. How can you support and motivate your child to do the right thing?

Is there a way to make the task fun? Can you plan something interesting to do afterwards? What preparations need to be made to the physical environment? How will everyone remember what they need to do? Do you need some rules? Should they be written down?

....

....

....

STEP 3: Chat Through
Choose a quiet time, away from the main issue. You know that criticism or pointing out what the children are doing wrong does not make them want to change their behaviour. If we blame, nag or lecture they will stop listening.

I will start with Descriptive Praise for:

....

I will empathise with:

....

What questions can you ask your child to draw out what he needs to do?

....

....

Refer to the chat-through in day-to-day conversation and alert them just before the situation arises – remember to ask questions, not just transmit information.

STEP 4: Show Time!
In the moment itself you will definitely need to use Descriptive Praise and Emotion Coaching. Don't wait until it goes wrong.

Setting up for Success in a nutshell

Set up for success to improve your child's skills and confidence and to make family life go more smoothly.

Use all the skills already in your tool basket, particularly Descriptive Praise to motivate and Emotion Coaching.

Use the micro-skills to train children to handle situations and develop good habits:

☺ Make sure expectations are realistic for this child at his stage of development and with his temperament

☺ Plan for individual situations and for training in good habits.

☺ Allow enough time and choose the time for training carefully

☺ Break tasks down into smaller components

☺ Prepare the physical environment

☺ Use the 3-Stage Approach when you give instructions

☺ Use Chat Throughs and Role Plays and engage the children in looking for solutions

☺ Develop a united front with your partner and others involved in the care of your child

☺ Look after the resource that you are for your family.

5

Skill 5: Family values

"The measure of our parenting success is not what our child does or achieves, but what kind of person he or she becomes."

– Mary Rice Hasson

When I was six years old I came to my mother after an afternoon of play with my best friend Hillary and I announced "Hilsy's mum and dad don't love her." My mother was quick to leap to their defence, saying "Of course they love her." She knew that their marriage was in difficulty. She asked me why I'd said that, to which I responded with all the wisdom of a 6 year old, "Well they don't have any rules in her house." At six I'd worked out that when you love someone you care enough to bother setting limits and providing guidelines. The truth was Hillary's parents were too distracted by their own problems and perhaps feeling guilty about the upheaval in her life to have any rules at home.

Values

It is part of our job in raising our children to teach them how to behave in the moment and to set up good habits for life. How we want our children to behave is dictated by the values we hold dear. As discussed in the last chapter there are many practical ways to encourage good behaviours and one of these is through the use of rules. You may just have had an adverse reaction to the use of that word! You may feel that rules are negative or constraining and stifle spontaneity and freedom. In this chapter we will look at how parents can use rules to help children get things right. This makes them pleasant to be around and is great for their self-esteem.

Part of my work is with children in an area of great social disadvantage in western Sydney. Their lives are characterised by uncertainty. Many of them are growing up without any rules at all as their parents are distracted by their very real troubles. But that doesn't mean they aren't acquiring values. If the parents of these children were able to focus on their kids they would not choose the values they are picking up. So let's be mindful about how values are acquired. Children learn values by observing their parents and making conclusions about what's important. **80% of parenting is modelling.**

The main points to remember are:

☺ Focusing on the values we want in our families is purposeful parenting. It enables us to think about what we're doing as we bring up our children rather than just going through life and the mountain of tasks that we have every day

☺ Getting clear about what we want to happen is the first step toward making it happen; focusing on what we *don't* want to happen doesn't get results

☺ Modelling is crucial, but it's not the only tool we have

☺ Formulating and communicating rules is proactive parenting

☺ Following through consistently gives children clarity and certainty. Yes, I know it's hard to do – read on!

What are your values?

What's important to you in your life? What are your strongly held beliefs to which you refer when making decisions and choices? What are your deeply held views about what makes life worthwhile? What are the governing principles by which you try to live your life? What kind of person do you want to be?

These are your values. These give us a clear vision of how we want to be as a family and enable us to parent in a more purposeful way. This is different from just making up rules in the moment. We need to think about our values first, and believe in them, otherwise it's hard for us to commit to any rules we make.

Some values are reflected in behaviours that you will be encouraging without having specific rules, such as being generous or kind; other values are made into specific rules. We expect our children to say please and thank you, and this may be clearly stated as a rule. Sometimes if the children are not behaving in line with your values you may need to make and uphold a specific rule. You may have an unarticulated value that family members treat each other with respect but your 9 year old is calling you names. A rule that reflects this value may be required, Example: Speak to others with respect.

When our children don't behave in line with our values, we are disappointed and we react accordingly, because it really matters to us. In the chapter following this we look at ways of responding effectively when they haven't behaved as we would wish.

Your turn

Time to get clear about your values. You could select from the list of values on our website (www.theparentpractice. com/book-resources#chapter-5) or just choose your own. Jot them down below or use the PDF on the website. Some families have chosen: honest, hard-working, respectful, creative, determined, considerate, responsible, solution-oriented, etc.

. . . .

. . . .

. . . .

. . . .

. . . .

Some families turn these values into a family mission statement. Having a mission helps you parent with a destination in mind and a route map, as Steven Covey says.[19] This always makes the journey clearer. There are commercial varieties of these available but you can easily create one yourself too. I've put an example from my family on the website page.

It's obviously not enough to just make a list of our values – we have to live them too. We have to think about how to encapsulate those values in behaviours. You'll be doing this with a lot of your values.

Family togetherness is a value for me so I made sure that we all ate together at the table (without TV) at least three times a week while my children were growing up and I tried to make it a positive time, i.e. I didn't raise problems there.

How do you currently live out these values in your family life?

. . . .

. . . .

. . . .

---

[19] *7 Habits of Highly Effective Families*, 1998

How to pass on values

Sometimes children may seem to be resisting or rebelling against our values in the moment. We need to take a long-term view – values are developed over time. (Sometimes it can feel like a long time!) To begin with, children do things in order to please us and then they often go through a stage when they seem to be resisting our values. Maybe you're experiencing that now? As they get older they are increasingly influenced by their peers but family remains a very strong influence. Children also pick up values from the media, especially around violence, commercialism, body image and attitudes toward sex, so we need to monitor what they are exposed to and make sure they get moderating messages. Our experience, derived from years of working with families, is that children who fiercely resist a rule in the moment often end up adopting the underlying value for themselves.

My now adult son mentioned the other day that he was glad we'd had a rule at home of only drinking milk or water at meals as he had developed healthy habits of drinking lots of water. As I recall there were some objections at the time – he had always wanted cordial or juice.

Jane's son Ned, having always fought against lists, checking, preparing the night before etc with much energy and volume in his primary school years, recently started secondary school and proudly told her about his new approach, which included making lists, getting everything ready the night before and checking in the morning!

Children will adopt the values we want for them if:

We are clear about what that value is

Work out what you believe in and what you want to happen.

Example 1: I don't want my children to whine when there's a problem but to look for solutions. (Value: resourcefulness)

Example 2: I want my child to not swear, at least not in front of me or other adults (Value: respect for others)

We talk about it often, in a positive context

It doesn't work to just point it out when they've done the wrong thing. Example 1: *"I hate it when you whine like that"*; and 2: *"don't you dare swear at me young lady"*. Lecturing and nagging only serve to alienate. Kids stop listening. Say what you *do* want to happen and descriptively praise when it does happen. Example 1: *"Could you please speak in a strong voice?" "Thank you for asking me in your normal voice."* Example 2: *"I want you to tell me how you feel without using those words."* Also comment favourably when others exhibit the value we want – 1. *"Jamie didn't just moan at his mum when she couldn't take him to the football on Saturday but he thought of who else could give him a lift."* 2. *"That was nice manners."*

Reinforcing the value shown by the behaviour is a key learning tool. When you see on the news that someone has made a long solo sailing voyage perhaps talk about the courage and tenacity that takes. When you're watching a David Attenborough documentary on TV allude to his curiosity, which sparked his quest for knowledge about the natural world. You might refer to people who've done well in business for their entrepreneurial skills or philanthropic endeavours like Richard Branson or Bill Gates. Or you might talk about people who've led the way in causes you believe in like Rosa Parkes.

Talk explicitly about your values. Why does it matter to you to show respect for another person's culture, opinions or feelings? Does good sportsmanship matter to you? What does it look like? You can start discussions by reference to what's on TV or in the press or in the books they're reading. Many children's books address moral dilemmas well. Family conversation starter cards can be great for stimulating interesting conversations and children of a very young age are capable of considering moral issues. They have a very heightened sense of what's fair in their own world and can be encouraged to think about this in a wider context. What are your values around the rights of women, workers, refugees, people with atypical sexual orientation, etc?

When you make decisions you'll do so by reference to your values. Be aware of that and articulate it for your kids. For example: *I told my children a story about when I was a teenager and applying for a Saturday job in a shop. I got talking to another girl while we were waiting for the interview and learnt that her father had been made redundant and her mother was ill. I was just looking for a little extra pocket money and some work experience but she really needed this job to support her family. So I went into the interview and asked them to give her the job.* This makes me feel as if I'm blowing my own trumpet but it's how kids learn about values in action, in this case the value that we should look after those in need when we can. (See Chapter 12 for more on this.)

When your child is making decisions himself help him to reference the family values by asking questions, not moralising. For example: *"Given that you said you'd go to Sharon's party how do you think she'd feel if you then pulled out to go to Darcy's sleepover?" "How would you feel about yourself if you let the choir down? You know they need girls' voices."*

Being able to understand and to care about someone else's feelings is at the heart of all these values. This is why it is so important to cultivate an atmosphere of compassion at home through emotion coaching.

We model it ourselves

Talk out loud about how you're looking for solutions and don't moan, complain or swear in front of the children.

Children form assessments of what's important on the basis of what we do rather than what we say… Bad luck!

So it will not ring true if we say to our children that they should be kind and non-judgmental but then they hear us passing judgment on our friends and relations. Our children learn that what we pay attention to is what matters and what we let go by doesn't matter.

Have a look at this YouTube video clip, Children see children do: http://www.youtube.com/watch?v=KHi2dxSf9hw. The link is on our website (www.theparentpractice.com/book-resources#chapter-5).

A woman came to Gandhi and asked him to tell her overweight son to stop eating sugar. She knew he would listen to this great man whom he worshipped.

"Madam," he replied, "Come back in two weeks' time."

Surprised at the request, she nevertheless returned with her son two weeks later.

Gandhi looked at the boy and said, "Stop eating sugar."

When the boy had left the room, the mother turned to Gandhi and asked why he hadn't said this two weeks ago.

Gandhi replied, "Madam, two weeks ago I myself was eating sugar."

Modelling is a very important part of parenting but children don't always adopt their parents' values just by observing them setting a good example. I have always eaten my vegetables but my children were reluctant when they were little. We need some additional proactive tools.

We require it of them

1. *When they do moan, empathise about the problem and then ask them to speak in a proper voice and offer to help them come up with some solutions – maybe refer back to a solution they used previously. Example: Child: "I hate carrying my stupid heavy school bag." Parent: "Sounds like you'd like your load to be lighter. What would make it easier? To leave some things at school in your locker?"*

2. *Once they're calm require them to rephrase without swearing.*

Rules help families make clear what behaviour is expected of everyone and they need to be upheld consistently. We know this is easier said than done but when you're clear about the reasons for the rule and committed to the value behind it, it becomes easier to follow through. My guess is when your children were toddlers you insisted on them holding your hand to cross the road even if they objected. This is because you were clear why you had that rule – their safety was at issue. If you are just as clear about other underlying values you may find it easier to be consistent about rules to do with manners, doing homework, sibling interactions, etc.

Example: If it is a value for you that all family members make a contribution to the family and you believe that children's self-esteem is assisted by contributing (and you don't want to be regarded as a servant) then everyone has individual responsibilities or chores. (See Chapter 13.)

Stages in learning values

You probably want your children to do what they're being asked just because it is the right thing to do and not because they will get praise or a reward for that behaviour. Well, for that to happen kids need to *believe* that it is the right thing to do. That doesn't happen overnight just because we wish it or because we tell them so! It comes about because of parental modelling and consistent upholding of rules and by giving attention and approval. Children progress through various stages in acquiring values. The *end* of this process is when he is doing something because he believes it is 'the right thing to do'.

1. Children learn by copying
2. They do what's required to get parental approval (provided parental approval is forthcoming)
3. Over time the behaviour becomes a habit
4. Eventually they internalise the value, i.e. they think this is the 'right thing to do'

At first we need to be modelling the desired behaviours and to be noticing and descriptively praising the first signs of those behaviours in the children.

Rules

Rules should feel more like a scaffold which supports than a vice which grips.

– Penny Marr

Why do we need them?

Children need boundaries and limits to keep them safe and teach them lessons for life.

A safe, secure and predictable environment provides the best conditions in which to bring up children with good self-esteem. Children don't need to keep testing boundaries when they feel secure. When we live with chaos we feel out of control, which is stressful and takes a lot of energy. The presence of stress chemicals inhibits the development of the frontal lobes – essential for self-control, rational thought and development of judgment and perspective. External structure provides the conditions under which the brain matures.

My own experience is that when we put in place more structure at home my children really flourished and I became calmer.

We have expectations of how we want our children to behave – it seems only fair to make our expectations clear to them rather than just telling them off when they fail to meet them. Knowing where the boundaries are is much less stressful than not being sure what's ok and what's not. If children consistently misbehave people, including their parents, don't enjoy being with them and often criticise, which is not good for the child's self-esteem.

In order for children to win approval they need to follow the codes of behaviour whether of the family unit or society at large. This is not to say that we want to raise mindless automatons – we want our children to be able to have opinions and express them – and we also want them to be able to function well in a community.

We adults need to use our experience and sense of perspective and our more mature frontal lobes to set the boundaries or children may well choose to go to bed whenever they like, eat as many sweets as they choose, or play computer games beyond levels we think are healthy and they would probably never do homework or make a bed and would thus miss out on forming good habits in childhood which would stand them in good stead in adult life.

In real life…

As you go about everyday activities, discuss with your children what rules apply and how these rules help (or don't help?!) make the activity work.

For example: *on the way to school, what might happen*

if cars could park anywhere, or didn't have to stop at pedestrian crossings?

Or: *at a sports match, how do the rules keep the game going, and make it fun? When playing a game at home, why does it make sense to take turns, and have limits?*

Misgivings about rules

Maybe you don't like rules. You may feel they will break a child's spirit or crush spontaneity and creativity. Kids have plenty of rules at school and many parents want the home environment to be more relaxed. This can be particularly true for working parents or separated parents who don't have much time with their children and who want the time they do have to be free of conflict. The biggest worry for many is that they won't be able to follow through. This assumes that children will break the rules and that parents will be faced with having to ignore or punish so they decide not to make a rule in the first place! Luckily with the right prep kids mostly do follow rules and when they don't we have effective non-punitive responses that I think you'll be ok with. (See Chapter 6.)

Most people develop these negative associations with rules because their enforcement is generally punitive and rules have become associated with anger, criticism, blame and punishment. If you think about our experience of rules in the wider world they're usually expressed in negative terms – *don't walk on the grass* – and our attention is only drawn to most rules when we've broken them. If you're parked neatly, parallel to the kerb and within the park space and for the allotted time you don't find a little note on your windscreen commending you on your civic-mindedness. But if you overstay at a meter by even a few minutes (in London at least) you will get a reprimand in the form of a ticket.

But rules don't have to be negative.

Negativity isn't intrinsic to rules. They can be positive, provided

☐ they are reasonable for that child, given their stage of development

☐ there is some input from the child

☐ the rule is framed in positive language

☐ the follow through is positive

So what makes a good rule?

The content of a rule should be for the good of the child (example: healthy eating choices or bedtimes or electronic gadget limits) or for the harmony of the household (household chores, ways of speaking to each other or resolving conflicts) rather than just something the parent wants (a *House & Garden*-standard living room).

Is there an area of your family life that isn't going smoothly at the moment? Consider whether you need a rule for it. *Example: do the kids always fight over TV programmes or where they sit in the car or is your son speaking to you in disrespectful ways or does your daughter keep leaving her homework till the last minute and then having a major panic the night before it's due?*

The restrictiveness of the rule should be minimised. *Example: tidy up the living room after use*, rather than *don't ever sit on the pristinely white sofa*.

If you are unclear whether you want a rule about something, such as keeping a tidy bedroom, ask yourself the following questions:

Is this a reasonable rule? Does it conflict with my child's basic needs, drives or tendencies? Is it consistent with their developmental stage or temperament? Is the rule likely to lead to conflict?

If the rule is about preventing a young child from making noise, moving around or expressing an emotion or an opinion, it's not going to help. In fact, it's going to make the situation worse. A rule like *you must love your sister* is unrealistic and unenforceable.

If I knew my child would comply without argument what would I ask her to do here? Often we are woolly about rules because we anticipate resistance to them and we convince ourselves that it isn't something we really mind about. Remember to ask yourself **if such a rule is reasonable for** *this* **child?**

Child's input. Rules will seem a lot less controlling if the child has contributed to the arrangement. The level of contribution will depend on the child's age of course. *Would you like to brush your teeth in the bathroom or the kitchen, before you put your shoes on or afterwards?* Getting your children's input makes it more likely they will accept the arrangement and it gets them used to problem-solving. *Now that we have a new puppy we will all need to take a share in looking after him. What jobs do you think will need to be done? Who is going to do each job?* (This conversation is best had during the exciting phase when the puppy is new and very cute.)

Start small. When we start with rules it's often tempting to spotlight the typical hot spots of bedtime, homework, screens, self-care, tidying up, mealtimes, etc. These areas do benefit from rules and routines but it can be better to start with less troublesome areas first. You can add more rules into other areas as you experience success with the first set.

They may not like it. Even if the rule is reasonable and for the benefit of your child, it's still to be expected that your child will not like the rule sometimes. You can explain the purpose of the rule once, and thereafter empathise that they wish it were otherwise. Use your emotion coaching skills to help the child learn to deal with disappointment, frustration and feeling powerless.

Do remember, **there is no one correct set of rules**. If that were so, you would have been given a rule book when you left the hospital with your baby. Every family has its own set of values. Some families will have absolute prohibitions on jumping on sofas and others won't allow sleepovers. Some families are relaxed about 'cheeky' language and table manners. Some families have strict rules about when and how homework is done and some will allow electronic gadgets in the bedroom. Others require their children to take a share of household responsibilities. This chapter is about helping you set your own rules and make them work.

How do I set them up?

Parents discuss FIRST

Start by discussing with the other parent what the rules should be and then include anyone else involved in the care of your children.

Presenting a united front (even when there are differences between you) is important as children are quick to detect and exploit any lack of consistency between parents. It may involve some compromise if parents find there are some points of disagreement between them but presenting a united front is more important than the actual content of the rule. If parents do not support each other with the enforcement of the rules it not only undermines the other parent's authority but it teaches the child you're not really serious about that rule. So take steps to bolster your united front – reinstate date night.

If you're not together with your child's other parent still try to achieve as much consensus as possible for the sake of the children. I know this can sometimes be difficult so don't worry if you end up with different sets of rules in different households. Children can cope with that. Just make sure you are consistent within your own household. If your child says *"we don't have to do that at Daddy's"* resist the temptation to give your opinion on Daddy's parenting methods and just say *"I'm glad you know what the rules are in each house."*

THEN involve the children
Sit down with the children and ask them – what are the rules here? Not what would they *like* them to be, but what *are* the rules or what *should* they be? Explain your values and what the goals are, such as harmony and good sharing of common resources, and ask them (according to age) for input on achieving this goal.

Children often know the rules even if they are not following them. They don't follow them because nothing much happens when they do, and nothing much happens when they don't... except scolding, which comes to be accepted as part of being a child and therefore loses effectiveness.

Conventional rules tend to be about what children can't do, and what they find hard, and they tend to be imposed on children without any input from them. Most are accompanied by the threat of what will happen when they are broken rather than when they are followed. No wonder rules seem negative and punitive.

But when children get to discuss the rules, and the rules include things they *can* do, they begin to see rules as things that will help them, rather than hold them back and frustrate them. This means they are more likely to take ownership of the rules.

NEXT record the rules
The rules are now more real because they've been verbalised, and made explicit. Writing them down helps clarify them further.

☺ When the rules are recorded clearly, in words and/ or pictures or photos, everyone will find it easier to remember.

☺ Having them in writing de-personalises them – it's not just the whim of a parent – it's the RULE, which has been thoughtfully considered. In developed societies the written word is respected so writing things down gives it extra credibility.

☺ The children can refer to the rules, rather than relying on us to ~~remind~~ nag them, which helps them develop independence. Get into the habit of referring the child to the rules rather than repeating what needs to be done. Take photos of a tidy room and say let's make it like that.

☺ We can refer to the rules to avoid making up what needs to happen on the spot, and to remind us to descriptively praise – what rules are the children following? (For some examples of DP prompts we made for my son see the website (www.theparentpractice.com/book-resources#chapter-5).)

☺ When the children write them down and decorate them, or take photos of themselves carrying out the rules, the rules become THEIR rules. And that means the rules are no longer YOUR rules which you make them follow.

Effectively, they are now rules for the family – which means you need to follow them too! Of course, there may be some differentiation within the family as to the actual detail of the rule but it should be a rule of general application that all family members get enough sleep – it's just that 4 year olds need more than 40 year olds!

Then be prepared to UPHOLD the rules... consistently
This means noticing when the children are following a rule and commenting on it, as well as taking action when they

don't get it right. Let's look at why we are inconsistent even though we all know it's unhelpful.

☺ **It takes effort to uphold rules.** Sometimes we have to get up from what we're doing (and we're not just pottering on Facebook – we might be dealing with another child's important issues) and go to the child to turn off the Xbox or redirect them from the chocolate biscuits. We have to make a stand about the way they talk to their father or their sibling. We have to support them to use their manners and do their homework. And it's every day... many times a day.

We need to make sure we have the energy for this challenging part of parenting by replenishing our own resources routinely.

☺ **We need clarity about our values.** Have you ever wondered when your child is having a meltdown about your screen rules why you have this rule in the first place? Especially if all the other parents seem to allow their sons to play Grand Theft Auto. Knowing the answer to that question makes upholding your rules much easier.

☺ **We may not feel able to deal with the upset** that results when we say No or insist that they go to bed. It takes so much time. Practise your emotion coaching skills so that you can acknowledge when your children don't like something you're insisting upon. All of the skills take time initially until we get proficient with them. But in my experience time spent using positive skills feels a lot nicer than time spent yelling at the kids. And over time it yields greater rewards.

We had a rule that the boys could have ONE ice-cream a week from the ice-cream man who parks right outside the school. The boys agreed with the rule, it was recorded and I said it could be on any day they chose. One day I collected Constantine earlier than Alexander and the ice-cream van was there. He asked for an ice-cream and I said yes, but reminded him that as it was only Monday, he may have to walk past the van for the rest of the week and asked him how might that feel if he couldn't have another one later in the week, especially if it was hot. He insisted he was OK with this even though his brother might have one on another day, and he couldn't have another. All fine, ice-cream bought, consumed and loved!

The following day, I picked both boys up at the same time and of course, the van was there. Alexander wanted an ice-cream, I said yes and Constantine says he wants one too. As I had suspected this may happen, I was prepared for it so lots of EC, asking him to remind me of the Rules and our conversation the day before, etc. He didn't take this news too well and had a full-on meltdown right outside the school gates, screaming "I want an ice-cream! Give me an ice-cream! He's got one and you won't let me have one..." etc – said how much he hated me, how mean and what a cruel mother I was etc! He was, by this stage, sitting on the pavement outside the school! Of course, to other parents, it must have looked like I was being unfair as his older brother was standing right next to him with an ice-cream! Several parents offered to buy him one, or lend me money to get him one – and I had to be really calm (internally I was screaming!) and say it was OK and thank you for the offer but it's not about the money etc! I used all the skills I could muster at that moment and eventually, he got up and, sobbing, walked to the car! Then lots of DP (slightly through gritted teeth!) that he made it to the car and we came home! Once home, he calmed down, had a snack and then later that evening, we went over it and he then decided that it would be better next time to have his ice-cream when his brother was there so they could do it together.

Victoria, mum of two

☺ We may want to have some flexibility. Flexibility poses an interesting dilemma – one person's adaptability is another person's inconsistency. Rules do evolve as circumstances alter – 12 year olds can stay up later and don't usually have to hold your hand to cross the road, and have to do more homework than 6 year olds. And sometimes a parent will alter a rule as a result of a reasonable argument made by a child – this is fine so long as it is because the parents are convinced of the validity of the points made rather than being worn down by whining. How much negotiation you are willing to enter into will depend partly on the age of the child (more as they approach their teens) and partly on your child's temperament. We know that some kids are very persistent and will take the proverbial mile when you proffer an inch. Children who are not very adaptable need a higher degree of certainty.

☺ Sometimes we just forget. So write them down. Have a pasta jar handy or post-its to help you remember to notice them getting it right.

What should rules look like?

KEEP the rules positive – about what they SHOULD do,

rather than what they must NOT do. For example: a rule at the table may previously have been *don't bring toys or electronics to the table*. A more positive rule would be *put toys in the box or leave electronics in the drop off zone*, which is easier for the child to follow.

Why?

☺ Our brains are not able to visualise negatives. So when rules focus on what we do NOT want – say, children running in the house – our brains concentrate on running... which is the opposite of what we want! A positive phrase conjures up the image of the desired behaviour taking place; a negative phrase conjures up an equally vivid picture of the wrong kind of behaviour taking place. The brain doesn't distinguish between the two. This is why if you tell someone not to think about blue elephants, they will think about blue elephants! After all when you get in a taxi you don't tell the driver where you don't want to go. In short, the rule should give rise to a mental image of whatever it is that you would like to see taking place. So rather than telling children not to run in the house, we phrase it positively – *walk in the house, run outside*.

☺ Having positively phrased rules helps us to re-programme our brains to notice the positive things the children are doing rather than pouncing on the negative ones.

☺ If rules are expressed in a negative way it places a restriction on a child. Children are naturally going to feel annoyed or frustrated or rebellious that they are being told not to do something. Even if you are normally well behaved it may make you feel resentful purely because you have been told not to.

Be SPECIFIC – this is to give clarity about what is expected.

Dropping belongings in the hallway

Elinor drops her belongings in the hallway as she comes home from school each day. This behaviour is frustrating – it makes the hallway look a mess, it means she can never find things the next morning and it means her new coat is getting dirty. When Mum picks up after her she feels resentful and anxious that her daughter is not developing good habits. She wants her coat and her bag hung up on the peg under the stairs, and her shoes put on the rack underneath. This will keep the hallway clear, and she will know exactly where everything is the following morning. And her coat will last longer.

RULE: As soon as Elinor comes in she needs to put her coat and school bag on the peg and shoes on the rack. (Mum needs to make sure she does this with her own belongings!)

REWARD: Notice and descriptively praise what Elinor does right. "You've put your coat on the peg. That shows me you've remembered the rule about what to do when you come in. You've done one of the three things you need to do. I wonder which thing you'll do next? I love it when you're responsible for your own things."

CONSEQUENCE: Nothing else will happen until everything is in the right place. The snack and game are delayed until the coat, bag and shoes are put away.

This structure works if Elinor has forgotten or is not yet in the habit of doing these things. If she is not hanging her coat up etc because she is upset about something, then that will need to be addressed first through emotion coaching.

Bedtime example

Having a rule that a child must go to bed at 7.30pm will have some effect. However, the rule will have MUCH more effect if it is surrounded and supported by the other skills.

When we set up for success, we can have a chat about why our bodies and brains need sleep. We can empathise that she feels she's missing out on something when she goes to bed. We can descriptively praise her for doing any of the different elements of the going to bed routine. We can let her know how much we like the bedtime rituals we share. In the morning we can notice how much energy she has. We can have written or picture reminders of her getting her pjs on and brushing her teeth so that we don't have to nag. And we can spend positive time with her so that all our interactions aren't about telling her what to do!

Rules make it easier for kids to know how to behave but they are a blunt instrument – **they are no substitute for relationship.** No one likes to be controlled but children will be willing to accept your control if the relationship is positive. Otherwise rules, rewards and consequences will just lead to resentment and rebellion. Even if your child has complied with your limits they will not have learnt self-control. Will they still do what's required when you are not there to enforce it?

Rewards

"Rewards and punishments are the lowest form of education."

– Chuang-Tzu

At The Parent Practice we believe there is a place for rewards but that they should be used with caution. When you are aware of the downsides of using rewards you will be able to use them effectively.

How do you feel about rewarding your child? Perhaps you are concerned that today's children are given too many treats and material objects. We worry about giving them any more just to get them to follow the rules. Surely, we ask ourselves, they should just do as they are told? And what's going to happen if we start rewarding them now, how long will this go on for? How will we be able to sustain the inevitable reward inflation to guarantee continued compliance? And, let's be honest, 'rewards' is just a euphemism for 'bribes', isn't it? Also if I offer ice cream for eating broccoli am I giving my child the message that ice cream is intrinsically better than broccoli?

We need to take account of these concerns – because unless we feel comfortable with the idea of rewarding positive behaviour, we will be inconsistent and uncommitted.

☺ **Use rewards mainly *after the event* to acknowledge children's behaviour.**

☺ **Set up some rewards for a finite period.** At first the potential of earning the reward may be the reason for the child behaving well. Then he is encouraged to continue the behaviour because he enjoys the attention and acknowledgment he gets for doing what's required, until it becomes a habit. Over time the child acquires his own set of values and behaves in line with these values. It feels right. (After all, not many 10 year olds are still getting chocolate buttons for peeing in the loo!)

☺ **Always point out the intrinsic benefits of the task** to prevent the reward becoming the only reason for doing something. For example: *"your teeth are shiny and your breath smells fresh and because you're looking* *after your teeth well it's ok to have sweets sometimes."* *"When you've done these fractions you will be more practised and they will be easier." "When your room is tidy you will feel satisfied and will be able to find your things more easily."*

☺ **Offer rewards which are closely related to the task** where possible. So when your child does her reading practice with you point out how lovely it is to read together and say how much you're enjoying the story. Then offer to read another story to her.

☺ **Don't offer rewards for your child's academic or sporting achievements.** The reward for improving in reading is her increased ability to access written material. Point this out to her. The reward for academic tests is the grade achieved as well as the improvement in proficiency. The win in a match is reward in itself. Rewarding outcomes rather than effort makes failure difficult and self-esteem fragile and it feels like parental approval is conditional.

☺ **Use non-material rewards mostly.** See below for some ideas.

☺ **Don't use food as a reward.** This runs the risk of setting up poor eating habits for life. Many adults are emotional eaters where we give ourselves food as a reward or as a comfort.

Bribes

☺ **Parents are often concerned that there is little difference between a bribe and a reward.**

☺ **A bribe is given in advance of the desired behaviour and is designed to influence that behaviour.** The words used are important.

> An example of a bribe is *"IF I let you watch TV now you must do your homework straight afterwards"*.
>
> ☺ Rewards acknowledge the desired behaviour after the event.
>
> ☺ If you say "WHEN you've completed your homework you will have earnt your TV" the language of 'when' vs 'if' is more intentional. There is no suggestion that doing what you've been asked is optional.

Examples of rewards

Below are some examples of possible rewards. This list is by no means exhaustive. The possibilities for potential rewards are limited only by an individual parent's imagination and I have been blown away by what parents come up with.

FIRST reward is always Descriptive Praise

Always descriptively praise your child – be creative and vary the delivery. You can phone grandparents or other relations and praise the child to them within your child's hearing, or accompany descriptive praise with a visual acknowledgment such as a token in a jar (pasta pieces/marbles/pebbles) or put a sticker on their forehead, have a presentation ceremony, slip a note under their pillow or send a postcard (or a text!). Sometimes children need to do things as their contribution to the family and they won't get a conventional reward for that but they should always be acknowledged for it to show that their efforts are appreciated. Your child will always value your approval and as you are using more Descriptive Praise, you may be noticing that it is becoming easier to do.

PRIVILEGES can be earned

It is much better to let the child earn privileges by good

behaviour than take things away for misbehaviour, which will cause resentment.

Children are much more appreciative of their pocket money, screen time, toys, outings, having friends to play, credits for mobile phones, etc if there is a system in place whereby they earn these privileges. Earning things also increases their self-esteem, confidence and motivation. Can you remember how proud you felt as a child when you earnt something through your own efforts?

ADDITIONAL rewards – for any and all ages!

Sometimes what determines whether something is a reward is the way it is presented. For example if you are excited about the idea of going on a walk with them, referring to it as our 'special time' together, and say that it is because they were so good at playing by themselves and not interrupting when you were on the phone that there is now time for a walk with you on their own, they will regard it as a reward. Here are a few ideas – there are many more on our website. (www.theparentpractice.com/book-resources#chapter-5) (For ideas about pocket money see chapter 13.)

- ☺ *Choice of meal – Friday evening, Sunday lunch, weekend breakfast*

- ☺ *Cooking, baking or 'grown-up' meals*

- ☺ *Extra stories or stories in 'special place' e.g. parents' bed*

- ☺ *Change of role – parent does child's jobs (not homework!)*

- ☺ *Pillow fights, rough and tumble, jumping on trampoline with you*

- ☺ *Water bombs/pistols, hosepipes and buckets – in the shower or garden*

- ☺ *Building caves, dens, forts*

- ☺ *Breakfast in bed, indoor picnics – under the table, in a den, in the bath!*

☺ *Outdoor picnics – not just summer – baked potatoes and sausages and wrap up warm!*

☺ *Playing cafés – be waiters, write menus and take orders*

☺ *Back rub, massage – for everyone – gentle stroking for younger children*

☺ *Beauty treatments (manicure, pedicure, facial, hair brushing) – for them and for you*

☺ *Playing traditional board games*

☺ *Home Disco – music, lights, prizes for best costume, silliest dancing*

☺ *Handing over money in shop /going to corner shop on own to buy milk*

☺ *Earn credits/money for mobile, iTunes account*

☺ *Having a lift instead of taking the bus/train*

Your turn

(Complete this here or on the PDF on our website (www. theparentpractice.com/book-resources#chapter-5))

Pick an area of family life that isn't going super smoothly at the moment. What do you want to happen? Discuss this with your partner.

....

....

....

Check your expectations – is it reasonable for your child at his stage of development, given his temperament? If it is what will your rule be?

....

....

· ·

Is it framed positively and is it specific enough? Practise making the following rules positive.

"Don't leave your room in a mess"

· ·

"Don't forget your PE kit"

· ·

"Don't snatch!"

· ·

What will you do when your child follows the rule?

· ·

Family Rules

Rules work so much better when they are generated by the children and they feel ownership.

When my son was around 6 (now 14), before the start of a new academic year, we were talking through the morning routine before school. He said "I have an idea mum. In the mornings you can't talk to me, even look at me, I can't eat or drink or step out of my room until I am fully dressed in my school uniform." As that was his idea and he was so proud of sticking to it, that is what he has got in the habit of doing ever since. Even as a teenager there have been no issues of getting up and ready for school.

Rachel, mother of four

Rules we have for our family...

Work on homework as soon as we get home from school – reward is 15 minutes on the iPad. This links to the value of being self-disciplined/independent/accountable.

Listen to others when they say STOP (for when the boys are play fighting) – reward is Descriptive Praise for that – links to the value of being controlled/considerate/respectful of others.

Joanna, mother of two

Lily got her first pasta-jar reward on Sunday (all day in her pj onesie) and is now filling up her second jar for her second reward – walking our neighbour's dog, which she loves.

Katy, mother of one

We chose a family pillow fight as the reward for filling the pasta jar. Before the jar was full, we had a chat-through about how the pillow fight would work. We agreed how long the fight would last for, what we could do if anyone wanted to stop and what we would do after the fight was over. I'm so pleased we did this – the pillow fight was fabulous! The children LOVED it and so did we. I recommend bashing each other with pillows as an alternative family therapy!

Gail, mum of two

Values, Rules and Rewards in a nutshell

Some values can be encouraged by modelling and by descriptive praise. Others will be captured in specific rules.

Rules are no substitute for relationship. Children may follow rules in order to win a reward or out of fear of a consequence but without all the other skills they will not develop self-discipline.

Rules can and should be positive. They need to be about what kids **can** do, not what they **can't** do.

They need to be:

☺ reasonable for that child, given his temperament and stage of development

☺ not too restrictive

☺ created with input from the child

☺ framed positively

Writing rules down gives clarity and helps consistency.

Rewards are useful but need to be used with caution and should be distinguished from bribes. Use rewards not to entice, but to acknowledge, and point out the intrinsic benefits of that behaviour to the child.

Use non-material, non-food rewards. The best reward is time spent with parents.

Further reading

Madeline Levine, *Teach Your Children Well*, 2012

6

Skill 6: Positive discipline

The object of controlling a child is to foster self-control.
The object of discipline is to foster self-discipline. If
parenting is not accomplishing that then all the rules,
all the consequences, are for naught. You will only foster
rebellion. Or resentment, or just plain pain.

– Dr Debby Schwarz Hirschhorn

Lily, age 6, often wants to have the last say. Her parents end
up negotiating with her about TV or the number of stories at
bedtime, or about whether she's going to do what she's told,
e.g. "I'm only going to do [that] if you do [this]." She tries to
boss her parents around, ordering them to do things for her
or saying "come here, Mummy" in a bossy voice. Her mother,
Katy, feels Lily is often trying to control them, especially when
they're trying to get her to do something she doesn't want to,
like homework or reading. Katy thinks Lily is determined not
to do what she asks, e.g. get in or out the bath or get ready for
bed. She'll just completely ignore her and stare into space, for
example (which really makes her mother see red). She ignores
every calm request, even when Katy points out that there'll be
no time for stories. Then when mum takes the stories away, Lily
cries as if it's all unfair and a big surprise. Her tactic is to then
promise to be good.

Does any of this sound familiar to you? When we
canvassed parents about their top ten issues cooperation was
top of the list. Other parents want to know what to do about

aggressive behaviours, unkind words, damaging property, breaking rules, lying, tantrums or disrespectful behaviour.

One mum reported that her 11-year-old son would shout at her angrily when she arrived a little late at school, "Where were you? You are supposed to be on time. I bet you have also forgotten my snack, as you always forget everything!" And then in the car driving home, "Why on earth are you braking so unexpectedly? I hit my head really hard! You should be careful taking corners, you NEVER pay attention when driving and ALWAYS hit the kerb!"

Parents clearly need to do something about these behaviours, for their children's sake as well as their own. The question is what? Katy clearly felt that what she was trying (and she had tried shouting, telling off, threatening and punishing as well as cajoling and negotiating) wasn't working and other parents may feel that a 'good clip round the ear' could work but that's not the approach they want to take. Nearly every parent I've ever met has said that they'd like to shout less. In fact one of our clients in New York state decided to take what she calls 'a vow of yellibacy': giving herself the goal of dealing with misbehaviour without shouting at her children.

Proactive steps

Our focus so far has been on skills which encourage healthy self-esteem and good behaviour and those proactive, preventative steps are essential, but of course they don't rule out completely the possibility that your children may occasionally get something wrong or behave in a way you don't like… just, maybe. So we do need effective ways of responding to poor behaviour. And when I say 'effective' I mean strategies that aren't just what we're conditioned to use because that's how we were brought up or because everyone says it's the thing to do, but tools that *really* work to teach your child how to behave, even when you're not there.

The main points to remember about positive discipline are:

☺ The best approach is to avoid poor behaviour arising in the first place. We know we can encourage good behaviour by fostering strong self-esteem and a positive relationship between ourselves and our children. Use Descriptive Praise to encourage good self-worth and to reinforce good behaviours. Listen and connect with Emotion Coaching thereby re-directing the feelings that might be expressed in misbehaviour. Set up for Success, including spending positive time with the children and building a strong partnership with their other parent. Use Rules so that expectations are clear.

☺ Take time to understand why your children are doing the things you don't like. Is it because of temperament or their stage of development or could the behaviour be driven by a feeling? In this chapter we look at other reasons why kids do things that push their parents' buttons. By the way it is NEVER because they are inherently evil or just trying to wind you up! All behaviour has a cause.

☺ You need some strategies for responding to poor behaviour that will result in your child learning something without damaging self-esteem (yours or theirs).

You're in the right place.

To be effective in responding to unwanted behaviour parents need to stay calm. This is the holy grail of parenting and the subject of a whole chapter on its own – chapter 7. Dealing with inappropriate behaviour without getting angry is essential if children are going to learn something from the episode. We need to STAY CALM and we also need to TAKE ACTION.

Reasons for misbehaviour

"There's no 'one-size-fits-all' solution for behaviour issues. We have to ask WHY the child is behaving this way. When we miss the WHY, we miss the child."

– Alfie Kohn

I'm going to refer to 'misbehaviour' throughout this chapter for ease of reference but there is no judgment attached to the term and the more we explore the reasons for behaviour the more compassionate we can be. You may be concerned with any behaviour on a spectrum ranging from lying or stealing or truanting from school to getting down from the table without asking or thumb sucking or refusing to look at someone when talking.

Your turn

What behaviours are pushing your buttons or needing your attention right now?

. . . .

. . . .

. . . .

Parenting author Bonnie Harris refers to this as 'mistaken behaviour'.

Instead of 'misbehaviour' which comes with assumptions about 'being bad' and 'on purpose' and all those thoughts that lead us to ineffective reactions, I am coining it "mis(taken) behaviour". We MISTAKE their behaviour as intentional when in fact it is the only thing they CAN do at that moment given whatever they are dealing with. It is in fact only a mistake, not a failure.[20]

All behaviour has a cause. Misbehaviour arises from a need that is not being met. The child is using an inappropriate strategy to meet his needs. So when faced with inappropriate behaviour we need to ask ourselves **what does he need?**

Example: the child who wants a toy and hits another child to get it. He's not wrong to want the toy but he needs to learn a different strategy for getting it. The child who expresses himself through inappropriate language may be trying to provoke a response from parents or calling attention to some need he can't articulate or letting his parents know he is feeling something.

The need will usually not be identified by the child – it may be a need for more structure or positive attention or consistent follow through. A child with aggressive tendencies may need a lot of Emotion Coaching to help his higher brain take control.

If adults just react to behaviour without addressing the underlying cause that need will manifest itself again in some way, at some time. It's a bit like mopping up the floor without fixing the leaking tap.

We're looking at these causes not to 'excuse' the behaviour but to work out the most appropriate way to deal with it.

---

[20] Bonnie Harris, http://bonnieharris.com/misbehavior-mistakenbehavior/

To do with the child

Sometimes it is simple. They're tired, bored, hungry or unwell. Sometimes a behaviour is just what you'd expect for that age, as when a 4 year old squeezes all the toothpaste out of the tube in order to hear it squelch or when a 10 year old wants to be on the iPad all the time. Sometimes the behaviour is as a result of temperamental traits. Impulsive children find it very difficult to slow down and think before acting. Introverts may want time to themselves but they're required to be in company. They don't mean to be rude and they're not anti-social.

At other times it's not so obvious but just considering the possible reasons for a behaviour already puts you into a calmer, more compassionate mind-set and you will be more effective.

They ~~want~~ need attention

Children have evolved to seek attention and they can learn that it is easier to get attention for negative behaviour than for positive behaviour, because we usually pay more attention when they are behaving badly than when they are behaving well.

They're full of emotions

Children can have quite intense feelings and swing between them. Many inappropriate behaviours have at their root anger, disappointment, frustration, inadequacy, jealousy, feeling out of control, overwhelm, disempowerment, isolation, confusion, loss, etc.

Fergus, aged 8, was aggressive with his grandmother, brandishing scissors in a dangerous way and he threw an apple core at her. It turned out he'd felt very left out at art summer camp; it hadn't been where he expected it to be and the friends he thought would be there were not. He had felt lonely and disappointed and his feelings came out when he got home.

Acknowledging and articulating the feeling helps the child feel heard and understood which helps improve behaviour.

They're living in the moment
Children have a very different tempo to adults. They can get absorbed or find it difficult to wait and don't seem to have any sense of urgency. For example: *They are fixated on finishing their Lego creation while you want them to get dressed.* When adults are faced with the pressure of a deadline we can end up nagging and shouting and threatening our children.

They're immature
Their undeveloped frontal lobes and lack of experience mean they are usually impulsive, forgetful, have poor self-control and lack judgment. They find it hard to know how to manage their feelings and delayed gratification is difficult for them. For example: *running indoors, interrupting, you are guests at a friend's house and a plate of biscuits arrives which they snatch, you ask them to find a shoe and they come across a really interesting comic, they rip the head off Action Man to see what's inside, they throw objects from a height for the fun of seeing them disintegrate and without regard to what may happen to anything underneath.*

They have a different agenda
They have their own priorities and they want to do what they want to do. Their agenda is just as important to them as yours is to you. *You want to get out of the house on time with everyone dressed and breakfasted and with all relevant kit. They want to read a book, play with a toy, save their hero from the monster or daydream.*

It is natural for children to want to have some power in their lives. They resist doing what they are required to do because they would rather be doing something else and/or because they don't like feeling controlled. For example: *you may get defiance from a child asked to clean up his toys when*

*it's time for dinner because he would simply rather continue
playing and he has been told what to do all day.* Being
sympathetic to his wish to continue with his game
lessens his resistance. Children need empathy for finding
tasks difficult, boring or not what they really want to do. Give
him power whenever appropriate. Invite his input whenever
you can. Our aim is to motivate children to want to do
what we are asking because of our positive relationship and
because it earns attention and approval.

*One mum found that her son became less reluctant to do
homework when he had some choice about where and how it
was done. She had to bite her tongue when he opted to do it
lying on his tummy on the living room rug but the work was ok
and there was no battle.*

They don't understand

Sometimes children don't understand what's expected of them
or they might think the task is too difficult for them. Sometimes
we assume that our kids know what's expected of them without
spelling it out and they don't actually understand either what
to do or how to do it. There may be too many instructions at
once. Up to the age of 6, a child can only hold 1 or 2 pieces of
information in short-term memory and they can't manage
more than 4 or 5 items until well into their teens. So *"go upstairs,
brush your teeth and hair, make your bed and don't forget to bring
down your library book and your trainers for gym, etc"* which can
be 8 or more instructions, is doomed. You'll probably find your
child sitting half way up the stairs having forgotten why he's
there. If a child does a job poorly it may be that he simply hasn't
appreciated the detail required for the task or he's forgotten
elements of it.

They identify as 'the naughty one'

A child may be used to thinking of himself as 'the naughty

one'. He may feel it is impossible to get approval for doing the right thing and so determines to be 'good at' doing the wrong thing. This takes time to shift. In order not to develop such thinking it is very important to avoid labels such as 'naughty' and to give lots of descriptive praise, particularly for cooperation.

One of the reasons the 'naughty step' or 'naughty corner' doesn't work is because it becomes a self-fulfilling prophecy – if a child believes he is naughty then he will behave that way. Children don't want to be naughty; they want to be good.

Your turn

Can you see any possible reason for the behaviour that you identified above?

....

....

....

Things parents do

Steel yourself for this bit.

Parental habits greatly influence children's habits and there are some things that parents do in response to children's behaviour that actually contribute to poor behaviour next time round.

We get more of what we pay attention to

When we focus on what they're getting wrong and we criticise, children's self-esteem is reduced. When a child feels badly about himself he behaves badly. He may be rude or uncooperative or unkind to others. If he is frequently punished he may feel resentful or rebellious and retaliate with more poor behaviour.

Sometimes misbehaving may seem like fun – it often gets a 'good' reaction. Many kids get hooked on the drama associated with misbehaviour. They like to provoke an explosion from the parent. We need to make sure we respond calmly to misbehaviour and give enough attention to good behaviour.

We don't spend enough time doing positive things as a family

The average British family spends about 49 minutes a day together. Nearly half of all parents questioned for a poll for National Family Week felt it was not enough and more than 1 in 5 children complain that they don't spend enough time with either of their parents.[21] Ouch! Many families find that the time they do have together isn't really positive time but more about getting stuff done.

Katy was surprised by Lily's very clingy behaviour after a school play when she refused to go back to the classroom with her teacher. She clung to her mother and made a big scene. Later that day, just as she was going to sleep, she suddenly said: "Why aren't parents allowed in the school with the children?" After some gentle probing on Katy's part, it came out that she felt there was never any time to see her parents because there was hardly any time after school. Bath time came round so quickly and then she was supposed to go to sleep, and then it was time to go back to school the next day!

It's so important that parents schedule some time to do fun things with the children that maybe other activities have to go.

If children feel disconnected from us they will not want to do what we want them to do. They may feel disconnected because such time as they have with us may have become about directions and criticism.

---

[21] The *Independent*, 30 May 2010

We ask too much or not at all

Or at the wrong time! An instruction might also be framed in non-authoritative language, or we may be giving too many instructions which ends up as nagging which children quickly learn to tune out. If we ask our kids to do things over and over we train them to pay attention only when we've asked them to do something multiple times.

If a child feels he is being bossed around all day he may feel powerless, which can lead to battles for power. The child may want to exercise control by refusing to comply and provoking parents into losing control.

We're inconsistent

Sometimes we follow through on a rule and sometimes we don't. Sometimes we remain firm and sometimes we give in. Adults often give in when behaviour escalates, the whingeing gets more persistent or the crying or shouting louder. If the parent gives in when behaviour gets worse the child learns to keep the behaviour going.

We model poor behaviour

Finally, we need to be careful that we model the behaviours we want to see in our children – after all, people in glass houses can't throw stones! We need to put our own house in order, and make sure we're not moaning or complaining, or swearing or shouting, if that is how we expect our children to behave. We need to model resolving conflict without bullying, keeping our tempers or taking constructive steps to manage our feelings when upset, having positive/can-do attitudes, exhibiting good table manners, treating others with respect, etc.

For a bit of light relief have a look at this video clip from the film *Kramer vs Kramer* on YouTube http://www.youtube.com/watch?v=5G_w8SI-cu0. (The link is also on our website, www.theparentpractice.com/book-resources#chapter-6 page.)

Your turn

Can you be brave and identify some behaviours of your own that contribute to your children's poor behaviour?

....

....

....

The outside world

It's not all our fault. There are some aspects of 21st-century living and influences outside the home that can encourage behaviour we don't want. Parents need to be aware of these and take steps to mitigate their effect.

Some behaviours are influenced by:

- ☐ **peer group** – As children get older they are more influenced by their peers and some behaviours are picked up from others

- ☐ **school** – School is a big part of children's lives and poor behaviour is often the result of feeling unsuccessful or unhappy at school either academically or socially

- ☐ **media** – This can be a big influence, especially violence and bad or disrespectful language, high consumerism, early sexualisation, negative body image, bullying attitudes and a quick fix/'I can have it now' mentality. A lot of time on social media can also contribute to lower self-esteem

- ☐ **diet** – Most parents are aware of the need for children to get a good variety of healthy food for the sake of their physical health. But what we eat affects behaviour too of course. Sugar, caffeine and many additives can have the effect of hyping up children's behaviour. One mum said she had to stop her husband from drinking coke because of the effect on him!

☐ **sleep** – Although experts suggest that primary school children require 10-12 hours' sleep a night, many get significantly less.

In a study of children aged between 10 and 12, children told to sleep 40 minutes less for several nights were then tested for memory, reaction times and attention and found to be the equivalent of two years behind their classmates, who got 35 minutes more sleep a night than usual.[22]

☐ **time in front of a screen** – While computers and other digital devices are very much part of our lives and can be an amazing resource, if children spend too much time in front of a screen this can result in tetchiness, a lack of exercise and fresh air, not enough time for other activities, including 'actual' socialising with others. Time on a screen in the evening can also interfere with sleep. (See chapter 11.)

☐ **not enough time in nature** – Richard Louv has coined the phrase Nature Deficit Disorder and says *"This has implications for a wide range of health issues, including ADHD, child obesity, stress, creativity and cognitive functioning."*[23] It also affects the pace at which lives are led, the loss of practical skills and an appreciation of our natural world.

What we can do

You can breathe easy now. Here are the tools you need to respond effectively to behaviour you don't like. How I wish

---

[22] Reported in *The Times*, 29 September 2012
[23] *The Nature Principle: Human Restoration and the End of Nature-Deficit Disorder*, Algonquin Books; Reprint edition 2013 and *Last Child in The Woods: Saving Our Children from Nature-deficit Disorder*, Atlantic Books 2010

I'd had all of these in my tool basket when my kids were younger! In this section I'm going to outline an approach to teaching kids how to behave that will be foreign to many readers. It will feel strange and you might think *but surely not!* A parent in one of our classes admitted that she hadn't thought these techniques would 'be enough' but was amazed when they worked. Do question the ideas but keep your mind open. If you raced ahead to this chapter go back and read the first few skills – you'll need them to make these ideas work.

There will have been times when you have disciplined your children in ways that were effective to teach them and other times when you've used ways that you know just didn't work! I will be advocating an approach here that might be quite different from some of the methods you've used before. If these ideas resonate with you please do adopt them but don't beat yourself up for having done it differently previously.

Positive discipline

"Misbehaviour and punishment are not opposites that cancel each other – on the contrary they breed and reinforce each other."

– Haim Ginott

When we hear an adult say *"what that child needs is some discipline"* we don't usually assume they mean that the child needs understanding and some coaching in problem-solving techniques; we would guess that the speaker was advocating punishment. The fact that we even need to put the word 'positive' in front of 'discipline' suggests that otherwise we'd conclude that we're talking about something negative.

In fact the word discipline means teaching, and if our discipline techniques don't result in some learning for our children then they've failed.

"If you get to punishment you've already failed."
– Camila Batmanghelidjh

When our children do something we don't like we need to regard it as a 'teachable moment'. We are our children's teachers and our role is to educate them. Discipline is different from punishment in several ways.

Discipline	Punishment
Involves problem-solving	Involves something that hurts
Delivered calmly	Delivered in anger
Purpose: to teach, to help child behave differently next time	Purpose: to be right, child is wrong, to get revenge
Goal is self-discipline	Goal is obedience
Based on respect	Based on fear, humiliation
Leads to improved behaviour and self-discipline	Results in resentment, rebelliousness, furtiveness and loss of self-esteem

Parents sometimes tell me they need to make the child feel bad in order to teach them that what they did was wrong. They may try to distinguish the behaviour from the child – the behaviour is what is unacceptable, not the child. In theory this should preserve the child's self-esteem but unfortunately it doesn't work that way because the *child* doesn't distinguish between himself and his behaviour. If he hears that something is bad or wrong or naughty he will think that *he* is bad, wrong and naughty. When a child feels badly about himself, he is not only unhappy but he doesn't behave well either.

Children can be made to stop behaving in a particular way through fear but at great cost to the relationship with the parent. And no real learning takes place when a child is afraid, feeling resentful or when their self-esteem has been diminished.

Positive discipline recognises that children will get things wrong because they are young and learning and that it is a parent's job to provide a framework and an atmosphere that helps the child to learn.

It can help to think about the child's motives – what did they mean to happen? Did they realise how others would feel? Are they developmentally able to consider others' feelings? If we understand that their intention is reasonable but their understanding of the circumstances limited, it is easier for us to respond appropriately.

Smacking

Without judging parents who lose it and smack occasionally, especially when it is done out of fear, such as when a small child dashes across the road, it is important to recognise that smacking is ineffective in the long term and sends the child very mixed messages. There are more positive ways to achieve the same result without the cost to the relationship between parent and child and without the long-term difficulties.

Studies[24] have shown that smacking leads to:

- ☐ Increased aggression in childhood and adulthood
- ☐ Less capacity for empathy
- ☐ Less ability to develop his own sense of right and wrong

---

[24] The Report of the Commission on Children and Violence 1995

☐ Increased probability of antisocial and criminal behaviour

☐ Increased susceptibility to mental health problems

Parents tend to smack when we have lost it, and our children are aware of this, so smacking signals our loss of control. Smacking does not teach children to behave better, nor why the behaviour is inappropriate and how they could behave differently. Smacking often stops the action only while the punisher is present and teaches the child to be furtive. He does not learn self-discipline.

Smacking also sends very confused messages to the child. When we smack, the child gets the message that smacking is ok and yet we are trying to teach our children not to smack others. If he thinks that it is not ok for *him* to smack but it is ok for adults to smack, this is a dangerous message to give. He will think that it is ok for him to use physical power to get what he wants in adulthood.

Of course there is much controversy around this issue and many will have different opinions, often based on their own childhood experiences. I am not an advocate of the criminalisation of smacking but a firm proponent of educating parents about other, more effective ways to teach a child to behave.

"When a child hits a child, we call it aggression.
When a child hits an adult, we call it hostility.
When an adult hits an adult, we call it assault.
When an adult hits a child, we call it discipline."

– Haim Ginott

Use, not abuse, of parental power

When we discipline we are teaching our children how to negotiate with the world. We may inadvertently teach our children to be bullies if we use our greater power to coerce them into doing what we want. Do we want them to learn to get their way by using force or manipulation? Instead don't we want to teach them to try to understand, use their words to negotiate and to problem-solve?

We always say to parents **don't pick your battles**. Don't use the language of battles at all. Battles are between enemies and the outcome is a win/lose one. Change this to a win/win model. This is what you get when you negotiate solutions.

The power of influence is greater than the influence of power.

– Michael Grinder.

Power is short term and focuses on the issue before you – *how do I get my child to pick up her toys?* It is result oriented. We want change to happen now.

Influence is long term and it focuses on the relationship – *how do I get my child to want to do the right thing?* It is more process oriented. We know that change will happen over time.

Adults do need to be in charge because we have greater experience, perspective and more mature frontal lobes. But if we are over-controlling we will create resentment and resistance. As with so many aspects of parenting it's a question of balance. If you're reading this book you're probably thinking a lot about how you want to parent. Be a boundary, not a bulldozer. Allow liberty, not licence.

Author and lecturer Alfie Kohn[25] emphasises that parents should always ask themselves the question, are we doing what we're doing in order to help the child or just to get them to obey? He thinks that many people adopt a controlling approach because of a mistaken view that the alternative to control is permissiveness. This is pendulum thinking. I found myself doing this when Christian was behaving badly as a little boy. I would try a positive approach and then conclude that it hadn't worked as he was misbehaving and so would come down hard on him with punishment. I'd then feel remorseful and try the softer approach again. Success came when I discovered that **I could be positive and firm at the same time.**

Parents find themselves on a spectrum between 'controlling or authoritarian' on the one end and 'permissive' on the other. Somewhere in between is the authoritative parent. This parent is in charge but is not over-controlling. The child has input but isn't ruling the roost. Being in charge doesn't mean the parent always has their way.

If we over-control our children the danger is that we may:

☐ Provoke rebellion as they feel manipulated and nagged

☐ Create dependency on us. They don't learn to think for themselves and they don't develop responsibility

☐ Create docility

Parenting works best when it is about encouraging, not forcing. If you want to raise a child to be an adult who can speak up for her own needs, solve problems and sometimes question authority then use the following discipline methods.

---

[25] *Punished by Rewards*

Strategies

What to do when something goes wrong

- ☐ Cool down
- ☐ Connect
- ☐ Constructive steps

Take cool down time

When there is misbehaviour, sometimes the adult needs to take immediate action to prevent harm to people or property. Then the child (and the parent!) will usually need to take time to calm down. This may take just few minutes or even a few hours, depending on what has happened and the strength of the emotions.

One mum needed to wait until the next morning to deal with her son (he had sensibly gone to bed) after he drew on the new carpet with marker pens!

It's a vital step to take before we turn to problem-solving. If we try to deal with the behaviour when we're upset we will be ineffective and may actually do damage. Cool Down Time is NOT a punishment but a chance to calm down. Very often a 'time out' involves sending a child to his room with the admonition to "*think about what you've done*". I can guarantee that all your child is thinking about is how mean you are. If you've been using time outs as a punishment then be sure to distinguish Cool Down from time outs. This will be credible if you take some time to calm down yourself. Cool Down Time doesn't have to be in isolation (don't withdraw if your child needs you) and doesn't need to be uncomfortable. Let your child know that you will address the misbehaviour later (not too much later for young children) once everyone has cooled down. Explain that this is because you can't deal with things effectively when you're upset.

Connect

Describe the feelings that were behind the behaviour and how you think she is feeling now. Assume that she will be feeling remorseful. Children usually do when they understand that something was wrong if they are not faced with judgment and blame and anger.

Christian would not take responsibility or show contrition while adults were shouting at him. He would lie, make excuses and blame others, refusing to look at his accuser. But when we took a non-judgmental approach and took steps to improve his self-esteem he was able to accept responsibility.

The adults need to bring the emotional temperature down and connect before the child's frontal lobes will be engaged for learning.

Constructive steps

When something has gone wrong our aim is to work out how to avoid it happening again and learn something from the episode. Our job is to teach our children and to support them to do better next time. When we only have punishment to deal with misbehaviour, parents sometimes feel reluctant to act – which means we hesitate, or try to ignore it, and then feel compelled to do something in a panic.

Here are three constructive approaches to misbehaviour: The Mistakes Process, Consequences and Problem-solving.

First of all assume that your child wants to get things right and has made a mistake. That doesn't mean that there wasn't some element of intentionality about his actions. But what was his intention? *Did he think that by putting his brother down and calling him names he would feel better about himself? Did she not know what to do with her feelings of overwhelm at the party? Was he angry that he had no say in the decision to move house and the consequent change of school?* They need to be shown another way to get what they need. We need to tell children why it is important that they pick their clothes up off the floor and why they cannot hurt someone else.

The Mistakes Process

Getting it wrong

All human beings make mistakes. How we deal with them is what is important. If we can accept that and not beat ourselves up about it when we slip up, it leaves us able to deal with the mistake more effectively. I have learnt more from my Low Parenting Moments than from when things go smoothly. We want to teach our children to take responsibility for their actions, to forgive themselves and to learn something from the experience.

What is a mistake?

A mistake is a negative or inappropriate action which is an attempt to meet a perceived need. It doesn't actually get you what makes you happy.

For example: putting another down is done in the unconscious hope that the person doing it will feel better about themselves in comparison but it doesn't address the real need to feel valuable. A child may hit another to get a toy or to express anger. Much negative behaviour by children is an attempt to get their parents' attention. Often the real need behind poor behaviour is for structure and security and approval.

When something goes wrong and there is poor behaviour our aim is to meet our children's real needs and to teach the child how to get what he wants in a way that doesn't hurt others. And how to clean up what he has done. The child who hits others can be taught a better way to get what he needs whether it is respect or his fair share or help with school work. He can be shown how to voice his feelings so that he feels heard.

We use the neutral term 'mistake' rather than using the words 'naughty', 'bad', 'wrong', 'crime' or 'sin' because when those words are applied children feel bad about themselves and find it harder to take responsibility. Being able to take risks and to take responsibility for making mistakes is an absolute prerequisite for learning and healthy development.

Feeling bad about oneself is an obstacle to learning. It makes us close down and become defensive. Shame is paralysing. A child often repeats the thing he has done wrong because he sees himself as a bad person. This is different from feeling true remorse – where the child regrets the action taken but doesn't view *himself* as bad. This is a feeling which can lead to change. Seeing *oneself* as bad doesn't allow for change – that is just who you are.

How to use the Mistakes Process
First connect with your child and acknowledge the feelings out of which the mistake emerged. If he is still in the throes of anger, upset, humiliation or fear and not ready to take responsibility for his actions he will first need to be heard. He may need some time to elapse before talking about what happened.

1. ADMIT what happened and that it was a mistake
Why was it a mistake? For example: *"You were angry with your sister and you pulled her hair. We need to help you tell your sister how you feel with words, because nobody should be hurt."*

Let your child say in his own words what happened. If he says he 'didn't mean to', instead of lecturing him on how 'that doesn't matter because the harm is still done', Descriptively Praise the child for not intending to do harm. For example: "*I'm glad that you didn't mean to. That shows me that you know it wasn't the right thing to do and you wouldn't have done it if you'd been calm and thinking of alternative strategies.*"

Don't expect your child to want to look at you when you're discussing something unpleasant. Descriptively Praise him if he does or for staying put or for not arguing and for the maturity and self-control this shows. If he does leave, don't follow but resume the conversation before anything else happens. Acknowledge the fact that the child may be expecting blame or criticism. That is probably what happened in the past and, if you acknowledge that, your child will not only feel heard but you will be demonstrating taking responsibility for your own mistakes.

Children need to learn that people can admit responsibility and come out unscathed and, even better, that their acceptance of responsibility can make them strong. (Descriptively Praise other people who do take responsibility for their mistakes.) Descriptively Praise them for the courage it takes to own up to something and empathise with the feelings of embarrassment they may have.

2. Make AMENDS – set wrongs to rights

The child may need to fix someone's upset feelings. This might include an apology but not unless the child is ready, that is, she really does regret what she did.

It may help to say: "*You're probably sorry inside your head – when you're ready you'll also need to apologise out loud. You're probably wishing you hadn't done this.*"

She will feel regret for mistakes much quicker if the adults are not blaming and judging her. It allows room for her own conscience to act. (For more on apologies see chapter 12.)

A consequence may be required to help the child not do the same thing again. Ideally involve the child in coming up with an appropriate consequence. *For example: a child caught playing with collectible cards some time after lights out when he should have been asleep may suggest losing the cards for a defined period.* The goal should be to help the child to sleep and to acknowledge that the cards are a distraction – not to withdraw something precious as retribution. See below for more on consequences.

3. ALTER – what can you learn from this? What can you do differently?

What would help your child not to do this again? *"If it makes you so angry that you hit your brother when he turns off the TV while you're watching it, how could things be set up differently?"* The child may need adult help setting things up to avoid disputes.

4. ACCEPT – forgive yourself

We want to teach our children to think *when I make a mistake I know how to clear it up.* The situation is complete if amends have been made so it should not be brought up again in reproach or as a nag.

There are usually plenty of opportunities for parents to model handling mistakes, to show that we are not diminished by them and that we can accept responsibility without losing face.

A common mistake is when we've had a hassled morning and we shout at the kids. Cleaning it up might sound like this: *"This morning I shouted at you guys when we were getting ready to leave the house. That was a mistake because it doesn't make anyone feel good, including me, and it doesn't make you go any faster. It's not a nice way to start the day off like that and I'm sorry. I realise that the reason I was so cross is because I was feeling tired so what I need to do is go to bed a bit earlier tonight."* (The children usually think that's a terrific consequence!)

This doesn't mean there wasn't poor behaviour on the part of the children. They are more likely to accept responsibility for their role if they see you taking responsibility too and if you don't criticise or nag.

The Battle of Macintosh

One morning on the journey to school it started to pour with rain. I insisted my boys put their pac-a-mac raincoats on but my 5-year-old son Luke refused. He wanted to take his blazer off first, he said, but I insisted he do as he had been told, as I felt it was important that he comply and not argue with me.

Luke refused and the battle was on… and the three of us stood in the rain getting wetter and wetter… He shouted at me that I was the worst mummy in the world and all I ever wanted to do was to make him cry on purpose.

Somehow, I managed to scrabble my thoughts and words together and realised I had made a mistake. I sincerely apologised for not listening to his first idea about taking his blazer off to put the raincoat on. I said it had been a sensible idea and I wanted to accept it now. I imagined he must be feeling cross with me, and hard done by. He, rather sniffily, agreed and we continued our journey. We were wet, we were late… But we were (relatively) calm.

Jill, mum of two

Consequences

Consequences are not just a euphemism for punishment. They have a very different role, being designed to help the child make amends, and to learn and get things right next time.

Natural consequences

ALLOW the child to experience the effect of their behaviour.

We often make it hard for children to see the outcome of their behaviour because we tend to swoop in and either sort the problem out for them, or remove them from the situation, often while delivering a scolding.

Obviously we try not to let our children get into any danger or struggle with difficulties that they can't cope with. However, we must not protect them too much from their mistakes or from feeling guilty, or regretful, or worried about what they have done. Instead, we can empathise with those feelings and take steps to help them sort out what has gone wrong.

For example: when a child forgets his homework, or lunch-box, or violin, we don't deliver it to school or write a note to the teacher and then ban him from watching TV that afternoon. Instead, he has to explain to the teacher what has happened, or he has to feel hungry. Where we get involved is afterwards; we might listen to how he feels about the teacher and we help him remember what he needs the next day – a post-it note on the front door, a reminder on his phone, or a note in his diary.

For example: when a child doesn't get out of the bath on time, we don't drag him out and tell him off and then continue with the bedtime stories as normal, delaying lights out. Instead, there is less time for stories. We can empathise that he wishes he had got out of the bath earlier and we help him learn how to manage his time better – an egg-timer in the bathroom showing him how much longer he has, going upstairs a little earlier so he gets lots of time to play in the bath, etc. Get ideas from him.

When a child does not carry out his responsibilities then he does not earn his privileges.
Many children feel that screens and outings and playdates and mobile credits are their rights – they get them just because they are alive. But that's because the adults have set it up that way. Instead we can set things up at home so that these privileges are earned. Then it becomes the child's responsibility to earn them in the first place, rather than the parent's fault for taking them away.

At Emma's school they have a system where children get 'privilege' time at the end of the day when they can choose whatever activity they want to do. 6-year-old Emma was mortified when she lost some of her privilege time for poor behaviour. Her teacher said Emma didn't really care but Emma cared very deeply and behaved badly for the rest of the day and when she got home. This punishment taught her nothing but made her resentful. She thought her new teacher was mean.

A much better system is to set things up so that screen time is earned by feeding the dog, finishing homework and packing the school bag ready for the next day, or by tidying away toys, etc. Then if this behaviour doesn't happen, they are not able to watch TV or play on the iPad or have a friend over to play.

Sometimes following through just means waiting until your child has done what he needs to do, and nothing else happens until he has done it. That doesn't mean you can't use Descriptive Praise and using Emotion Coaching would definitely help.

Fixing consequences

HELP the child put it right.
Consequences should be as immediate and relevant as possible. When something has gone wrong, it needs to be put right. When our children make a mess, or break something,

or lose something, they need to be involved in sorting it out, as far as this is possible given their age and abilities.

This is different from waiting until the weekend and missing a swimming party because you lost your school shoes, or not being allowed to have pizza on Friday because you didn't help put the shopping away. Unless consequences are connected to the behaviour it's hard for children to view them other than as a mean-spirited whim on the part of the parent and hard for them to get the learning we intend.

Charlie, aged 10, and some friends were kicking a ball in the garden of a rented holiday house. They had been warned to kick the ball away from the house. The boys didn't heed this advice and the ball went through a window. The parents didn't get angry but expected the boys to take responsibility for what they'd done. The consequence was the boys needed to use the internet to find some local glaziers, ring them up to get 3 quotes and arrange for a glazier to come around to fix the window. They had to be there when the glazier came and they each had to contribute to the cost of the repairs.

Zack, aged 7, had woken up in the night and tried to get his collection of superhero figures down from the shelf above his bed. In doing so he made a noise and woke his 5-year-old brother and of course his parents. It took a long time to settle everyone back to sleep and next day both boys (and parents) were tired. Zack's consequence was to play quietly with a tired Aaron and keep him entertained. Bed was a bit earlier that night and there was also a conversation about what Zack could do if he woke up again in the night.

USE Take Twos
Take Twos are a useful consequence for minor misbehaviours – we simply require that the child does what he needs to do in

the correct manner here and now. There's no need to be angry or add any threat.

Take Twos give the child a second chance to do what's required and get it right.
They are then left with a memory of having made amends rather than a memory of getting it wrong and being scolded.

For example: when a child whines and pesters, we say *"It's hard for me to listen to that voice, and I can tell you have something to say. Please use your strong voice so I can hear you."*

For example: when a child leaves a trail of discarded belongings in the hallway as they come home from school, we say *"I can tell you're relieved to get home. There are a few things that need to be put away properly and then we can have a drink and a snack and I can hear about your day."*

Sometimes you'll need to address the feelings behind the behaviour before doing a Take Two. You may need to acknowledge the feelings that prompted rudeness before requiring the child to rephrase what they said. *"For you to speak to me like that shows you're really mad about something."* Listen to the problem and when things are calmer, *"In this house we speak to each other with respect even when we're upset. Please can you tell me how you're feeling politely?"*

Problem-solving

Problem-solving means the matter is discussed calmly and without judgment, from the assumption that the child wants to get things right and made a mistake. It may take the form of a Family Meeting or with an individual as part of The Mistakes Process.

Example: This morning you took the kids to the park and they raced ahead down the footpath on their scooters and bikes without regard to other pedestrians and nearly knocked over an elderly lady. Instead of punishing them you make necessary apologies in the moment and then have a meeting when you get home to discuss why this is a problem and what can be done about it next time.

Your turn

Go back to the behaviour you identified at the beginning of this chapter. What will your actions be now? Do you need to do anything more than allow your child's feelings to be heard? If so, what steps will you take to help them learn? Will it be a Take Two or some other kind of consequence? If you need to have a problem-solving conversation what will that sound like?

....

....

....

Broken eggs

Last Christmas, our friend kindly let us stay in his apartment in Miami when he wasn't there. I walked in and the first thing I noticed was 3 ostrich eggs in a bowl on a coffee table. I should have put them away in a cupboard!!! Within 45 minutes, my son had accidentally knocked one on to the floor and it smashed into hundreds of pieces. It took all my strength not to lose my temper – it wasn't ours to break. I didn't judge or blame but very calmly told him that it was up to him to put it right. He spent almost a day of his holiday trying to source another egg that was the right size and colour. I had no idea there were so many colours and varieties! One problem was he couldn't find a tape measure to work out the diameter of the other 2 eggs as they were all similar in size. He was very resourceful and downloaded a ruler onto his laptop and used headphones instead of string to measure up. He had to take photos of the other eggs and send them through, etc. The other issue was that it was over the Christmas/New Year period and lots of places were closed. I was insistent that it had to be sorted and the new egg in the flat before we left. He eventually sourced one in Chicago and arranged for it to be sent over. He then had to pay us back. This was a great learning experience and so much more powerful than a punishment.

Rachel, mum of four

Positive Discipline in a nutshell

☺ The best way of dealing with misbehaviour is by making it less likely that it will occur in the first place by using the proactive skills of Descriptive Praise, Emotion Coaching, Setting Up For Success and Rules.

☺ When kids get things wrong parents need to respond calmly – it helps if we understand the reasons for the behaviour.

☺ Positive discipline is different from punishment and must involve learning. When your child gets something wrong think of it as a 'teachable moment'.

☺ Take time to consider the cause of the misbehaviour. Consider temperament and the age of your child. Is there something you're doing that exacerbates the problem?

☺ When something goes wrong:
   ○ Take time to **Cool down**
   ○ **Connect** by acknowledging the feelings driving the behaviour
   ○ Take **Constructive steps** to teach your child how to make amends and get it right next time. Use **the mistakes process, natural consequences and fixing consequences or a problem-solving conversation.**

Further reading:

Dan Siegel and Tania Bryson, *No Drama Discipline*, 2014

Bonnie Harris, *When Your Kids Push Your Buttons And What You Can Do About It*, 2005

7

Skill 7: Keeping calm

"Between stimulus and response there is a space.
In that space is our power to choose our response.
In our response lies our growth and our freedom."

– Viktor E. Frankl, Holocaust Survivor and author of *Man's Search for Meaning*

When my sons were young their fighting really pushed my buttons. Christian could be so mean to Sam. He would provoke him mercilessly, saying "you smell" or "you're ugly" at any opportunity and play his music loudly when Sam was doing his homework. He would tease, call names and sometimes push, shove or hit him. Sam, in turn, could whine for Britain. He would come and tell tales on his brother, seeking to get him into trouble. These behaviours made me see red. I looked at these two kids whom I'd brought into the world and raised, and thought, 'where did I go wrong?' I thought Christian was mean and aggressive and would never have any friends and I imagined a future where I would be visiting him behind bars! I thought Sam was manipulative and would never learn to stand on his own two feet. These boys would never have the relationship with each other that I had envisaged for them. I'd obviously failed as a parent. I felt powerless and enraged and desperate. So I punished them, sending Christian to his room with a resounding character reference and withdrawing privileges and telling Sam off with a good lecture about tattle tales. I now know how ineffective those knee-jerk reactions are. Of course the minute my back was turned Christian retaliated against Sam and Sam didn't learn anything about resolving disputes. Had I been able to stay calm I might have been able to access some of the skills I had in my tool basket. But I had lost it and my skills went right out the window.

When we 'lose it' several things happen. We turn from that lovely, kind, empathetic parent into That Other Person and we say things that later we regret, like "*I don't want to be your mummy anymore.*" Where is that other parent coming from? We answer that question in this chapter.

When we lose it what happens physiologically is that our muscles tense, our blood pressure and rate of breathing go up, the levels of the stress chemicals cortisol and adrenaline increase and our attention narrows, with our ability to hear and see reduced. The red mist descends and our ability to access the rational part of our brains is reduced. This is not ideal. If we're in conflict situations our ability to see and hear the other is crucial.

When we lose it with our children they know we have lost control. The effect on our kids is that they may lose respect for us or be fearful of us or they may learn that they can provoke us into irrationality. Often when we lose it and have a knee-jerk reaction we regret it later and we may over-compensate out of guilt.

We know how important modelling is for children's learning. What are they learning from us if we're screaming like a banshee or hurling put-downs or sarcasm? Have you ever had that uncomfortable feeling when you've heard 'your' words coming out of your child's mouth?

Jemima, aged 6, was overheard talking to her sister: "Jessica, did you know Mummy and Dad have their Parent Practice course tonight? It's fantastic. They're learning how to speak calmly to us, because if you get cross, your children get cross too and that doesn't help anyone… But I could have told them that a long time ago."

Keeping calm in the face of children's provocative behaviour is the holy grail of parenting.

Keeping calm

The main points to remember in order to keep calm are:

- ☺ We need to understand what makes us crazy
  - ○ What makes kids do what they do
  - ○ What makes us react the way we do
- ☺ We have to take steps to reduce our stress levels and to look after ourselves
- ☺ We need strategies to teach our children to behave differently

Knowing you have positive and effective strategies for dealing with behaviour ready to use helps you to stay calm. It's not knowing what to do next that can make us panic and causes us to default to ineffective knee-jerk reactions. One parent described this sensation thus: "*I feel like I've tried everything and I'm paralysed by my own inability to think of solutions, my own incompetence and guilt.*"

We explored several different tried and tested strategies in the last chapter. Here we will look at the thought processes that often lead us to lose it. I am deeply indebted to Bonnie Harris, author of *When Your Kids Push Your Buttons And What You Can Do About It*[26] and creator of workshops of the same name, for many of the ideas in this section. These ideas will help you get the most out of the rest of the skills – keeping calm is the coat hanger on which you'll hang the other skills.

---

[26] Piatkus Books 2005

What makes us crazy?

Our expectations of our children

In order to STAY CALM we need to REVIEW EXPECTATIONS and UNDERSTAND the causes of misbehaviour. We need to take the time to understand why our children do what they do. In chapters 1, 3 and 6 we've been looking at what makes our children tick. We've looked at how temperament and the stage of development your child is in can explain behaviour which winds you up. We've explored how so much 'misbehaviour' is driven by very strong feelings that children don't yet know how to manage. And we considered many other causes like tiredness, feeling unwell, boredom, lack of understanding and different priorities, not to excuse the behaviour, but to help us understand it.

When we act on the assumption that our children misbehave because they are bolshie, difficult, trying to wind us up or 'out to get us', manipulative, lazy, mean or selfish, we won't be calm. And we close off possibilities to help them behave better.

If your expectation is that your 8 year old, who finds homework difficult or boring, will be resistant when you say it's time for homework you won't be surprised when that happens. Many parents say it is a revelation to them to think "Of *course* she doesn't like homework." With this thought, one of Harris's key concepts, you have a greater chance of staying calm and employing strategies to support her to get it done. If you understand that the reason he's just snapped at you is that he's had a rotten day at school you may be calmer about dealing with that behaviour. If you understand that your child is tentative about new situations and his refusal to join in the karate class wasn't just obstinacy or an attempt (a successful one) to embarrass you, you have a greater chance (embarrassment aside) of staying calm and supporting him.

What doesn't work is just to wish they wouldn't be like that (or to blame your partner's genes).

Sometimes our expectations of our children are unrealistic or inappropriate. Sometimes our expectations about ourselves are unrealistic. Indeed, some say that *"Expectations are resentments waiting to happen."*

We are re-evaluating our expectations in this chapter, not because we're going to abandon our goals or standards but because it will help us to be calmer if we're realistic about what's possible now. And we'll be more effective if we know that our input is required to help our children achieve those goals. **Expectations are what we're <u>hoping</u> our children will do now whereas goals are what we're <u>aiming</u> for them to do in the future with our support and training.**

If my 3 year old doesn't share his toys with his brother I may be calm about it because I know that's something he hasn't learnt yet. If he doesn't share his toys with a friend in the presence of the friend's mother my reaction may be a bit sharper because I'm embarrassed. If my 10 year old doesn't share I may get really cross because my expectation is that 10 year olds should be able to share and if he hasn't learnt to do so I blame myself.

The trouble is that expectations can become self-fulfilling – when you expect that your son will be 'lazy', or your daughter will be 'demanding' or that a child will be 'difficult/stubborn/rude' you will notice whenever they seem to be those things. It is called 'the Golem Effect'. These labels preclude the possibility of constructive parental action – you think your child just 'is' a particular way.

Have a look at your expectations. (Hold on tight – squirm alert.)

> **What were you expecting your child to do that she did not do?**
> Imagine (if you can) that your child is not doing what you want her to.
> Do you expect that your child should do what you say...
> Straightaway? Without argument? In exactly the way you wanted it done? Willingly? Always?

At what point did this expectation become unrealistic? This will depend on the age and temperament and personal history of the child. We need to keep asking ourselves whether our expectations are realistic for *this* child, at *this* stage of development, in *this* situation, considering *his* agenda.

Rather than: *'my child SHOULD be doing this'* (this creates guilt and is un-motivating)	Say: *'My child COULD be doing this when I train him, when I have given him enough support and when he is ready'* (this creates possibility)

Deciding that our expectations are unrealistic may not affect *what* we require our children to do but it will alter our approach.

Is it realistic to expect that your daughter is going to agree with you that it's a good idea to have limits on computer time and chocolate consumption and be happy about these restrictions? Is it reasonable to assume that your 7 year old can focus on getting dressed in the morning if the TV is on? Probably not!

Sometimes what our expectation had been isn't clear until we look at it afterwards. For example: *My child was disrespectful or hit and I expected him to be able to tell me what he wanted politely or explain why he was angry. Or I expected him not to feel so angry.* Sometimes when we articulate our expectation we can see its unreasonableness.

I realised that I had an unrealistic expectation of Sam when he was about 10 only after an exchange when I'd got really fed up with him. Asking myself what I'd expected of him I realised that I had just told him that I was going to change my approach to arguments between him and his brother. I had decided that it didn't help that I had got involved in their battles in the past and had taken sides and punished the one I perceived to be at fault. When I told Sam about this I hadn't realised that I had subconsciously been expecting him to agree that this was a good parenting technique and to go along with it! Not altogether surprisingly he had preferred it when his brother got told off when they argued. Realising this helped me to accept that Sam wasn't happy with the change and to have the courage to pursue my new approach anyway, knowing I was the adult and needed to make the decision and that I could help Sam by empathising with how he felt about it.

Other expectations parents often have are: I expect my children to get on well together; I expect my child to be polite and considerate; I expect my child to be able to delay gratification; I expect him to know that he needs to behave really nicely in front of granny; I expect my child to be happy/appreciative/positive/respectful/ independent/brave/careful/responsible/ truthful… always; I expect my child to wear a coat/go to the toilet/go to sleep/wake up/eat or not eat what and when I say.

We also have **expectations of our own behaviour.** For example: I should be patient/understanding, put the children's needs first, always be available, raise children who are polite/kind/respectful/ hardworking/well behaved/do well at school/are sporty/musical, etc, etc.

Our own thought processes

Sometimes our children will do things that really push our buttons. We know this because that's when we lose it and we look back afterwards and wonder where that response came from. When our buttons have been pushed we tend to shout, blame, nag, punish or use sarcasm, labels or threats.

Typical button-pushing behaviours including whining, complaining, crying, rudeness, physical fighting or bickering between siblings, biting, scratching or hitting another child or parent, selfishness, eating too much or too little, poor table manners, refusing to look at the person talking to them, ignoring us, not doing as they're asked, swearing, throwing food, spilling milk, painting on walls or furniture! These are all examples we hear about in our classes and  workshops. Some behaviours are obvious *mis*behaviours while others (like annoying snuffling or humphing noises) just get under our skin.

What pushes my buttons may not be the same as what pushes yours. You may find your partner is more tolerant of noise and mess than you are but can't bear it when your children don't seem grateful when given a treat.

When our children do something that 'makes us' crazy we assume that their behaviour has 'caused' our reaction. They made us do it. Honest, guv.

But actually **we need to take emotional responsibility for our responses.** This means understanding why our buttons get so pushed.

"You can tell a lot about a person by the way she handles these three things: a rainy day, lost luggage, and tangled Christmas tree lights."

– Maya Angelou, poet

In other words there isn't just one pre-ordained way to respond to rainy days, lost luggage and tangled lights or indeed to uncooperative children. **We can choose how we respond.** Being able to choose our response depends on our stress levels as well as having some different strategies. For a graphic representation of what affects our responses see our website (www.theparentpractice. com/book-resources#chapter-7 page).

When our children 'misbehave' that is certainly the event that triggers our reaction. It is the stimulus to which we respond. But the causation is not as direct as the diagram below would suggest.

In fact when our children behave in certain ways it triggers in us *feelings* that drive our responses. Our emotions cause our reactions, not our children's behaviour. When our children ignore or disrespect us it can trigger feelings of worthlessness and powerlessness that lead to shouting or harsh actions in our efforts to be noticed or to have some impact. Be understanding of and compassionate towards yourself – **no wonder you reacted that way if that's how you were feeling.**

Usually we think we can't control the feelings that arise in us but should be able to control our actions. And indeed with our more mature frontal lobes we should in theory be able to choose our actions rationally. But this depends on us being aware of what our feelings are. Otherwise they will control the actions we take. So when you feel yourself getting heated, push the pause button and ask, what am I feeling?

We may also be able to influence what we feel. Our emotions don't just come from nowhere. They are a result of the thoughts and beliefs we have about our children and about ourselves. This is where our expectations play a big part. The feelings that generate our responses arise out of what we think about what our child is saying or doing, or who we fear our child is or will become, and what we perceive about our role in that behaviour. We can reframe our thoughts and beliefs so that we feel and act differently. This is difficult to do because we think our thoughts and beliefs are the TRUTH. We need to be open to the idea that **there is another way of thinking about our children's behaviour or our role.**

"Is there a way to change how we experience the hair-pulling challenges of mothering? Can one truly alter her feelings in the midst of the supermarket trip from hell?... There is always another way to see the situation, a way that potentially offers greater peace, comfort, acceptance, and balance than our initial response."

– Bethany Casarjian and Diane H. Dillon

> *"Events and emotions are usually out of our control.*
> *To change our reactions, we need a different emotional*
> *state. But to change our emotions, we need to change the*
> *assumptions we make."*[27]

When my child acts stubbornly and persistently about everything he wants I feel angry, impotent and scared and I often react by punishing him and sending him to his room while shouting at him to leave me alone.

Let's look more at those feelings and the thoughts behind them.

My thoughts about my child when I see this behaviour are that he will <u>never</u> take no for an answer (we often think it's never going to be any different from how it is right now), that he will never listen and nobody will like him, hence my fear, which leads to anger. (Maybe I recognise my brother in him – he never listened to me either.)

My assumptions about myself are that I will never have control over him and I will never get a moment's peace. I have no idea how to handle him. I feel inadequate. I am a hopeless parent.

I can change my thoughts to be more accurate and constructive if I say to myself that my child doesn't like to be told 'no' or to be told to do something he doesn't want to do but actually he responds much better when I calmly say what he can do instead and when I acknowledge how he feels.

*When my 11 year old doesn't do his revision **(behaviour)** I feel anxious about his future and that I don't have control. I feel disempowered **(emotions)** and I react by nagging **(response)**. My beliefs about him are that he is lazy, doesn't*

---

[27] Bonnie Harris, *When Your Kids Push Your Buttons And What You Can Do About It*, 2005

care about his future, he isn't prepared to work, is after an easy life, won't develop self-discipline and won't amount to anything. My thoughts about myself are that I'm a bad parent and I haven't passed on my values about working hard (thoughts and beliefs). My expectations are that he should work hard, no matter how he is feeling. He should want to do well at school and he should understand that his future depends on what he does now. He should be able to put his desire to play on the computer to one side until his work is done.

Another way of thinking about this is that he's having a hard time getting motivated about his work. He's not inspired. His lack of success and struggles to date are making him feel there's no point in putting in any effort as it doesn't seem to get him anywhere. It's hard for him to care about the future as he lives in the moment. He doesn't have the experience or perspective to understand how his current behaviour will impact on his future.

Post script: this child has now graduated from university top of his year. He became completely motivated and worked harder than he ever had in his life. He wanted to achieve and learnt what he needed to do in order to get good grades.

Sometimes parents think that their children are deliberately trying to manipulate or control them or run the family or wind them up. Rarely is this assumption true. (If it is so it means something is making the child feel very angry and powerless and that needs to be addressed.) Children don't usually feel good when they have more power than the parents. When they fear that their parents are not in control they feel they need to take control themselves – this is scary for children. When we assume the child is 'just trying to wind me up' we get involved in power struggles and miss the real causes of the misbehaviour. Without identifying those, we can't target improving the behaviour.

Some re-framed assumptions[28]

My 5-year-old daughter isn't eating, again. She uses food to get at me. She's defiant.	She senses my anxiety around food. Mealtimes have become very tense. She feels criticised. She wants to have some say over her life – adults tell her what to do all day long.
I feel anxious that she will be unwell, that I will have failed in one of the basic elements of parenting – nurturing your child. I am hopeless at getting her to obey me. My mother is right about my parenting.	She is in the normal range for weight. I can teach her to develop better eating habits over time.
My 9-year-old son is really disrespectful to me. I know he gets upset about things easily but that doesn't excuse him calling me names. I really don't think he needs to get so emotional.	He has a hard time controlling his emotion-driven impulses. He has an immature brain. He needs a lot of emotion coaching for his brain to develop so that his frontal lobes will take control of his behaviour, not his feelings. I can help him learn to manage his feelings and his behaviour.

---

[28] For more on these ideas and to explore parental expectations and reframing assumptions see Bonnie Harris, *When Your Kids Push Your Buttons And What You Can Do About It*, 2005

He's so mean to his sister. She's so sweet. I don't understand how anyone could be so hateful. I didn't have another child so that she could be a punch bag for him.

I've been too soft on him.

He has a hard time controlling himself around his sister. She gets a lot of attention for being sweet and he probably thinks everyone prefers her to him. That makes him feel bad about himself which drives his behaviour towards her.

I can help him feel good about himself and to tell me when he feels jealous. I can let him know that I love him and that he is important to me. I can teach him some more appropriate ways to channel his feelings.

One mum found her buttons being pushed when her 4-year-old daughter was playing with the light pull in the bathroom.

Her daughter would pull and pull it, turning the lights on and off as the bath was running, and despite trying to be calm the mum just couldn't make her stop. She found it such a flashpoint – after working hard all day and rushing home to make sure she got quality time with her daughter, knowing she had more work to do after the girl had gone to bed; she felt under huge pressure to have a lovely time. She felt resentful that her daughter wouldn't just stop pulling the light switch. And underneath there was a guilt that she didn't spend more time with her...

And the light-bulb moment (sorry!) came when the mother realised her daughter was trying to say "let's have more fun, this is fun, let's play" – she wasn't trying to make her mum feel worse, but trying to make her feel better. It really opened her eyes to the fact that all her interactions with her daughter were focussed on getting something done, a meal, a journey to school, even the more fun things had become jobs to get through. She promised herself there were going to be more bubbles and cuddles...

Pushing the pause button

Steven Covey suggests that between the stimulus and our response we need to push a pause button so that we can access our skills and respond effectively.[29] What enables us to push the pause button and increase the calm in our lives?

We need to look at what we can do away from the trigger moments and during the trigger moments.

In the background

Look after ourselves

It is really essential that we are looking after ourselves so that we are physically and emotionally up to the task of dealing with everything our children throw at us (sometimes literally).

"When we truly care for ourselves, it becomes possible to care far more profoundly about other people. The more alert and sensitive we are to our own needs, the more loving and generous we can be toward others."

– Eda LeShan

You are an important resource for your family – your family needs you. Think of yourself as a bank account – if you don't make deposits you can't make withdrawals.

When you're over-tired, overwhelmed, under-exercised

---

[29] *7 Habits of Highly Effective Families*, 1998

and under-appreciated, when you are due out for a rare evening with friends, but you still have an important call to make, the washing machine starts leaking and your 5 year old wants another story... how do you behave? Will you say and do effective things? Are positive results likely?

For some of us, the idea that we need to take care of ourselves if we're going to be effective parents will be really obvious. For others, it may not be something you have really thought about or maybe you would concede it is a good idea but it may not be much of a priority. For many parents it can seem an absolute impossibility to take time for oneself out of an already overburdened schedule.

As parents we often make sacrifices for our children's sake and we frequently put our children's interests first. We are not suggesting this is the wrong thing to do but it can become habitual. If our children see that we do not sleep or eat well, that we neglect our friendships, and that we don't get to do activities we enjoy, then they may expect that for themselves. Or if we slave for our children without any care for our own welfare they may develop that sense of entitlement we worry about and treat us accordingly.

Taking good care of ourselves is not being selfish or self-indulgent – it is taking care of our needs so that we are better equipped to support our families. Try thinking of it as on-going professional development for your job as a parent. Compare being a parent with running a really smooth car, maybe an Audi convertible. If you had that car you would ensure it had enough fuel and oil and you would get it serviced regularly and (to begin with at least) you'd wash and maybe wax it. That's what it means to be looking after ourselves; it's the difference between the car running smoothly or chugging along and eventually breaking down.

When we're calm, we can access the parenting skills we already have, and the ones we're learning and working on. So in order to parent the way we want to, and enjoy our children, we need techniques for 'creating calm'.

So how can we do it?

When we're thinking about looking after ourselves we need to be looking at not only our physical needs but our intellectual, social, emotional and spiritual health also.

What do you already do for yourself, perhaps not often enough, that you know makes you a nicer, kinder, calmer parent? Many parents say that having some time away from the kids helps. Rather than just leaving this to chance, and hoping it happens again soon, commit to taking some small steps towards looking after yourself in each of the following areas. You probably know much of this, but the trick is *doing* it. You may feel guilty because you do know, but don't do. Don't worry, in a minute we will find ways to get into action.

PHYSICAL

☺ We all know the importance of maintaining a healthy, balanced diet and what a huge impact nutrition has on mood, energy levels and overall wellbeing. You will probably know already that diet affects brain activity too.

☺ Getting sufficient sleep is another area we know about but don't really prioritise – can you go to bed early once a week or learn how to power-nap? Research shows that a good night's kip boosts our immune system and regulates the hormones, helping us maintain a healthy weight, as well as regulating our mood, combating feelings of stress, anxiety and depression. If you have trouble sleeping, experts say a regular 30-minute wind-down period is a good way of sign-posting to the brain that sleep is on its way. Don't look at a backlit screen in this time and of course avoid stimulants such as caffeine and alcohol! Reduce the light in the room and make sure you're not too hot or cold.

☺ Incorporate regular exercise into your daily life. We know it's not easy so it will need to be prioritised. Exercise in groups can be social and fun – one mum joined an Irish dancing class – exercise, music, friends, all at once! Experts often suggest incorporating activity into daily life such as getting off the bus a few stops sooner and walking the rest of the way.

☺ Spend time outdoors in the natural world – fresh air and sunlight (or just fresh air if you live in the UK) are just some of the benefits.

INTELLECTUAL

☺ Find ways to stimulate intellectual growth and creativity – take courses, join book groups, visit museums and galleries or just read some books that challenge your brain.

☺ Kill two birds with one stone by incorporating reading into your wind-down routine at night. You'll either read a lot of your book or you'll sleep well. Sleep is of course essential for brain activity too.

☺ Maybe do brain puzzles like Sudoko or other brain teaser challenges. There are plenty online. Doing something that is a bit of a stretch for us, something not in our usual comfort zone, encourages the neuroplasticity of the brain and wards off Alzheimer's! Doing something that is a struggle – such as memory activities – enhances learning and makes the brain grow.

SOCIAL

☺ Make time for your partner. The couple relationship

needs to be nurtured as it is the bedrock on which the family is built. Stress in that relationship spills over into the rest of the family.

☺ Spend time with friends. Many people say this is important to them but don't do it. Think of ways to make it happen for you. One father had a to-do list for each week that incorporated social things and because there was a section on the page that made him think about it he did remember to get in touch with friends and family.

☺ Seek out fun and laughter – have a monthly film club or poker night! Joining a group or having a regular activity like a theatre subscription or watching sport means it is more likely to happen.

☺ Spend more time interacting with people in real time, either face to face or on the phone or skype, than in social media.

EMOTIONAL

☺ Descriptively praise yourself – positive self-talk is shown to increase how happy and in control you feel. Write down or say out loud three DPs about yourself – you should do this every day! We know that some people will find this idea cringey but the more descriptive your praise is the easier it is to take. For example: *"I was cheerful when I woke the children, even though I'm not a morning person; I planned the menu ahead of time so I had extra time to play with the children; I remembered to call my father who was lonely and it really perked him up; I did my first set of exercises which didn't hurt as much as I expected so now I'm more motivated to try again; I came home from work in time to see the kids 3 nights out of 5 this week"*. Identify the underlying characteristic it shows about you. Do it with and for your partner too.

☺ Find (or train) someone to be *your* emotion coach.

☺ Give yourself occasional treats – from a beauty treatment to a walk on your own at your own speed, rather than stepping on every line on the pavement!

☺ Spend time with people who make you feel good about yourself, and do activities that make you feel relaxed and competent (I draw, as I find it calming and it's satisfying to see skills improving).

☺ Write down what you are grateful for in your life.

SPIRITUAL

☺ Nurture your inner soul, whether this is through attending religious services or meditating, yoga or personal development courses or spending time in nature. Anything that helps you to connect with something bigger than yourself and helps you find peace will work.

Making it happen
To make sure you get into action:

TAKE one small step – rather than applying to run the marathon next year, join a local fitness class or download some running tracks and set off for the local park.

COMMIT money – if we pay up in advance, we're less likely to back out on the morning.

SCHEDULE it – the act of writing it into our diary makes it more likely to happen.

FIND a friend – either persuade a friend to join you in your run or trip to the museum, or ask them to act as a 'stand' for you which means you give them permission to call you and find out how it went.

> *I often ask Paula to be my 'stand' and I promise to go to sleep at a reasonable hour when my husband is travelling... Recently she made me do a 'pinky promise' for this – you curl little fingers and shake... she said her daughter will say "BUT Mummy, you made a pinky promise... you HAVE to do it." It made me laugh AND it made me do it!*
>
> **Sue, mum of three**

SET up for success – and don't let things get in your way. Ask your children, partner, friends, work colleagues to respect the time you've set for yourself, by not arranging other activities at these times, or interrupting you during your You Time. This will take perseverance. Acknowledge your family if when they do this.

Have a look at our website (www.theparentpractice.com/book-resources#chapter-7 page) for a worksheet that helps you to commit to small steps toward looking after yourself.

Reducing stress in your life

Setting priorities at home in everyday life
We can readjust our day-to-day priorities to take charge of our lives and to create a calmer, happier home.

Step back and look at your day-to-day priorities. The main reason we don't take better care of ourselves is because we run out of time, after doing all the other things we commit to and feel responsible for.

One suggestion from Steven Covey[30] we've always found helpful is to categorise the areas of your life into 4 quadrants: Urgent/Important; NOT urgent/Important; Urgent/NOT important; and finally NOT Urgent/NOT important as per the grid below. (See also the great TED talk by Rory Vaden on time multiplying. https://www.youtube.com/watch?v=y2X7c9TUQJ8 – link on our website. (www.theparentpractice.com/book-resources#chapter-7 page)

Important/Urgent	Important/Not urgent
No clean sports kit	*Taking proactive steps to take care of yourself and your family: planning ahead, creating routines and systems to make life flow better, investing time in improving skills and maintaining relationships, creating community where you live by 'hanging out' with neighbours*
Empty fridge	
Child unexpectedly needs to be collected	
Illness	
Car breakdown	
Dog is sick on the rug	
	Renew passports
	Book dental appointments
	Schedule date nights
	Car maintenance

---

[30] *7 Habits of Highly Effective Families,* 1998

Not important/Urgent	Not important/Not urgent
Phone ringing during meal/ special time	*This will NOT be the same for everyone – but if there is something you do and then later feel it was a waste of time, and you wish you had NOT done it, then you need to ask yourself 'What did I need or want then' and find a better way to satisfy your need.*
Checking /responding to emails/texts	
Saying yes to requests from others that aren't a priority for you	

Our first goal is to decrease the amount of things that are urgent – i.e. things that control us and determine what we do, and when we do it. When parts of our life get into urgent mode we feel overwhelmed and out of control. And when this happens, we tend to feel incompetent and inadequate – and that makes us snappy, or resigned, or depressed.

Our other goal is to reduce the things that are not really important to us, according to *our* set of values. (In this case, we're focusing on us as parents, and our family life.) In order to do this, we need to work out what is important to us and learn how to say no to other things.

Don't feel bad about saying no because in doing so you are saying yes to you, to your family and to your priorities. You can say to the person who's asked you to organise the school fundraiser that you'd like to say yes to the request but you have to say no to the overwhelm you get from saying yes to too many things.

Everything that we do to reduce time in the other quadrants, means we get to spend more time in the area of non-urgent importance – doing the things that matter to us, and taking our time about them. The less we do here the more that things move into the urgent quadrants.

In the moment

Act sooner

We need to become more aware of the immediate lead-up to misbehaviour and train ourselves to deal with it in the early stages rather than waiting until the full performance. We think we're giving our children a second chance when we let a behaviour go but fall into a pattern of 'accommodate, accommodate, accommodate... explode!' When we feel we've been reasonable we expect our children to comply, and then we lose it if they don't.

> *"Every time I find myself yelling at one of my children, I realise that the fault is mine. Not only that I am yelling, but that I didn't intervene in an effective way before yelling was necessary. My five year old didn't turn off the computer when I asked, and now will be late to bed. Obviously, she needed me to help her do what was too hard for her to do alone – exit the fun program and go brush her teeth. Then I find myself yelling at her, because it's the fourth time I've asked and it's twenty minutes later. Anytime you've asked that many times, you aren't being effective, and a different, more involved approach is necessary... If you end up screaming, they just feel picked on. They learn nothing useful and much that is harmful about how to handle their own feelings when they watch you indulge yours at their expense."*[31]

---

[31] Dr Laura Markham, www.ahaparenting.com

Use a calming technique

When our buttons get pushed, or circumstances conspire against us, we need to have something to help us stay balanced. Different calming techniques work better for different people – take some time and try them out. You will soon find which type suits you best, and which particular technique is most effective for you. These 3 'V' techniques work for children when they're steamed up too.

VISUALISE – SEEING (good for visual people)

Visualisation techniques are highly effective ways to let off steam.

You can either visualise the stress and get rid of it (imagine a pressure cooker releasing steam or a raging bull – watch it pawing the ground and blowing air through its nostrils and then make it charge off into the distance as you watch it get smaller and smaller) or visualise something very calm and soothing (a special memory you have, or a beautiful place you know).

When my kids were young I was able to stay calm in public, and when we had guests or family visiting... but when I was alone I'd 'let my hair down' and found it all too easy to start shouting or worse at my kids. Then one day I pretended that my beloved mother-in-law (lucky me that's how I felt!) was in the room with us... and it worked! I would NEVER lose it in front of her. Indeed, I felt a lovely sense of being supported and not so alone. I could also 'see them through her eyes' as she was their ultimate champion.

Sue, mum of three

VERBALISE – SAYING (good for auditory people)
Use a mantra to help you calm down.

Examples from parents include:
"I can be the adult," "Right now doesn't matter," "Choose sanity," "Am I being effective?" and *"Breathe and relax."* Also *"Slow Down,"* not only said out loud, but written on brightly coloured post-it notes all over the house. And even *"My child is actually NOT a sabre-toothed tiger,"* and *"There's no blood on the floor!"* Counting to 10 also works.

MOVE – DOING (good for kinaesthetic people)
A very effective technique is the kinaesthetic or 'moving' method. Don't underestimate the effect of changing your physical state to change your emotional state.

☺ Take deep breaths – stretch your neck, breathe from the abdomen. This releases calming chemicals while shallow breathing from the chest releases adrenaline.

☺ Do something physical like going for a quick walk – if you can't leave the house, walk into another room or upstairs.

☺ Splash cold water on your face or hands or drink cold water to bring down the temperature!

☺ Put on music or knead your shoulders or neck – get the children involved. Sue's daughter gives her a head massage. Get some massage balls and roll against a wall or the floor with the balls between you and your back, shoulders or neck.

☺ Kids can punch a pillow, tear up paper or do a scribble drawing and so can we! *Diana had taught her daughter to use angry drawing to vent. One day they came home and found the repairman had NOT come to fix the fridge. Diana was upset. Her little daughter disappeared and returned with pen and paper and said "Mummy would it help to do an angry drawing?" She did and it DID help!*

☺ Leave the room – with no blame towards the child. As one mother said "*When I get stressed by the kids I follow the advice on a bottle of aspirin: 'Take two and keep away from children!'*" Recognising our limits and taking time out away from the child to calm down is a great practice to help us be calm. If we verbalise that this is what we're doing then we're also being a good model for the children of how to handle feelings.

My friend, her husband and two children were staying with us in Yorkshire. Her youngest (5) was exhausted! They had travelled up from London on the train, they had been cooped up in a car driving around the countryside and the little girl didn't want to do something. I can't remember what it was... but she quickly got into full-on brain/emotion hijack and was having none of what Mum and Dad were trying. I went downstairs to get her a glass of water. When I returned with the water, she took a few sips and immediately calmed down. It was the perfect example of 'change in physical state leads to change in emotional state'. My friend thought I was a magician!

Ann, mum of one

Knitting Stories

Mei Lee was struggling with her reading. She was falling behind in class, and becoming more and more reluctant to try. Her mother, Teresa, was getting increasingly concerned and desperately wanted to find a positive way to help her daughter, as she kept falling into criticism and threatening. She realised that she was anxious for her daughter and, if she was honest, embarrassed by her lack of progress. Teresa recognised that she had assumed her daughter couldn't be bothered to try because she lacked drive. This was a big button pusher for her as she had always wondered if she'd been held back in her career by her own lack of determination (really a lack of self-confidence). She didn't want her daughter to make the mistakes that she had made. She resolved to reframe her assumptions about Mei Lee.

She told herself that her daughter had been feeling tense and criticised and that she needed to do something to change the atmosphere to something more positive. Now that her buttons had been defused Teresa felt much calmer and could think creatively.

After some thought, Teresa dug out her old wool collection and started to crochet a blanket – a huge one, that would take months to complete. Mei Lee was very tactile, and so her mother knew she would be drawn to the blanket. Each time the girl sat with her mother on the sofa and read, Teresa would get out the blanket and start crocheting. Crocheting the blanket kept Teresa calm and meant she was in a good, positive frame of mind to give descriptive praise. And the daughter found watching the blanket grow was wonderfully motivating and pleasurable – it was tactile and visual and she knew it was especially for her.

Teresa, mother of two

Your turn

Complete this here or on the PDF on our website (www.theparentpractice.com/book-resources#chapter-7 page). Adapted from Bonnie Harris's Workshop workbook.

Identify a BEHAVIOUR that winds you up.

For example: not listening to me/doing what I ask.

....

....

....

How do you REACT when you see this behaviour?

For example: shout, nag, criticise, give up, complain.

....

....

....

How do you FEEL when you see this behaviour?

....

....

....

Identify your EXPECTATIONS about your child's behaviour.

For example: I expect him to pay attention when I'm talking to him. I expect him to do what I say when I say it.

....

....

....

Identify your THOUGHTS and BELIEFS about your child and about yourself.

For example: he's so rude, he's a spoilt brat who never thinks of anyone else. I'm a hopeless parent, I have no control – my children ignore me – they should pay attention to me, I'm not teaching my child good habits for life.

....

....

....

How can you RE-FRAME these thoughts and beliefs?

For example: He's easily distracted and absorbed with other things. He's not yet in the habit of making eye contact when I talk to him. He is tired when he comes home from school and sick of being told what to do all day long. He wants some power in his life.

....

....

....

Keeping calm in a nutshell

Keeping calm is all about altering our thought processes.

☺ We need to review our expectations and make sure they're realistic for this child at his stage of development and with his needs, including temperament.

☺ Understanding why they do what they do really helps us to stay calm.

☺ Understanding why we do what we do helps us to be compassionate towards ourselves and to

☺ alter our thought processes to something more constructive – we can reframe our assumptions and our expectations about our children and ourselves.

☺ To be calm we need some strategies:
  ○ Outside of trigger moments we need to be taking care of the resource that we are for our families and using tools to work out our priorities and reduce stress
  ○ In the moment we need a calming technique (which we need to practice in non-stressful moments)
  ○ We need to know what to do about our children's behaviour (that's why you're reading this book)

Further reading:

Bonnie Harris, *When Your Kids Push Your Buttons And What You Can Do About It*, 2005

Steven Covey, *The 7 Habits of Highly Effective Families*, 1998

Part Two

Applying the skills to everyday parenting challenges

8

Their world of relationships

"Family is just accident.... They don't mean to get on your nerves. They don't even mean to be your family, they just are."

– Marsha Norman

"The family. We were a strange little band of characters trudging through life sharing diseases and toothpaste, coveting one another's desserts, hiding shampoo, borrowing money, locking each other out of our rooms, inflicting pain and kissing to heal it in the same instant, loving, laughing, defending, and trying to figure out the common thread that bound us all together."

– Erma Bombeck

You're half way through this book! Hopefully you're practising the 7 essential skills for bringing out the best in your children and now in this chapter we'll look at how these skills work together to help our children develop positive relationships between siblings and between friends.

Sibling relationships

Charlie (6) is very jealous of Alex (8). He always wants to be able to do what his older brother can do. He wants to be older, to be faster, to be better at reading, to be able to stay up later and have sleepovers. He thinks Alex has more stuff and gets more attention. On a recent visit to their grandparents' house Charlie counted how many photos of him there were compared with the number of Alex. Alex, on the other hand, thinks Charlie gets away with murder. The boys bicker and complain about each other and use possessions to manipulate each other: "if you don't do what I want I'll take my soldiers away." But they also laugh a lot together.

The main points to remember about sibling relationships are:

☺ Parents can INCREASE HARMONY between brothers and sisters by addressing the cause of the friction and by using 7 strategies to help them get on better

☺ Parents can help DECREASE FIGHTING. Stay out of low-level conflict and when intervening, mediate and support without judgment

☺ While some conflict is to be expected between siblings and can even provide opportunities to learn important life lessons, parents need to pay attention to determine whether it has turned into bullying

Sibling fighting

"Those who love each other fight with each other."

– Ukranian proverb

Conflict is normal in families, in fact in any close relationship. Although we may accept that brothers and sisters fight, and we may try to reassure ourselves that they are learning about conflict resolution, sibling conflict still drives us mad! It is frequently mentioned in our classes as a major button-pusher because the squabbling and bickering really gets on parents' nerves. Sometimes the name-calling and taunting or the hitting, hair-pulling, kicking, elbowing and taking possessions away can get too much. If you are an only child and all you wanted was a brother or sister you may feel particularly dismayed. We want our children to learn how to express their needs in acceptable ways, how to share and compromise and problem-solve, how to stand up for themselves without taking themselves too seriously, and to respect differences between people. And we can help them learn all this!

Why does it happen?

When children make friends in the playground they can choose their playmates. They'll look for someone with similar interests to themselves, usually someone of their own age. But with brothers and sisters there's no choice and, apart from multiple births, there are differences in ages. These factors of themselves can lead to friction. Older children often have to accommodate younger children's lack of skills and younger ones are frequently frustrated by not being able to do what their older sibling can. The lament *"when will I be as big as him?"* is played out in many households.

A clash of temperaments can sometimes lead to difficulties too. The kids just don't understand each other. If you have an extrovert in the family who talks nineteen to the dozen and likes to play music loudly and a child who is more introverted and just wants some peace and quiet there can be tension. One child may be jealous of her sibling's achievements or popularity or the ease with which she appears to negotiate the world while she has a more cautious or negative approach. *One mum reported that her older son just can't understand why her younger son can "just be so happy all the time, for no reason."*

As usual there are the many transient causes of misbehaviour that can cause one sibling to lash out at another such as tiredness, feeling unwell, boredom and hunger. Many squabbles are over possessions or shared resources such as the TV or computer or favourite seats in the car or at the table!

Other reasons for sibling fighting are:

☺ A bid for parental attention. In busy families a guaranteed way to get your parent's attention is to annoy or even thump your sister.

☺ At a deeper level some of the rivalry between siblings is for their perceived share of parental approval and love. Some children may think that a sibling is getting more love than they are; that mum or dad prefers their sibling to them. This may be measured by how much time is spent with the 'preferred child' or by what privileges or possessions they are given or how little they get told off compared to the other. This is a big issue for families where one child demands a disproportionate amount of attention either because of poor behaviour or because of special needs. When a child perceives that his parent prefers his sibling he feels a painful lack of belonging and his brain suffers from opioid withdrawal. This is a form of grief and as strong as heroin withdrawal.[32]

☺ All of us bring home our issues with the wider world. Home is where we feel safe and we can vent. That may mean that children who are struggling with life take out their feelings on a sibling. Feelings of inadequacy, powerlessness, frustration or anger may be vented on another child with put-downs, name-calling, teasing or aggression. He thinks he will feel better if his brother feels worse. When a child has poor self-esteem he may

---

[32] Professor Jaak Panksepp quoted in Margot Sunderland, *The Science of Parenting*, 2006

pick on a younger brother or sister because he doesn't know what else to do with his feelings or because he can't bear to be the only one feeling this way.

Although sibling arguments are commonplace you may still be concerned about the frequency and intensity of the fighting. You may be asking yourself, 'when does it become bullying?' That's an uncomfortable question to ask and a complex one to answer. Your own experience of childhood fights with siblings may colour your views. Was an older sibling allowed to bully you? Did you feel abandoned by your parents? Or did you fight with your brothers and sisters but become good friends in adulthood? Do you still feel there is a legacy from those times, perhaps difficulty in asserting yourself and a tendency to avoid conflict? Do you believe that children who get away with bullying at home go on to be bullies at school, and in the workplace, and in relationships?

Some studies have shown that sibling bullying puts children at greater risk of developing depression and anxiety that can last into adulthood[33] as well as having lower academic scores and general health concerns.[34] Repeated bullying can result in emotional shut down or over-reactivity and aggression.[35]

So how can you tell the difference between normal fighting and something more serious? It's not straightforward. We need to consider the child's intention (to cause harm or not), the power imbalance between the two and the frequency and duration of the behaviour.[36] When interviewed for studies into sibling bullying children were told that bullying meant *"when a brother or sister tries to upset you by saying nasty and hurtful things, or completely ignores you from their group of*

---

[33] Corrina Jenkins Tucker, Associate Professor of Family Studies at the University of New Hampshire, published June 2013 in the journal *Pediatrics*.
[34] US Center for Disease Control and Prevention
[35] Margot Sunderland, *The Science of Parenting*, 2006
[36] Amanda Nickerson, director of the Alberti Center for Bullying Abuse Prevention at the University at Buffalo

friends, hits, kicks, pushes or shoves you around, tells lies or makes up false rumours about you".[37] Whether or not sibling fighting amounts to bullying, parents can and should intervene to teach children better ways of expressing their needs, of solving problems and to help them to share, take turns, tolerate differences and generally rub along together more or less civilly.

What parents can do – 7 Strategies to Foster Harmony

Parents can do a great deal to help their children get along better and interact peaceably. We can actively work to change the emotional climate at home so they are less driven to squabble with their siblings.

1. Give POSITIVE ATTENTION and build SELF-ESTEEM

We've seen that a big reason for fighting is if children feel badly about themselves. Another is their need for parents' attention, approval and appreciation. Usually when our children are getting on well together we don't even notice it and just get on with our own lives but we give them plenty of attention when they start fighting! This teaches them that an easy way to get our attention is to wind up a sibling and provoke a fight.

The most effective way to improve sibling relationships is to improve each child's self-concept and to give them positive attention. Use Descriptive Praise to ensure your child feels noticed, valued and good about himself. Make sure you never compare one child with another, even favourably. If you're praising one child in front of others be mindful of how the ones not getting praised are hearing it. Be aware of whether one child consistently gets more praise than others,

---

[37] Dr Lucy Bowes, Professor Dieter Wolfe and others, published in the journal *Pediatrics* Oct 2014

or if that's how the children see it. If so, acknowledge how that feels.

Use Emotion Coaching to really connect and to show that you value their feelings and listen to their opinions and ideas.

Give children age-appropriate responsibilities so that they can feel competent and confident.

If your child is feeling unsuccessful at school, either socially or academically, this needs to be addressed or he may well take out his feelings of inadequacy and frustration on his siblings or friends (see Chapter 9).

2. ENCOURAGE POSITIVE INTERACTIONS

Descriptively praise your children for getting on, for some aspect of team work or for problem-solving ten times a day, even if they're just leaving each other alone.

☺   *Just then you asked Sanjiv to move over in a polite way.*

☺   *When Tom and William were making a noise while you were listening to your story you didn't say anything hurtful. You should be proud of yourself. Keeping calm isn't easy!*

☺   *Even though you both wanted to play on the computer at the same time you hardly argued about it at all. You started thinking of solutions. I appreciate that you were both willing to compromise. That's very mature behaviour.*

☺   *You shared your ice cream with Adeela when she dropped hers. It was very generous of you.*

Remember the pasta jar from Chapter 2? Have one pasta jar for all the children to minimise competition. If Luke mentions that Sarah has done something deserving of a pasta piece then Sarah gets a pasta piece but so does Luke for drawing attention to it.

Reduce competition further by allowing children to pursue different interests if you can and don't race children against each other, even if it makes them go faster in the morning!

Some families will have a ritual for appreciating each other, for example at the dinner table, where everyone says something they appreciate about the person sitting on their left.

☺ *"I appreciate that Toby let me borrow his racing car set."*

☺ *"I appreciate that Daddy made spaghetti Bolognese tonight"*

☺ *"I appreciate that Toby and Sadie found a solution to the problem of who can sit in the front seat of the car."*

☺ *"I appreciate that Mummy helped me clean my room."*

3. Provide for TIME ALONE and TIME TOGETHER

Set up opportunities for positive interactions together. Keeping them separated may reduce fighting but it wouldn't teach them to get on, even if it were possible! Having fun together is important if siblings are to see the point of each other. They have more to lose if they fall out with a good playmate.

At first, this may need to be in small bursts and under supervision. Set up for success by doing an activity that you know they'll all enjoy for a short amount of time and taking part yourself. Choose the times carefully – not when they're tired and hungry. Chat through in advance and descriptively praise them for all positive interactions.

Tell stories of shared memories so that children can remember they belong together.

In addition, it is crucial that each child has some **Special Time** alone, ideally with each parent. When children get our undivided attention, at least at certain defined times, they are less likely to compete with their siblings for our attention. Refer to the fact that special time is in the diary and that you're looking forward to it. Special Time doesn't need to be very long. Do something you both enjoy such as playing a game, reading a story, kicking a ball, cooking, going for a walk or just having a conversation. Homework is not Special Time! Many parents use staggered bed times as an opportunity for one-to-one time with each child.

Apart from your scheduled Special Time, can you think of any opportunities to catch some one-to-one time wherever you can? Maybe when you're waiting with one child while another child has Saturday football?

One mum grabbed 20 minutes of impromptu special time with her daughter on a trip to a museum with another family when her son went off with his friend and the other mum. They had a lovely time doing a quiz together.

Another dad took the opportunity provided by a long queue in the butchers to play some word games with his son. He told his boy that they were having special time together and he was so pleased it was just the two of them.

Blackberry time
Paul's sons asked if they were 'in' his Blackberry and he said, "You guys are much too important to be in that." Their little faces fell. So he got it and said, "Of course you can be in my Blackberry," and made an entry for their special time. Both boys starting dancing around the kitchen singing "We're in Daddy's Blackberry!"

Girl uninterrupted
Linda set her first special time for 5pm and asked her best friend to call at 5:05pm so she could easily say to her daughter, "Oh, I'm not answering that... this is our special time!"

4. Teach children to MANAGE FEELINGS and ENCOURAGE EMPATHY

We now know that when we **acknowledge how our children are feeling** – angry, jealous, hurt, frustrated, disappointed, inadequate, left out, unappreciated – they learn to identify and process feelings, rather than take them out on others. Being able to empathise is essential to their ability to get on with siblings and with others. This means understanding, and caring, about how someone else is feeling. Our focus on feelings helps shape our children's understanding of emotions and ability to 'read' other people's feelings and thoughts.

Acknowledge others' feelings and discuss feelings generally in the family. Comment on why a person may be feeling and acting as they do and what may help. *"Oliver seems cross at the moment. Brothers and sisters sometimes get angry with each other when they're really upset about other things. I wonder if he didn't have a happy day at school today. Maybe he needs a bit of time on his own."*

Encourage them to tell you how they are feeling rather than scolding them for having 'bad' feelings. Don't say *"Of course you don't hate your sister. That's a nasty thing to say."* Do say *"I'm glad you were brave enough to tell me. I think you need a hug."* When she says, *"You love Oscar more than me – you always go to his football but you never come to my ballet,"* don't say *"That's not true. I love you both the same."* Instead say, *"I hear you'd like me to watch your ballet. How can we arrange that I wonder? I love that you enjoy ballet. It requires strength and grace at the same time. You are a girl who can be strong and you can also be gentle."*

More examples of how to encourage empathy:

☺ *"You would like to be noticed for the special things that you do and have all the attention for that."*

☺ *"I know you really hate it when Sarah speaks to you like that – maybe it makes you feel that she's treating you like a baby."*

☺ *"I can see you were really angry when Josh knocked over your plane that you'd spent ages building. It took a lot of self-control not to hit him then."*

☺ *"You wish you could stay up as late as Ahmed. It feels unfair that you have to go bed half an hour earlier."*

☺ *"Sometimes I bet you wish you didn't have a brother or a sister."*

☺ *"When you say you hate Katie I can hear that you're really mad at her. Sometimes when our feelings get hurt we feel really angry, even towards people we love. When you're ready I'll help you to tell her how her words hurt you."*

Practise using self-calming techniques. For example: drawing, ripping up (appropriate) paper, or visualisation strategies such as imagining your anger is a big red balloon and popping it or letting it float away. Children can also use other forms of physical release such as punching a pillow, running up and down stairs, jumping on a trampoline, deep abdominal breathing, cold water splashed on their face or hands or getting some fresh air – anything that changes their physical state will impact their emotional state. And listening to relaxation CDs can help. Model this yourself.

Afterwards, when calm enough, use **Take Twos** (Chapter 6) to require children to express themselves in words

5. Teach and train children in WAYS OF INTERACTING POSITIVELY

Some children pick up on essential social skills easily but some need to be taught them explicitly (and take a while to get good at them). This takes time but it can be fun and incorporated into play. In the section on friendships below are several ideas for teaching children social skills which will also be relevant to siblings.

For sibling harmony it is particularly important to teach them negotiation and problem-solving skills, how to ask for something, trading deals, taking turns and sharing as well as resolving conflicts.

☺ Many families have the rule 'one divides, the other chooses' which ensures fair divisions

☺ *"I'll let you play with my Tumbling Stuart now if I can borrow your stunt car later."*

☺ *"If we watch Peppa Pig for 15 minutes first then I get to watch Frozen for the rest of TV time, ok?"*

☺ *"Please, Charlotte, kindest sister in all the world, can I use your new felt tips to do my drawing? I promise I'll put all the lids back on tightly."*

☺ *"I know you want to go on the computer but so do I. You had first turn yesterday so it's fair if I go on it first this time. How about you play with the Lego underwater thing while I'm on it and then you can have your turn later?"*

Descriptively praise them when they use constructive strategies (even if they're different from yours) or show fairness, generosity, kindness or forbearance.

6. Provide RULES FOR FAMILY LIFE

☺ **Accept and acknowledge the feelings kids have for each other and set firm limits on actions.** *"You're really cross with Jason. Nobody likes to be called a 'retard'. That hurt your feelings. You can tell him how you feel and I will help you. You may not hit him."* Kids may need self-calming strategies for releasing feelings before using words.

☺ **Be clear about your family values.** *"In this family we treat each other with respect. So no name-calling. When you've calmed down you will need to make amends to Victoria."* Make sure this applies to the adults too. *"I'm sorry I called you 'Eeyore' this morning. Although I didn't mean to be unkind I can see you didn't like it. Let me make it up to you by playing some UNO after dinner."*

Some rules regarding property which many families have found useful are as follows:

☐ Each child is the owner of his own property and does not *have* to share it with others. However, if a child gets attention and approval when he is willing to share, he is more likely to be generous again.

☐ Special belongings are kept in the child's own private space; everything in the common space is to be shared.

☐ Help children work out ways of sharing common resources such as computers, TV, the trampoline, the train set or even the shower! Some families have the rule that the first person who gets to play with a toy gets 10 minutes and the child who waits for the second turn gets 15 minutes.

☐ Explain clearly what rules about behaviour apply when friends come to visit. For example: the older child shouldn't be expected to always include younger ones when he has friends around.

☐ Set a routine for taking turns to get privileges like sitting in a special chair or sharing chores like feeding the fish or setting the table.

☐ Remove the object of the quarrel while the children work out a way of sharing it. This isn't a substitute for teaching children to share.

☐ Many families find it useful to have rules about private spaces (when one child can go into another's room or the bathroom), about the doing of homework (to ensure that older children get the space, quiet and attention that they need), about bedtimes (so that everyone gets enough sleep and that each child gets one-to-one time at the end of the day and you get some adult time), about chores (everyone makes a contribution according to their ability) and limits on the use of electronic gadgets.

☐ Many families give older children responsibilities and privileges. Some responsibility for younger children can build bonds between them but don't overdo it lest it cause resentment or leads to too much bossiness.

☐ If children spend less time on screens there are more opportunities for interaction with other children, they learn to socialise better, they get the physical outlets they need for releasing energy and their language development is improved. If children are playing games with violent content many parents observe that children become more aggressive. *For my own part I always noticed that if they'd had a long time in front of a screen my children were just much more tetchy and uncooperative.* (For more, see Chapter 11.)

7. MODEL what you want to see

Children who grow up with positive discipline tend to get along better with other children. Punitive discipline teaches children to give way to greater force, not wisdom. They learn about dominance and submission. If parents are aggressive towards each other or to the children, the children are more likely to be aggressive. Punitive discipline results in the child absorbing tension that must be discharged and it may be against another child at home or at school. This kind of discipline can also result in a child hardwired for stress who develops a very short fuse.

We send mixed messages if we punish children physically when they fight or shout at them when they're shouting. We need to match what we say to what we do for it to have any impact.

After reading Chapter 6 you will be modelling negotiating and problem-solving in your own interactions with the children, rather than just punishing! You can also set examples around apologising and making amends, speaking politely, being respectful, tolerating differences, managing emotions and looking after yourself. No pressure then!

What parents can do – to resolve conflict

Conventional wisdom had it that parents should stay out of sibling fighting since that would be to give it the attention it was designed to attract. We now know this advice to be too simplistic. When parents refuse to get involved it can give licence to bully and tells the ones being picked on that they don't matter. Fighting may stop but this is because the weaker one gives way to the more powerful one. *When I stopped intervening in my children's battles my younger son felt abandoned and it seemed I was sanctioning my older boy's conduct.*

We do need to help our children resolve conflict but our involvement should not be of the 'step in and sort it out' variety. Rather we need to help children resolve the problem themselves. We often unintentionally appoint ourselves judge and jury and decide who is at fault. This immediately puts all participants into intractable roles with the children identified as perpetrator and victim. What's worse is that this becomes a default setting – we can get caught up in positioning one of our children as the aggressor and the other as the victim. And if they become accustomed to these roles, the situation continues.

Minor squabbles

We can stay out of squabbles of a minor nature. Phew! This is ok if the power difference between the two children is not too great. (Just remember that what the younger child may lack in brute force he often makes up for in low cunning.) Send the children to a designated 'solution place' and tell them you trust that they can resolve it and you'd be interested to hear what solutions they come up with. For example: *"I am going to wait here until you have reached a solution… It might be that you decide to take turns, or one of you might decide to do* something else, or you might both decide to do something else… *Just tell me what you decide."* This is not a punishment; instead it's a new way of dealing with their low-level disputes.

We used to keep a 'solutions' book that the children could refer to and I would write in it the solutions they thought were successful.

Pop your head in after a while and descriptively praise them for their efforts to find solutions. If their solutions seem a bit imbalanced in favour of one child you might ask questions to help them to assess the fairness of it.

More heated or repeated arguments

When we get involved it should always be to:

☺ help the children **define the problem** and **identify any risk** – "*Only one computer and two boys who want to play different games on it.*" Or "*Lizzie, you want to play your CD and Oscar, you'd like peace and quiet. You're both so mad with each other that there's been yelling and door-slamming. We need to calm down or someone might get hurt.*"

☺ **acknowledge how both sides feel** without judgement or blame. "*You're both really angry about this. Henry wants to have first turn on the computer and Alex feels pushed out of the way when there is no discussion about it. Alex feels unfairly treated and resentful.*" "*Lizzie and Harry it sounds like you both feel the other one is being bossy and unfair about this. You'd both like the other one to consider your point of view.*"

☺ help them **find solutions**. "*How can you sort this out in a way that is fair to both of you without hurting? I'd love to hear what ideas you've got.*" If it's quite heated stay with the kids.

If you have habitually acted as arbitrator you will need to prepare them for the fact that you will not be sorting out their problems now. "*I know in the past I have got involved in your fights and sometimes taken sides. You are old enough now to sort out your own fights. From now on I am going to help you find your own solutions to the problem.*"

For a detailed example of a dispute-resolving conversation see our website (www.theparentpractice.com/book-resources#chapter-8).

Dangerous levels of conflict

Your first task is to take action to put a **stop to dangerous behaviour** (while keeping calm yourself). Separate the children, physically, if necessary. Then define the problem – state the risk in the behaviour or the rule it is breaking. "*This isn't safe. There is no hurting in this family. You both need to cool down.*"

Next, **take 'Cool Down Time'** immediately as a strategy, rather than a punishment. "*I'll listen to both of you when you're calmer.*" It may take some time for tempers to cool. The difficulties may still not have gone away especially if it is a long-running or recurring dispute.

When parents and children are both calm you will need a family meeting to help each child voice his opinions and to suggest solutions. Talk through what happened, the effect of what one child did on the other child, and ask how they could behave differently next time.

Your role is to mediate and guide non-judgmentally rather than impose solutions, to focus on constructive discussion rather than blaming and to give each side the opportunity to state their case.

Family meetings

Explain why you're having the meeting.

☺ Explain the ground rules – no interruptions when someone else is speaking. Maybe use a talking stick (see our website).

☺ Acknowledge everyone's feelings.

☺ Listen to each side's point of view without judgment.

☺ Reflect/summarise each view point – *"So Adela you wanted to use the computer and Joe you think it's your turn."*

☺ Describe the problem – *"It's hard when two people want the same thing. This problem keeps recurring."* Or ask the children what the problem is. *"Are your disagreements mainly about who's boss or have you any other ideas?"* You may say *"It sounds like there were mistakes on both sides. What did you each do that contributed to the problem?"*

☺ Invite solutions – mention dispute resolution skills such as compromise. Ask each child, *"What would you like your brother/sister to do differently in future?"* and *"What will you do differently?"*

☺ Either leave the room to let them come up with a solution or stay if their negotiating skills are unequal, especially if you think one child will force the other into compliance.

☺ Agree a solution – maybe write it down. Brainstorm with them and guide as necessary as to what dispute resolution techniques will work.

"Say what you need or want without attacking the other person."

"Pretend you are the other person and say what their point of view is."

"If you say something disrespectful, apologise."

"Ask if you need some cool down time."

"Don't bring up past arguments. Don't say 'You always' or 'You never'."

☺ Agree when to review it to discuss how the solution worked.

When I was a child I used to steal my sister's things all the time because she would never let me borrow them and I really wanted her to like me enough to share her things with me. My stealing was designed to make her like me... That's what psychologists call a maladaptive strategy! Of course it will take parents' help for children to be able to understand complex matters like these.

Football fight

Jerome felt he had had a 'light bulb' moment following a class on Siblings with the idea of the roles of Judge/Victim/Perpetrator. Phoebe and Ben were playing football in the garden and he could hear Ben smacking the ball against Phoebe's legs. Instead of doing what he normally would have done (steaming on in, making Ben the perpetrator and Phoebe the victim, snatching the ball and sending Ben inside), he asked if they could find a way of adjusting the game so Phoebe wouldn't be hurt. He left them to it and went inside. When he looked out, he saw Ben with his arm around Phoebe comforting her and they worked out new rules for the game where Ben went in goal instead!

Your turn

How can you respond to these common sibling comments, addressing the child's real needs?

"You always give him the biggest slice"
Rather than: *No, I don't, I give you the same, don't be silly.*
Say: *Are you still hungry? Would you like another slice?*

"Mum, it's so unfair; she always sits in that seat!"
Rather than: *Well, she's older and she asked first.*
Say: *It seems you would like to sit in the front next to Daddy sometimes.*

"You spend hours with Jimmy doing his homework."

....

....

"You love Sylvia more than me."

....

....

"I hate Jamie. He's so stupid."

....

....

One child deliberately knocks over/spoils the other's game/picture.

....

....

Only children and multiples (with thanks to Ann, Becky, Jeralyn and Flora)

Parents of only children say they have to be their child's siblings as well as parents and sometimes find that they battle with their child on a childish basis. Many of the above strategies will be applicable when you find yourself in disputes with your child.

It is just as important to remember to set aside special time for your only child lest all your time together is about 'getting stuff done'. Remember to schedule fun times. Only children will obviously need opportunities to spend time with other children if they are to learn social skills. Ann advises ensuring your home is a welcoming place for kids.

Parents of only children need to be particularly careful that they are not over-protective of their children and let them try things, take risks and make some mistakes. Parents of twins and triplets are of course dealing with more than one child of the same age so life is very busy. The temptation to compare is great, especially where the children are of the same sex. Advice from our parents of twins is as follows:

☺ Don't make comparisons and definitely don't label them, e.g. *the organised one* or *the forgetful one.*

☺ Celebrate their uniqueness through Descriptive Praise. Point out the positives of their temperaments, skills and qualities.

I love how you enjoy life so much – you're a really positive person.

I really appreciate how cautious you are. You analyse things very carefully before committing to them. I'm confident that you'll be safe.

☺ Allow them to be different – let them have separate birthday celebrations if they want, different sports and hobbies and separate rooms where possible. At school see if they can be in different classes. Different schools may suit different personalities and strengths. Encourage them to have different clothes and hair styles if they want.

☺ Don't overdo it and end up discouraging togetherness.

☺ Multiples can be obsessed with fairness so be clear that fairness doesn't necessarily mean being treated exactly the same. After all you don't get glasses for all the children because one of them is short-sighted.

Mary was driving with her 2 children in the car when Ben started throwing up! Mary had to pull the car over and stop and in the middle of it all Phoebe started saying, "You love him more than me because he's being sick and getting all your attention" (or words to that effect). Mary was able to stay calm and whilst cleaning Ben up, give Phoebe a tissue, saying she'd noticed how bad her cold was and that she really needed a tissue for her nose!

Friendships

Friendships can be lovely – affirming, supportive and nurturing; they can bring a child out of themselves and challenge them to try things they wouldn't on their own; friendship groups can give a sense of belonging; friends can provide emotional support; good friendships provide an opportunity for a child to air their views and work out what they believe in. Being with friends teaches trust and intimacy; negotiating with peers teaches communication skills; learning how to break up and make up is also useful. Friends can help kids through tough times.

Friendships can also be troublesome if they don't go well. Children fall out with each other, some kids find it hard to make friends and some are bullied.

Parents tell us the problems their children experience around friendships are:

☺ Being excluded

☺ Teasing/bullying, unkindness, meanness, name calling, put-downs – children say things like *you can't be my friend, you can't hang around with us, you're not in our club.* There can be quite personal slants – they call each other weird, fat, stupid, beanpole, shorty, gay, and criticise or make fun of their friends' clothes, hair, the fact that they wear glasses, have freckles, a funny nose etc

☺ Betrayal of confidences

☺ Being the subject of rumours

☺ Peer pressure, inappropriate friends/behaviour

☺ Children being too bossy or aggressive, or not assertive enough

☺ Children may have developed behaviours which aren't conducive to forming friendships – insensitivity to others, inability to read cues, coming too close, shouting too loud, grabbing, not knowing when to stop talking, moaning or complaining, being too needy/pleading, having a strop when things don't go their way.

We can foster good friendships by:

☺ **Providing opportunities for children to be with other kids their age** – neighbours, relatives, friends from activity groups. School will be the main meeting ground but if things go wrong in your child's school peer group it's good if they have friendship groups outside school too.

☺ **Involving children in groups outside school** – sporting clubs or youth groups, groups doing physical or creative things or community involvement. *"Having a good friend will lessen the harmful effects of bullying. If you are excluded by the general peer group but have a friend who is saying, 'you are not so bad as they say you are,' this can be enough to satisfy your need to belong. You will not be damaged if somebody* *special is valuing you, even if you are not valued by everyone.*"[38]

☺ **Modelling being with our own friends and being friendly with our partners.** Model loyalty, commitment, empathy, self-respect, taking into account the other's perspective, constructive dispute resolution and managing your feelings. Children who grow up with anger and upset can find it difficult to be good friends.

☺ **Helping the children develop social skills** – see below.

☺ **Not criticising 'unsuitable friends'** – this may make them more appealing. With younger children you can probably limit your child's association with other children but as they get older this is harder to do. Your children are more likely to adopt your values and be influenced by you if they get plenty of positive input from you. Point out what you don't like about the friend's behaviour rather than saying you don't like *them*.

Boys and girls have different styles of friendships in the primary school years. Boys tend to play in groups while girls have small clusters of friends and best friends. Boys' play tends to be more active and physical whereas girls may spend time talking as well as playing games.

Your turn

If your children are struggling with friendships it might help to start by asking 'What makes a good friend?' Help your

---

[38] Dr Michael Boulton, child psychologist, Keele University, quoted in Jan Parker And Jan Stimpson, *Raising Happy Children: What every child needs their parents to know*, 2004

child put together an 'advertisement' for a friend, and name all the qualities they are looking for.

Wanted: good friend

....

....

....

This exercise brings to your child's attention those qualities that they need to be cultivating too, in order to be a good friend themselves. Now you have a list of qualities to be looking out for – this will help you to descriptively praise your child when you see any sign of them.

Children we asked said that a good friend is one who:

☺ Is fun to be with – has common interests/views

☺ You can talk to (they listen)

☺ Shares and takes turns

☺ Likes you for who you are/doesn't pressure you to be different

☺ Keeps your secrets

☺ Sticks up for you

☺ Won't laugh at you, doesn't talk about you behind your back, won't lie about you

☺ Doesn't get mad/upset easily but talks to you instead

☺ Trusts that your intentions are good

☺ Believes you when you say sorry, forgives

☺ Apologises when she's wrong

☺ Can compromise

☺ Is dependable

☺ Is happy for you even if she feels jealous

☺ Comforts you when you're sad

Training in social and communication skills

We can help our children to feel comfortable in the company of others, and to be able to enjoy group situations. But we need to remember that each child has their own temperament and this will influence how they approach social events, and other people. *For example: a child who is reactive will hang back in any new situation and be unwilling to throw herself in until she is ready. Rather than push her forward, and try to 'train' her by dropping her into different environments in the hope that she will get used to it, we need to help her prepare for such situations.* Is your child an introvert? She may prefer to be by herself or with just one friend rather than a crowd or she may need downtime after social events.

Use **Descriptive Praise** on an on-going basis to help your child value himself and to highlight specific qualities that will help in friendships.

Play games with your children to encourage skills such as listening, turn-taking, being a good sport, i.e. using self-control, handling their feelings, considering other people's feelings, following rules and instructions, looking for solutions and developing strategies for dealing with problems. See our website for a guide to using games to teach children these vital skills and some suggestions for games to help train specific skills.

Role play how to join a group of children, different ways to say hello and ask to join in. *Hi, my name's...what's yours? I like your top, is Arsenal your favourite team?* You can laugh about funny ways to say hello in the process of finding a way that works for your child. You could pretend that different family members are strangers and say hello to each one in different ways. Training in small steps means practising in non-threatening areas first. Practise also what to say if the child says "No, you can't play".

You can also use role plays to help your child work out how to look after their needs without hurting anyone else. Practise saying something like *"I don't like it when you take my things. Stop that!" "I want to play with you but I don't like this chasing game – it hurts when you get slapped."* Experiential learning is the most effective – children can visualise and remember themselves doing it right.

Role play is also a good way to teach children to read **social cues** from words and body language. We can teach our children to gauge their impact on others and adjust accordingly, including the amount of space a person needs. See the role play on reading body language and facial expressions on p.132 for some ideas.

Sharing demands a level of social understanding which comes with maturity. Sharing means the child cares about what the other child wants as well as what he wants. Don't expect too much of this from younger children. Show children how to take turns by playing games and by example. Sharing toys provides the first experience of negotiation. First, recognise ownership so the children feel the situation is properly understood. For example: *"I know it's your car and it's for you to decide. And Hannah's really sad. If you'd like to play with her toys sometimes maybe you could let her play with yours?"* Then let them sort it out as much as possible. *"Sam's really upset. Can you think of anything else he might like to play with to cheer him up?"*

Descriptively praise sharing and turn-taking whenever it occurs. Express confidence in a positive outcome. *"Lucy, will you let Emma know when you're ready to share?"*

Model sharing. *"I'm going to let you have some of my ice-cream because you dropped some of yours and I can see you're sad."*

Saying sorry

I'm sure you will have been in situations where an apology has seemed necessary and you've insisted on it. How did that go? Forcing a child to apologise before they're ready to will result only in that kind of hollow "Well FINE then, SOR–RY!" that everybody knows is insincere. It will teach the apologiser nothing and won't benefit the person to whom he is apologising. It's meaningless, and it's actually not enough.

We need to wait until the feelings have subsided before anything useful can happen. This may require cool down time and will definitely require connection – describe how your child was feeling when he did the 'wrong thing'. He is more likely to feel real remorse if you do this without anger and judgment. It is that fear of being made wrong that makes a child push away responsibility and prevents contrition. (For a really effective form of words for apologies see Chapter 12.)

Technology and friendships

For older children social media can really increase the speed and intensity of gossip, humiliation and drama. It can enable fighting or meanness in ways that wouldn't happen face to face. Its reach means that home is no longer a safe haven, out of reach of cruel behaviour. It can also be addictive, which may mean less real-life interaction. For ideas on dealing with their digital world see Chapter 11.

Bullying

If your child is being bullied outside the home you can help by:

- ☺ **Listening** to and taking seriously what your child tells you and how they felt about it. Discuss with them (i.e. get lots of input from them) what bullying is (behaviour intended to hurt, whether isolated or persistent – distinguish from banter), where it might happen (hot spots), how to minimise opportunities for bullying, and what they can do if bullied.

☺ Let your child know that showing bullies you are frightened or upset encourages them and retaliating will escalate the situation. (The child could get seriously hurt, it reinforces the idea that might is right, it can make a child feel abandoned to fight his own battles and can turn the bullied into bullies).

☺ **Practise in role play** what the child can do – **don't just talk about it.**

Kids can:

- ○ run/walk away
- ○ seek adult help (although teachers often don't take effective action, which is why the child needs their own strategies)
- ○ assert themselves verbally – practise a good form of words and body language with them, e.g. *I don't like that, stop it*
- ○ when someone makes hurtful remarks:
  - ▪ Visualise insults not reaching you because they are swallowed up in enveloping fog/ bounce off a protective shield. Nothing touches you.
  - ▪ Reply with something short and bland, e.g. *that's what you think* or *really?* Then walk away. Get the child to come up with the words where possible.

☺ They need to understand **it is not their fault.** Some children feel they are causing trouble by reporting it. They must be able to tell a parent or teacher or other trusted adult. (But if adults don't take *effective* action reporting may backfire on the child and lead to retaliation from the bully so the bullied child will not want to tell again.) A child may get very embarrassed if their parent 'makes a scene'. We need to deal with the matter calmly and discreetly. Descriptively praise a child for telling you about bullying. If bullying is ongoing keep a record of incidents. Write to the school as well as speaking to them. When going in to the school both parents should attend.

☺ Let your child know it can happen to anyone and **no one should accept it**. Don't describe your child as a 'victim' or they may behave like one.

☺ **If your child is bullying** it takes courage to consider what the causes may be. He may be feeling inadequate or unloved (this doesn't mean you don't love him), he may be following the crowd, he may have been bullied himself or he might not have learnt to negotiate or compromise. Could he have had his own way too much?
   o Keep calm
   o Assure your child of your love even though the behaviour is unacceptable, say why it is unacceptable but don't label him/her as a 'bully' lest it become part of their self-image.
   o Explain what bullying behaviour is and how it can hurt and frighten.
   o Talk about the feelings of your child and the child who has been bullied. Make sure your child has regular opportunities to talk about his feelings.
   o Ask your child for ideas on how to stop the behaviour and make amends.
   o Does your child need to learn skills of communication, negotiation or dispute resolution? Practise ways of handling difficult situations in role play. Show him how to get positive attention, how to win friends, assertion vs aggression.
   o Provide opportunities for channelling aggression and teach self-control through sport, rough and tumble and martial arts.

○ Can you be brave and look at your own behaviour honestly? Are you modelling intimidating, humiliating, threatening or aggressive behaviours?

Children also need to learn when to trust or believe someone and to understand that people can be deceptive for their own reasons. When they are let down we can acknowledge how it feels to be betrayed.

Betrayal

My daughter Holly (7) had a friend over to play who told our neighbour's little girl Laila that Holly didn't like her, which isn't true, but Holly had said that Laila sometimes made quite a lot of noise in the flat above us which could be annoying. Laila was upset and so were her parents. Initially I wanted Holly to apologise but I didn't want to force an insincere apology and Holly thought that was unfair as she hadn't done anything wrong. I thought about it from my 7 year old's perspective and realised that it was a big ask for her to understand the unintended impact of her words. I acknowledged that she felt betrayed by her friend's breach of confidence and she decided to tell her friend (gently) about the effect of her words. Holly could see that sometimes words have unintended hurtful consequences and I said that saying sorry in this case was not an admission of wrongdoing but an acknowledgment of hurt caused. We compromised with Holly spending the afternoon happily with Laila keeping her entertained. Parents soothed, children happy, something learnt. Result!

Sharon, Mum of one

Playdate

When Sophie was in Year 1, she really wanted a play date with a girl in her class. The day finally came around and the girls were playing happily in the living room. All of a sudden I realized that Sophie wasn't in the room. She had gone off into her own bedroom and was playing by herself. At first I was a bit cross with her as she had asked for the play date for a long time, and it seemed like unkind and rude behaviour and I told her to go back in to the room and re-join her friend. After the class on temperament, I realized that I have a child that needs time alone in order to be able to fully be with her friends.

Ann, Mum of one

Relationships in a nutshell

Parents can help siblings to get along by:

1. Building self-esteem and giving each child individual positive attention

2. Noticing and commenting on positive interactions between brothers and sisters

3. Providing opportunities for fun together and alone

4. Encouraging empathy and acknowledging each child's feelings

5. Having rules to govern how family members interact and dealing with hot spots like possessions

6. Teaching children good pro-social habits

7. Modelling positive dispute resolution techniques

When brothers and sisters fight parents should stay out of it if it is low level and the power difference between children isn't too great. Parents need to watch out in case normal sibling fighting turns into bullying. Use a 'solutions place'.

For more intense disputes a parent should not be a judge, but a mediator. Involvement should be to help children:

☺ Identify the problem and any risk

☺ Have their feelings and point of view heard

☺ To come up with solutions that are fair to everyone

Parents can support children's friendships by providing opportunities to be with other children and by teaching children social skills like sharing. Parents can empower children to deal with bullying powerfully. Role play is a very effective tool here.

Further reading:

Laura Markham, *Peaceful Parent, Happy Siblings: How to Stop the Fighting and Raise Friends for Life*, 2015

Jan Parker and Jan Stimpson, *Sibling Rivalry, Sibling Love*, 2002, *Raising Happy Children: What every child needs their parents to know*, 2004

Adele Faber and Elaine Mazlish, *Siblings Without Rivalry: How to Help Your Children Live Together So You Can Live Too*, 2nd edition, 1998

Rosalind Wiseman, *Queen Bees and Wannabes: Helping Your Daughter Survive Cliques, Gossip, Boyfriends, and the New Realities of Girl World*, 2009

Patti Kelley Criswell, *A Smart Girl's Guide to Friendship Troubles: Dealing with Fights, Being Left Out, and the Whole Popularity Thing*, 2013

9

Their intellectual world

"We worry about what a child will become tomorrow,
yet we forget that he is someone today."

– Stacia Tauscher

"When you are inspired by some great purpose, some
extraordinary project, all your thoughts break their bonds:
Your mind transcends limitations, your consciousness
expands in every direction, and you find yourself in a new,
great, and wonderful world. Dormant forces, faculties and
talents become alive, and your discover yourself to be a
greater person by far than you ever dreamed yourself to
be."

– Patanjali

Thomas had been at a very good London primary school and
had been near the top of the class from the age of 5. All this time
his parents had told him how clever/talented he was. He was
a nice, happy child who got on well with his parents. At 11 he
sat exams and gained a place at a very prestigious secondary
school. Within 2 months of being at the school he had lost all
confidence and no longer wanted to go to school, complaining
of tummy aches and other ailments. He was also being very
rude and aggressive with his mother. Now he was at a school
where he was a similar academic ability to all the other boys
– no longer the 'clever' boy. He had no tools to deal with this.

Education Stress

Our children spend a great deal of time at school, and their success, or otherwise, at school greatly affects their happiness and confidence in the present as well as playing an important role in their futures. But school-based education is not the only place where the intellect is developed and the mind nurtured. Curiosity, creativity and passion for learning are more likely to be fostered at home.

Recently there has been much concern amongst educators about the stress that children experience at school through the pressure to perform in tests. Too much academic measuring sucks the joy out of learning.

"When we want the elephant to grow we feed the elephant. We don't weigh the elephant."

– unknown Indian teacher

Studies show that the more people are encouraged to chase results the less interest they take in the task itself. *"If school is too much like a race you get tired and enjoy it less. I know I learn things best when I am enjoying myself."* Jari, 13, quoted in Carl Honoré's book *Under Pressure*.[39]

Cheating in school has become commonplace, students become disengaged, stress-related illness and depression are increasingly widespread by the time they get to secondary school, and many arrive at university and the workplace unprepared and uninspired. Much of the pressure comes not just from the educational system, but from us too. This can be a very difficult area for parents these days. We mean to encourage but end up putting so much focus on our kids' achievements that we make it impossible for them to not

---

[39] Carl Honoré, *Under Pressure: Rescuing our children from the culture of hyper-parenting*, 2008

achieve. Children can be so stressed that they give up and become risk-averse.

Honoré refers to 21st-century parents bending their lives around children in a way never done before – we move house to be near schools, more and more both parents work to pay for housing, childcare, education and holidays, and we sacrifice sleep and leisure time to get children to all their activities. In some ways this is a good thing but the greater the investment in the children the more there is an expectation of reward, i.e. their achievements.

In times of financial insecurity we invest more in our children's future because it feels uncertain. We feel we need to give them an edge – to get ahead and beat the rest. We fear that our children will get left behind if we don't take action to maximise their potential. We worry we may be letting our children down if we don't push them more, that we are short-changing them if we don't aim at anything less than the absolute pinnacle of success. So we urge them on at school and we enrol them in enriching activities outside school that will look good on their CVs, sometimes forgetting whether the children actually want to learn the violin or Mandarin. Honoré tells the story of Jo Shirov, Human Resources manager and mother of twin boys. Jo says: *"If you think the corporate world is competitive, you should try being a mother today. You feel like everyone is judging you, and – this is a horrible thing to admit I know – but sometimes you end up doing stuff just to impress other moms rather than for the sake of your child... I enrolled the boys in a Mandarin class because everyone was saying how important it was, but they totally hated it. We dropped it pretty soon after, but it still took me a month to tell the other mothers we'd given up."*

I believe there are things parents can do that will help kids be motivated and creative learners and happy and confident people. Part of that is cultivating a healthy attitude toward success and failure. You can encourage your children to be ambitious, do their best and work hard but not to define themselves completely by their grades and certificates.

Success

The Collins and Oxford dictionaries both define success as the attainment of wealth, fame or position. But what about happiness?

What do you think success involves? Parents in our classes are saying that success needs to be about more than just particular attainments. If our children are to be successful long term they need to be fulfilled and contented and living worthwhile lives, not just having achieved grades, passed exams, obtained qualifications or jobs. Many adults have all of that and are still not happy.

"Happiness is achieved through fulfilment, through hard work and through leading a virtuous life. Politicians, administrators and educationalists who are shaping schools around the world are profoundly wrong in believing that exam success is the only metric of value. We are developing generations of dysfunctional and misguided products from our exam factory system."

– Dr Anthony Seldon, Headmaster of Wellington College[40]

When the families taking part in the 'Child of our Time' longitudinal project, aired on the BBC under the series of the same name, were interviewed at the children's birth in 2000 they all agreed, as every parent would, that *"happiness was the greatest gift they could have."* But Dr Tessa Livingstone, child

---

[40] http://www.huffingtonpost.co.uk/dr-anthony-seldon/happiness-isnt-superficia_b_3004653.html

psychologist and author of the project, has observed over the course of this study that *"our children and their parents may wish for happiness but they aim now for success, with material goods and money as their goal."* [41]

When your children have grown up, what do you hope they will have got out of their schooling and qualifications? And what qualities do they need now in order to do well at study and at work? Parents in our classes suggest that they need confidence, perseverance, resilience, motivation, to be good communicators, to be able to listen to and to learn from others, to be creative, risk-takers, hard workers and passionate about what they do.

We need to think carefully about success and what it means for our individual children. There is a Hasidic teaching that says, *"If your child has the talent [and the passion] to be a baker, don't ask him to be a doctor."* [42] One of our facilitators mentioned this to a parent and her response was: "Oh no, MY son will be a doctor!" Let's be careful we don't live out our dreams or unfulfilled ambitions through our children. Do ask yourself why you want your child to do competitive ballroom dancing and be in the swim squad and play piano and do extra maths. Is it really for him? And if so, what are the benefits? Do these activities outweigh the advantage of being able to spend time with the family and alone, to be able to play and be a child?

When I left school I wanted to be a teacher but was persuaded by my father to study law because he rated that profession more highly and would have liked to have become a lawyer himself. I enjoyed law school and don't regret my years of study but in practice I wasn't well suited for the confrontational aspects of life as a commercial solicitor and gave it up when my youngest

---

[41] http://www.kddc.com/Simpler-Pleasures.aspx
[42] Quoted in Wendy Mogel, *The Blessing of a Skinned Knee: Using Jewish Teachings to Raise Self-Reliant Children*, 2008

child was born. If I'd had the courage to follow my heart I would have got to a fulfilling career in education sooner than I did.

"Everyone is a genius. But if you judge a fish on its ability to climb a tree, it will live its whole life believing that it is stupid."

– Albert Einstein

(See the Animal School video on http://www.youtube. com/watch?v=o8limRtHZPs. Also on our website. (www. theparentpractice.com/book-resources#chapter-9))

If children are to do their best in whatever path they choose they will need to be confident and self-motivated, to be prepared to try hard and not give up, to be willing to try a different path than that taken by the majority, to have courage and believe they are worthwhile. They will need to be able to think for themselves. They will need to pick themselves up after failures, not be defeated by them but embrace them as opportunities for learning.

There are several ways parents can help children develop the above qualities and stimulate curiosity, creativity and a love of learning.

What gets in the way

Stress

Neuroscientific research tells us that the developing brain is very vulnerable to, and key brain structures may be altered by, stress. When stress chemicals are activated in early life the brain may remain in a stressed state. An oversensitive stress system means that the child overreacts to small upsets (even a broken Kit-Kat!) and is vulnerable to anxiety and depression.[43] Chronic stress inhibits learning. When the

---

[43] Margot Sunderland, *The Science of Parenting*, 2006

lower brain is activated by stress, stress hormones actually turn off the parts of the brain that allow us to focus attention, understand ideas, commit information to memory and reason critically.[44] Kids have to feel safe in order to learn which means they need to know it's ok to fail.

We can help our children feel less stressed by making sure our expectations are realistic for that child, by setting up for success, by focusing more on process than results and by listening to their worries rather than dismissing them. If we are calm and consistent about daily routines it helps kids be less anxious. It can be difficult for parents to accept that their child might suit a less academic environment or that the child needs more support for the environment they're in. We can also teach our children stress-reducing techniques such as those mentioned in Chapter 7.

Criticism, nagging, etc

Jory was doing homework on a Saturday morning and had to create an A3 page all about the life cycle of a newt. As Dad walked in the house he could hear that his wife was berating him for the messy handwriting and was forcing him to re-do the work as the teacher would be completely disappointed in his efforts. Jory then turned the paper upside-down and said that he could say the life cycle without looking at the page... and started to do so. She cut him off by saying that it wasn't a test and that he needed to get on with the presentation. He quickly got angry with her and decided to re-do the work on Power Point. She then told him that he should do it on paper as that was what the teacher had asked. He started to re-do it, and she continued telling him that he should get a ruler and make lines on the paper so his work would be neater. She took the sheet away and drew the lines on for him. And... he got the work done. BUT... Dad realised there was not an ounce of praise

---

[44] William R Stixrud, PhD, http://learnnow.org/topics/stress/reduce-stress-to-increase-learning

and that he might have used a similar approach himself in an attempt to get his son to 'do it right'. Because it was not him in the hot seat he could see that it was total criticism and he felt so bad for his 9 year old because that had been the approach in their household...until that moment!

Reading this story may have been uncomfortable. We know that what will not inspire our children either to do their homework in the moment or to develop a love of learning over time is nagging, criticism, put-downs or labelling. And yet many of us find ourselves slipping into this, usually out of anxiety that our children will not succeed. Guilt is only useful if it motivates you to make change. Let's resolve to start afresh.

Specific Learning Difficulties

There is no reason why a child with a specific learning difficulty such as dyslexia or dyspraxia should not do the best that they are capable of. The nature of their difficulties may mean that they need extra support and their progress may not be the same as their peers but the biggest obstacles to their success are the definition of that success, unrealistic expectations, a failure to look behind behaviour to see whether there is a learning difficulty and the child's loss of confidence. Many children with learning difficulties, like my son, suffer huge loss of confidence and may seek to distract from their struggles through behaviour which then gets them into trouble in the classroom. This further compounds their problems. They often believe that they are stupid or naughty but the difficulties thrown up by these conditions have nothing to do with intelligence and their behaviour is a reaction to unmet needs.

How to motivate and encourage without causing our children stress

Use Descriptive Praise

As you know by now, Descriptive Praise is your main tool for motivating and encouraging your children.

How do you ensure that your attempts to bring out the best in your children don't cause stress that could actually inhibit their learning?

Keep your Descriptive Praise focused more on process and progress than outcome. Comment on your child's efforts, the strategies he is using, the attitude he brings to the task and any improvements on his last attempt rather than focusing on the results. This is the best form of praise in all contexts, not just when you're talking about school work. This can be a difficult idea to accept as many of us were brought up with the view that results were everything but when we focus on process the outcomes take care of themselves.

"It was a good idea to look up that information about Einstein in Wikipedia. You found out more than was in your book that way."

"You know it works well for you to walk up and down outside where you won't be disturbed when you're learning your lines for the play. You've figured out strategies that work for your own style of learning."

"You kept on trying with these sums even though you didn't find it easy. I call that persevering. Your efforts have paid off – five out of six are correct. I wonder if you can work out how to correct the sixth one."

"When your first tactic didn't work with that experiment I noticed you modified your method a bit. That's a really scientific approach. How's it going now?"

"When you look over your work for any improvements you can make, that shows that you're willing to do your best. That's a great attitude to your studies."

"Look at your handwriting now compared to just a few weeks ago. You can form your letters so carefully now and most of them are sitting on the line. Do you think that's because you've been practising?"

Don't call them 'clever'

Many parents, in the hope of building confidence in their children, will say things like 'clever girl' or 'you're so smart'. But studies by Professor Carol Dweck, psychologist, have shown that praise which focuses on talent is actually damaging to children.

Dweck's research has shown that when children are praised for their intelligence they develop a **'fixed' mindset.** They think that a person is given a fixed amount of talent and intelligence at birth, and whatever results they get simply demonstrate the 'cleverness' that they possess. They think that if they are 'clever' they shouldn't have to work too hard at something. People with a 'fixed' mindset tend to avoid exploration and challenge. They take the easy option rather than running the risk that they will prove that they are not in fact 'clever'.

"Praising intelligence takes it out of the child's control and provides no recipe for responding to failure... Mistakes crack their self-confidence because they attribute errors to a lack of ability, which they feel powerless to change. They avoid challenges because challenges make mistakes more likely and looking smart less so." [45]

In contrast others have a **'growth' mindset**, which means the belief that a person's natural capabilities and talents can be developed through application and effort. The risk-taking that is inherent in all learning is therefore not regarded as

---

[45] Carol Dweck, *Mindset: How You Can Fulfil Your Potential*, 2012

frightening, and more real learning can take place. When faced with mistakes or failures, growth mindset people believe that they can overcome through perseverance. When we praise our children for hard work, effort and application they develop a growth mindset. Have a look at this YouTube video clip which shows the effect of effort-based praise in Dweck's studies: https://www. youtube.com/watch?v=TTXrV0_3UjY (also on our website (www.theparentpractice.com/book-resources#chapter-9)). She takes two groups of children and gives them puzzles to do. One group is told *"you've done really well – you must be really good at puzzles"* whereas the other group is told *"you've done really well – you must have tried really hard."* The children are then offered a harder set of puzzles to do. You'll see that the group who were praised for being smart at puzzles declined whereas the group who were praised for their effort opted to do the harder set. Effort-based praise helps children develop a growth mindset.

My friend's son is suffering from fixed-mindset thinking as he approaches his final year of schooling – he simply believes that he shouldn't have to apply himself if he is clever. The result is he's not doing as well as he could be and he now thinks he's not so clever.

Embrace struggle

We can talk to our children about fixed and growth mindsets and let them know that intelligence is malleable and that they can grow more by their efforts. Let them know that struggle is a predictable part of the learning process and encourage them to embrace it because it is through struggle that brain cells grow.

Be careful that you don't communicate to your children that their success is attributable to how smart they are. Two conversations between parents and children with different cultural backgrounds noted by Professor Jin Li[46] demonstrate different approaches to success. The first is between an American mother and her son. The boy is a good student who loves to learn. He tells his mother that he and his friends talk about books during recess, and she responds with: *Do you know that's what smart people do?* Li compares this with a conversation between a Taiwanese mother and her 9-year-old son. The boy won first place in a piano competition, and the mother is explaining to him why. *"You practised and practised with lots of energy. It got really hard, but you made a great effort."* In the latter conversation the emphasis is on the boy's perseverance and effort rather than his innate talent.

Research shows that when students struggle to find an answer, active engagement in the process makes it more likely that they will retain the learning and they will feel good about themselves.[47] *One young boy was heard telling his dad delightedly that he could feel his brain growing as a result of his struggles with his reading.*

Don't ask them if they won
When your children have got a test back or have taken part in a sporting or other contest what should you ask? I'm not saying that doing well doesn't matter but if your first question is *"did you win?"* when they come home from a hockey game this will undoubtedly convey to them that winning is most important, whatever you may say to them otherwise.

Focus on small successes
Set up for success using all the skills from Chapter 4 and

---

[46] Professor at Brown University quoted in an article 'Struggle for smarts' by Alix Spiegel in NPR Shots in November 2012 http://www.npr.org/sections/health-shots/2012/11/12/164793058/struggle-for-smarts-how-eastern-and-western-cultures-tackle-learning

[47] Rapid Learning Institute October 2012, http://rapidlearninginstitute.com/training-insights/learners-struggling-to-find-answer/

notice and comment on small successes to grow confidence and allow your child to tackle bigger challenges.

"You have got off to a great start – I can see you've got your student planner out."

"You've already written three sentences."

"I like the way you've sounded out that word. You broke it into smaller sounds and then put it together."

"You persevered until you figured out how to embed that video into your Power Point presentation."

When children have early experiences of success they continue to do well, feel good and keep trying in a cyclical way. For those who haven't felt particularly successful to date we can help by keeping our focus on the small stuff, the building blocks.

Make sure your praise isn't comparative or creates unrealistic expectations

We want our children to feel appreciated for themselves and their own efforts. We don't want them to feel we are comparing them with anyone else. Comparisons invite competition whereas there is much evidence that children learn better in collaborative environments. You don't want your child's experience of success to be at the expense of someone else's failure, or vice versa.

Take care that your praise doesn't inadvertently create an expectation that they must *always* be able to do what you've just praised them for. Instead of *"Oh Sarah, you're such a kind girl,"* say *"When you saw that Amara was sad this afternoon you put your arm around her and played with her rather than going out to play with Gabriela."*

Although it's not the worst thing a parent could say to a child, *"I'm so proud of you"* can sometimes convey the idea that it is a child's job to make the parent proud of them. Instead say, *"you must be so proud of yourself."* Feel free to tell your child's other parent or grandparents how proud you feel!

Show interest in what they are learning

And how it is relevant in their lives by demonstrating how maths skills are used in cooking, shopping etc, how science helps us understand what is going on around us, or history can explain why it is we do what we do today. Visiting museums and galleries can help bring alive what they're learning at school and showing your interest is likely to inspire theirs.

Foster resilience

Listen to their feelings

When we accept, acknowledge and validate our children's feelings it has a positive impact on their self-esteem and resilience – the ability to bounce back and try again after a knock.

Emotion Coaching helps children respond better to stress, competitiveness and challenges as well as helping them with failures. When we release feelings we can access the logical parts of our brains to work out what to do.

Research has shown that children with good emotional intelligence have better academic achievements[48] because:

☐ Their logical brain (frontal lobes) and the connections between it and other parts of the brain are more highly developed

☐ Their minds are unencumbered by unresolved emotions

☐ They are able to sustain attention for longer

---

[48] Professor John Gottman, *Raising an Emotionally Intelligent Child*, 1998

For example: *"When you get stuck on a sum I think you sometimes feel a bit stupid – maybe it feels like you can't do what everybody else seems to be able to do."*
"It takes courage to try something if you're worried you might not get it right. Do you sometimes think you might look silly if you make a mistake?"
"It can be hard to get started on something if you feel you're not going to do well at it."
"You don't feel like doing your homework right now as you'd rather be playing. You're finding the new sums very challenging."

When your daughter says unkind things about her friend who's moved on to the next book in the reading scheme before her, *"I know you really like to do well and you like to come first so you're disappointed that Amy has moved up to red level before you. I love that you want to do your best and you have been reading every night so you will keep improving. Maybe in a little while you'll feel better and can be pleased for your friend."* As opposed to *"that's not a nice way to talk about Amy,"* or *"just get on with it and stop moaning, you know you have to do your homework."*

Listen to their ideas

If we want to encourage children to be independent thinkers and to challenge ideas we have to allow them to have opinions that are different from ours. Oh dear! That doesn't mean we can't require them to express themselves respectfully and nor does it mean that we will necessarily change our minds about what they need to do.

Parents in our classes say that it is important to them that their children have ideas, and that they are prepared to present them and stand up for themselves. Sometimes you'll need to respond *"I hear this is important to you, and you've clearly thought it through. I appreciate your view... Today we need to do it this way. I'm sure you're disappointed."*

It may take more time but if we're going to foster creative thinking and problem-solving skills we also need to be sure we're inviting input from them rather than just dictating what, where, when and how everything should happen. Brainstorming with children for solutions also produces great ideas.

Encourage independence

When we encourage children to do things for themselves we give them the message that we believe they are capable. But often we do things for them out of habit and because it puts us in control. It also feels like the stakes are high and we can't afford to let our children make mistakes. *I know we did too much for our youngest son around his exams because we felt it was so important that he get the grades he needed for the next step in his education, his passport to successful adult life. But when he feels his parents are there to catch him he doesn't put so much effort in himself. When we do too much of his thinking/planning/organising he doesn't do it himself. He also gets the unintended message that we don't think he can do it and his confidence suffers.*

For parents there is a fine line between Setting Up For Success and helicoptering. We will look at how to 'help' around homework and encourage good organisational habits below.

One of the ways we can help children think for themselves is by not always providing ready answers to their questions but encouraging them to think or find the answer for themselves. Consulting Dr Google is a lot quicker than when I was a child and had to look up things in our set of World Book encyclopaedias!

Is competition a bad thing?

The well intentioned 'prizes for all' philosophy adopted by some schools may not be equipping our children for the real world. Behind this refusal to allow competition seems to lie a suspicion that competitiveness is inherently evil. When is competition a good thing and when can it be a problem? Being competitive is not always the same as being ruthless. But it can put friendships at risk if children see their success as linked to someone else's failure, when proving your worth is about being top of the pile. When self-esteem is dependent upon coming first it is a fragile thing. Research shows that in the classroom collaboration is better for learning than competition. And competition can add to a child's stress.

"Instead of competing with each other we can compete with ourselves which is the best way to learn things." **Patrick, 13**
"Hockey is just more fun when winning isn't everything."
Thomas, 13 [49]

It's alright to know there are people who are better than me at things if I believe I can improve my own performance through effort and I can do my best and be satisfied with *my* best. Remind your children that **doing your best is not the same as being the best.**

So we don't need to shield our children from competition but we do need to teach them how to manage and benefit from failure.

How to fail well

"At a time when we place so many restrictions on our children, we need to give them the space and confidence to explore the new, to become independent, and to take risks.

---

[49] Quoted in Carl Honoré, *Under Pressure: Rescuing our children from the culture of hyper-parenting*, 2008

298 | Real parenting for real kids

You learn more from making mistakes than from getting everything right."

– Heather Hanbury[50]

Thomas Edison was a famous American inventor, scientist and businessman who developed many devices that greatly influenced life around the world and is attributed with inventing the commercial electric light-bulb – but not without making a few mistakes first. He said: *"I have not failed. I've just found 10,000 ways that won't work... Genius is one percent inspiration and ninety-nine percent perspiration. Accordingly, a genius is often merely a talented person who has done all of his or her homework."*

Author Alfie Kohn has argued that many educational practices in our results-oriented systems ensure that our children have multiple experiences of failure. Competitive environments ensure that children can only succeed by others failing; the use of standardised tests cause more competition and pressure; the setting of homework requires the working of a second shift when they get home from a busy day at school; and the use of grades by definition compares one child with another.[51] All this despite much evidence that children learn better in collaborative rather than competitive environments.

There has been much discussion in recent years about failure, with many respected writers making the claim that schools and parents don't allow children to fail, to their detriment. The argument has been made that if a child has no experience of failure they will not be able to cope with it in later life; that shielding a child from failure prevents the development of grit, resilience and responsibility.

---

[50] Then Head of Wimbledon High School, speaking in London on the panel of a screening of the film *Race To Nowhere* hosted by The Parent Practice in March 2011
[51] Interview on the 'Great Parenting Show', September 2014. Kohn is the author of *The Homework Myth: Why Our Kids Get Too Much of a Bad Thing*, 2007

But the premise that the experience of failure itself tends to be beneficial is inaccurate.

Failure *per se* does not lead to success. Failure leads children to experience themselves as incompetent, with loss of confidence. This makes it more likely that they will fail again the next time or that they will avoid exposure to failure and become risk-averse.

The route to success is via small experiences of success and having the emotional intelligence to enable one to keep failure in perspective.

It's not enough just to let kids have the experience of failure, to drop them into situations where they will fail or to cover their work in red ink. We have to **build resilience through Emotion Coaching** and we have to be mindful about approaching **failure as an opportunity to learn.** You can encourage your children to see themselves as successful in overcoming adversity. They need to see that they can make mistakes, solve problems, struggle and come out triumphant, and that their value as human beings is not contingent upon their achievements.

Model handling failure/mistakes well yourself

When you make a mistake don't beat yourself up about it but acknowledge the mistake and why it was a mistake. Then, where appropriate, take steps to remedy it or make amends. Articulate what you are learning from your mistake and show that you are not diminished by your mistakes but can profit from them.

For example: *Yesterday when we were doing homework I was very critical of your efforts. I'm sorry. I thought about it afterwards when I was calm and realised that it was because I thought you weren't trying very hard. I worry that if you don't do your best you won't pass your exams at the end of the year. But I know that when I nag you and point out all the mistakes it makes you feel bad and you don't want to do your homework. Today I am going to try to notice all the good things you do during homework. Will you help me?*

Draw attention to good examples of learning from failure

We can highlight (rare) examples of public figures handling defeat well like Nadal by Djokovic in the 2011 Wimbledon finals when he said: *"First I would like to congratulate Novak and his team for his victory today and his amazing season. It wasn't possible [for me] today in this final. I tried my best as always. Today one player played better than me. I will try [again] next year."*

In that gracious statement Nadal acknowledged that Djokovich won and Nadal lost and was happy for Djokovich and what he accomplished. He acknowledged that he was beaten by the better player on the day. He says that he played his best, and he understands that on that particular day, his best wasn't enough to win. He left with an increased commitment and motivation to learn from his loss, to look at what he could have done differently and to refine his game and improve so that next time there would be a different result!

This is such an important lesson to instil in our children – the ability to win with grace and humility and the ability to lose in the same way. Defeat can shut you down so you no longer want to try or it can be a source of inspiration and learning.

Give your children the opportunity to practise and learn from your example of winning and losing by playing games with them (see our website (www.theparentpractice.com/book-resources#chapter-9)).

Point out where children are learning from their mistakes

"You realised that sentence wasn't right and rubbed it out. But

I love that you didn't get so mad that you screwed up your work like you have done in the past. You are learning to accept that we all make mistakes."

"When your experiment didn't work the first time you learnt something valuable about what happens to clay when it dries out."

"Now that you're calmer you can probably see that the way you spoke to your brother didn't make him want to help you. You've learnt something about how to speak to people when you want cooperation."

Your relationship with the school

For your child to do well at school you also need to have a positive relationship with his teachers. You need to be seen to be supportive of school policy. If you don't like something speak to the school about it rather than complaining in front of your child. I made big mistakes in this area when Christian was little as I thought their approach to discipline was terrible. If you do disagree with the school's approach work to change it with the school or remove your child, but to speak disrespectfully or to undermine the school's authority in front of your child will make life hard for him.

Teachers are human beings too(!) and so will respond well to Descriptive Praise and Emotion Coaching. Let them know what you appreciate about the job they're doing and empathise with the difficulties of looking after 20–30 children with individual needs and temperaments. If you are trying to get your child's teacher to adjust their approach don't tell them how to do their job but instead say something like *"what we're finding works at home is..."* Maybe say *"we tried punishing – I was really good at it – but it didn't work..."* Humour can help, provided you don't patronise!

After school

Homework

What are your memories of homework? Did you rush through the door after a long day at school and happily settle down to it? I didn't mind it but I was a nerd and I didn't have nearly as much as my children got. Don't expect your child to love doing homework after a long day at school. Many kids hate it because it impinges on their own time or because they feel unsuccessful at it or because the atmosphere around homework has become very tense with much nagging, ordering around and criticism.

One mum said this was her breakthrough: "Of course my son doesn't want to do his homework..." She stopped making him wrong so her tone of voice changed and her support and encouragement became more genuine. He does not yet like homework, but they are having fewer battles.

Many parents hate homework as much as their children. Get clear on your own beliefs about the value of homework or it will be hard to make it work. If your child is attending a school that sets homework you will need to support the school's policy or work to change it, or move schools. **Empathise** with your child, without agreeing that homework sucks. *"It's tough after a long day to sit down to do homework."*
Get their input. Doing homework is non-negotiable but how and when homework is done can be agreed with the child and giving them some control can make a big difference.

Prepare a comfortable environment for homework and try to minimise distractions, both clutter and noise. Research says that children who associate reading with a warm, comfortable lap become avid readers.

Prepare a child for doing homework independently by using **Chat Throughs**. This means having your child explain to you what he has to do, in detail. If you feel he hasn't quite understood it or you anticipate areas of weakness, **ask questions** to clarify. *"How will I know where the beginning and end of each sentence are?"* By asking questions rather than supplying the answers he gets into the habit of doing his own thinking. If he doesn't know the answer to something ask him where he could find the answer or point him in the direction of where he can find out.

Descriptively Praise any willingness to engage in this process, especially taking guesses. Children sometimes find this process of 'chatting though' their homework tedious but don't be tempted to skip it until they are in the habit of working well on their own and producing work of a satisfactory quality. You can empathise with how they feel.

Once he has explained what he has to do **leave him to get on with it** for a short period at first but for increasingly longer intervals. Young children (or children not used to working on their own) will need parents to be present, perhaps doing some paper work (not screen work) of their own.

Do I need to say **don't do it for them**? Remind yourself of the point of homework – it's not so the teacher knows how well you can do a science project, better than the next parent. Or indeed showing your child what a 'good job' looks like. Homework is for exploring responsibility and doing something by themselves.

After a while **Descriptively Praise** behaviour such as concentration, sitting still on his chair, not fiddling with things, working independently, an improvement on previous efforts, strategies employed and anything about the work itself. Make sure you're acknowledging good qualities or behavioural traits such as commitment and creativity as well as being able to spell well or do fractions.

Ask him to **find something to improve** (or maybe a set number of things, half his age is a reasonable target). Descriptively Praise his willingness to do so and any improvements made. If he doesn't find for himself something that you can see needs to be changed ask him questions to direct his attention to it or make suggestions about how it might be improved. For example: *"You've got 6 of the 7 letters in 'because' right. Can you see what needs to be added?"* If you do this habitually they will get the idea that we can always make our work better and not hear our suggestions as criticisms.

Don't rescue. If homework is not done it should be your child's responsibility to explain why not to the teacher, unless you had decided that he was just too tired to do it or a grandparents' visit took priority.

Extra-curricular activities

What is the point of extra-curricular activities? Many parents enrol their children in a large number of activities because they want them to have accomplishments (that will look good on a future CV) or they didn't have those opportunities themselves when young. But if the child doesn't have a choice about or interest in the activities he will become resentful.

Extra-curricular activities can be great for:

☺ Doing something that isn't school based and providing a chance to socialise with non-school children (particularly if your child isn't feeling successful there)

☺ Opportunities to engage more in sports or the arts for which there isn't much time in the curriculum

☺ Giving a sense of belonging, feeling part of a team

☺ A chance to sample activities that require non-academic skills that might become a passion

Be wary of over-scheduling your children. What are you and your child losing as you rush from one scheduled activity to another? School-aged children need time to play and connect with parents and siblings. They need opportunities to have the down time in which ideas come and to sleep. When parents are rushing children from activity to activity they spend so much time in the car they get little exercise, unless it's structured sport, they share few good meals together and parents end up rushing and nagging. It was one of the best things we ever did when we cut down on the children's scheduled activities.

Play

"To stimulate creativity one must develop the childlike inclination for play."

– Albert Einstein

Play is a vital part of childhood. It gives children joy, but it is also where learning happens. It helps develop creativity and teaches a child social skills and to use the imagination as well as helping her to discover her own interests, strengths and weaknesses. Children need to be able to share, empathise and follow instructions at school which they learn through play.

Time for play is an essential antidote to the busyness of the school day. Allow Protect time for unstructured child-led play so that children can de-stress. Otherwise learning will be compromised and behaviour will deteriorate.

One child said in response to a survey on the children's website CBBC: *"Adults can be very stupid at times. Kids should be allowed to experiment and try things. Otherwise when they grow up they'll make very stupid mistakes from not getting enough experience in childhood."*[52]

Protect sleep

We all know from experience how vital it is that our children get the sleep they need. Without a good night's sleep children will not perform well at school (attention, memory and processing information are compromised), they will be crabby and at risk of depression and weight gain over time. In the 4–12 age group, children need 10–12 hours' sleep at night. Even if parents have rules around bedtimes children may have trouble falling asleep and often this is because of the nature of pre-bed activities. *Theo, aged 10, found that once his family set up a no-electronics rule for the hour before bed time he was falling asleep straightaway whereas previously it was taking him up to an hour to fall asleep.* Sleep experts say that a regular routine aids sleep and all agree that no electronics before sleep is a good idea. Other things that can get in the way of sleep are noise, being too hot or cold, exercising too close to bed time or food intake. A heavy meal just before bed time can make sleep difficult.

Encouraging focus and organisational skills

Stress, lack of sleep, diet and emotions all affect your child's ability to focus as well as her age, temperamental propensity to impulsivity and distractibility or conditions such as ADHD. All things being equal children can focus on a learning task for approximately the same number of minutes as their age, plus one. So your 5 year old should be able to focus for 6 minutes on a challenging task. She can focus for much longer

---

[52] http://www.telegraph.co.uk/news/uknews/2059471/Child-Of-Our-Time-Whatever-happened-to-our-childrens-playtime.html

if it is fun and she is very engaged, so motivation is key. Break work segments into manageable blocks. Even adults can only focus optimally for periods of 90 minutes. Children lose the ability to sustain concentration if they have little experience of doing so. If they spend all their time engaged in activities that require no sustained thought, such as most TV programmes and computer games, then focus suffers. Counteract this by providing construction toys, jigsaw puzzles and craft. Play listening or memory games like Simple Simon or My Grandmother Went to Market or make up your own versions. For more games ideas see our website (www.theparentpractice.com/book-resources#chapter-9).

Consistent Emotion Coaching helps build the frontal lobes, which are responsible for logical thinking and controlling impulses.

Active kids will also need to have opportunities to be physical and release their energy.

Use Descriptive Praise to draw attention to the moments when they're focused. If you pay attention to it you'll get more of it. If you don't want to break the spell then wait until they break focus themselves and praise them for having just been concentrating.

Most parents are pretty organised people – we have to be! You can help your child to get organised too by using tools like schedules, planners, lists or post-its around the house or in the car or alerts on a phone. As they get older make sure that they do the thinking and work out what will help them remember things and plan their time. It's tempting to rescue them if they forget their library book at swimming training but better to help them work out how they can get it back. If they ask for a lift that's fine but don't work it out for them.

How do they see you keeping organised?

Cultivating curiosity and passion

This is all about modelling, modelling, modelling. Do we

have interests of our own or have we given these up in the hurly-burly of family life? If you cut down on your child's schedule and pick up an interest of your own you will be helping your child in two ways. When you see something beautiful do you express wonder? When you read something interesting do you share it with them? Have your children seen you engaged in study? Do they see you getting fired up about issues? Getting cranky with them is not the same!

Descriptively praise them for their passions and comment favourably on curiosity when you come across it in the wider world. Curious children are dirty and noisy – we have to be willing to let that happen. We also have to be careful that as parents we are a non-anxious presence, that we are not cautioning them all the time with *"Don't do that,"* or *"Be careful,"* or *"Just do what you've been told to do."* This makes them fearful and unwilling to take risks.

Parents can also stimulate passions by providing opportunities for kids to explore what they're interested in, not necessarily what you think they might excel at.

Homework choices

I had such a homework breakthrough this afternoon.

I decided to give him choices. Firstly, when we got home I offered him the choice of going to the park and doing homework after tea, or homework first and TV after tea. He chose park (which I was kind of hoping he would as it was a lovely afternoon, but also slightly dreading as the tireder he is, the more problematic the homework usually is). Then when it came to homework time, I asked him if he was happy to do it at the kitchen table (the usual place) or if he would prefer somewhere else. He said he would like to kneel at the coffee table in the drawing room. I was pretty dubious but I could see he was so delighted with his choice as he immediately, without prompting, rushed off to go and get his homework folder and came back carrying the folder and pencils and rubber etc (usually really a struggle to get all the equipment assembled).

Masses of descriptive praise for that and he knelt at the table and did all his homework in one sitting (about 40 mins) and was hardly jiggling around or chatting about other things at all. I just sat next to him with a running commentary on how well he was sitting still/ concentrating/holding his pencil/reading the question etc. I don't think it was the change of position per se that made the difference but the fact that he had been allowed to make choices as he said a couple of times how happy he was that he had been allowed to choose where and when to do it and the fact that I was constantly praising him instead of nagging him.

Anyway, I am still rather surprised at how such straightforward changes on my part made such a huge difference to him.

Lucy, Mum of 6-year-old boy

Piano tantrums

My 10 year old and 8 year old had been throwing tantrums every day for two years when it was time for them to practise the piano. I'd tried sticker charts, a prize box, warning them in advance that it's almost time for practice and nothing had worked. They were being very disrespectful to me as well. After the Positive Discipline class I sat down with my husband and thought about why they were behaving like this. I got that they didn't like to practice but that didn't excuse the rudeness.

Eventually we decided to sit down together with the kids and talk about piano practice calmly. We started with the fact that practice doesn't seem to be working for any of us. We acknowledged how much we knew they didn't like my nagging. Well that opened the floodgates. They said they felt bossed around and that piano was no fun anymore. And I was no fun anymore. Ouch!

I managed to stay calm (just as well my husband was there) and told them how frustrating it was for me when they didn't practise and how I felt responsible for making that happen. I asked them where they would like to be in 5 and 10 years – more proficient at piano or not knowing how to play after having given it up. They both said they wanted to be able to play as well as Eleanor (their older cousin). Then my husband piped up: "How can we make this work for all of us?"

Well that was fascinating.

They said I wasn't to nag and that I should put a pebble in the jar each time I nagged or criticised. Each pebble would mean one minute less practice. (I think my older girl is headed for the UN!) They said they wanted to have some downtime in the afternoons and all their time seemed to be filled with activities. We agreed that we would look at the schedule and cut down on the number of after school activities. I committed to only opening my mouth to say positive things about their practice. They decided when they would do their practice and instead of me reminding them (which felt like a nag) we would set an alarm.

> *It's been two weeks now and piano practice has been transformed. And actually they are generally being so much more respectful to me.*
>
> **Connie, mother of three**

Your turn

What obstacles to your child's learning will you address at home? Can you reduce the stress in his life? Do you need to reduce the number of extra-curricular activities he's doing? If you're honest have you been nagging?

....

....

....

How will you adjust your praise to make sure it isn't adding to your child's pressure?

....

....

....

What will your approach to failure be?

....

....

Have a rethink of homework. Get your child's input into making it work well. How can you signify that things are going to be different now?

....

· ·

· ·

Write down some Descriptive Praises you can use during homework time. See the website for inspiration.

· ·

· ·

· ·

Their Intellectual World in a nutshell

☺ Children in the developed world today are subject to significant stresses, some of which are down to the results-oriented education system, and some of which are caused unintentionally by parents. This has a significant impact on their brain development.

☺ We can encourage and motivate our children without pressuring if we're careful to use Descriptive Praise. Don't call your child 'clever' lest you create a fixed mindset but instead focus on effort, strategies, attitude and improvements. Embrace struggle. Don't compare one child with another and when they come home from a match don't let your first question be, "did you win?"

☺ Use Emotion Coaching to build resilience and to help free children's minds to focus on their work.

☺ Encourage independent thinking and actions.

☺ Much can be learnt from failure but it's not enough for children just to experience it. We need to coach them to regard failure as normal and helpful. We need to model learning from failure.

☺ Provide a pleasant environment for homework but don't expect kids to like it. Empathise. Use Chat Throughs to help them work independently and don't do it for them. Descriptively Praise their efforts and strategies.

☺ Balance homework with extra-curricular activities, play time, family time and sleep.

☺ Model a passion for learning.

Further reading:

Carl Honoré, *Under Pressure: Rescuing our children from the culture of hyper-parenting*, 2008

Alfie Kohn, *The Homework Myth: Why Our Kids Get Too Much of a Bad Thing*, 2007

Carol Dweck, *Mindset: How You Can Fulfil Your Potential*, 2012

10
Their physical world

"Perfectionism hampers success. In fact, it's often the path to depression, anxiety, addiction, and life-paralysis."

– Brené Brown

6-year-old Anna is explosive. She is very sensitive and intense and a day at school for her is exhausting as she struggles to follow instructions, do her work and interact peaceably with her peers. Even the walk home from school is difficult as their route across the park means she is likely to meet scary dogs and the even scarier much older sister of her friend Amy. She has piercings and wears lipstick and tries to talk to Anna! Every day is full of new skills to master, ones that her brother Ben takes in his stride, like tying shoe laces, riding bikes, reading... so many opportunities to mess up! She has after school activities four days a week where she needs to master further skills in gymnastics and violin and earn badges in Brownies. She gets little peace as she shares a room with 4-year-old Emily and by the end of the day all of her emotions find their way out in a tantrum. She cries and rages and flings things around the kitchen and hits her mother.

Being physical

When our children are young, from babyhood through infancy and toddlerhood, their world is predominantly physical. They experience the world through their senses of course and as babies they explore by touching, putting things in their mouths and smelling them. They respond to visual cues like your face and react differently to unfamiliar or soothing noises. Their emotions are expressed physically through smiles and laughter and through tears or screaming as they don't yet have words. As they get older their frontal lobes develop and their vocabularies expand and with support they learn to use words to manage their emotions and to ask for what they need.

According to parents in our classes the issues that seem to arise for school-aged children around physicality are as follows:

☺ They're still expressing emotions physically and sometimes in violent ways. This seems to be more of an issue for boys, but sometimes applies to girls too. I'm not being sexist – that's what parents tell us and research confirms.

☺ Some children have VERY high energy and parents are at a loss to control it. It's wearing.

☺ Obesity. Parents are concerned about the extremely high prevalence of childhood obesity in the developed world and want to take preventative measures.

☺ Body confidence, or lack thereof. This is becoming more of an issue for boys as well as girls and it is increasingly something that concerns younger children. It needs to be addressed as early as possible.

Emotions and actions

As we've seen there is a very close link between how a child feels and how they behave, and for younger children or those who have not yet learnt to regulate their emotions their big uncomfortable feelings can come out in hitting, biting, pushing, kicking, pulling hair or pinching. This is expected for young children — they are in the motor stage of development. Some children will express those feelings through withdrawn behaviours or through mean verbal behaviours, all of which needs addressing too. Here we're focused on physical behaviours but the solutions are the same for all unwanted behaviours.

You know by now that Emotion Coaching is the answer to any behaviour that has at its root a feeling. Emotions are like water – they will find a way out somewhere. So the solution is to put into words the feeling that your child is having and teach him to connect that sensation with the words you give him. And maybe you'll require him to make amends, say sorry or to do a Take Two. But what *is* that feeling?

Let's have a look:

When your child does this:	Maybe he's feeling:
Hits or punches another child or adult	Angry. Yes, but what's behind the anger? There will usually be a fear of some kind. Fear that he's not going to get his share of or a turn at something, that he's not going to get the peace he needs, that he's not good enough to join in the game, that he never gets to say what happens in the playground, or at home, fear that he won't measure up in some way.
Pulls someone's hair	Powerless – is this an attempt to show that she can control something?

Disrupting a game by upturning the board or taking away the ball	Like he can't keep up
Pinching someone in class	Jealous? Perhaps of the attention given to that child by the teacher, of the apparent ease with which that child does her work or makes friends. Hurt that the other child doesn't like her. She should like me – I'll show her. The feeling of hurt has become anger.

Example: Christian's ability to deal with taunts or teasing was limited. His self-esteem was so fragile that his tolerance for such verbal parries was low and his impulse control was undeveloped. So when a child provoked him he would hit out physically. Needless to say he got in a lot of trouble, which did nothing to help the underlying problem.

In Celia Lashlie's book *He'll Be OK*,[53] she identifies that the only emotion most boys feel able to display by the time they get to their teens is anger. Other emotions such as hurt or sadness are often transmuted into anger and processed through hitting something or someone. The boys she interviewed felt that distancing themselves from emotions lessened their power over them and talking didn't help. What they wanted was time to let the emotions settle and for them to make sense of them. Most saw crying as unmanly. Most agreed they had received messages of disapproval when they had cried as younger boys.

---

[53] Celia Lashlie, *He'll Be OK: Helping Adolescent Boys Become Good Men*, 2011

Boys need to have an acceptable outlet for those emotions – if not talking, then some other constructive form of release. As part of our Emotion Coaching we need to give children alternate outlets for their feelings until their frontal lobes are sufficiently developed to control their physical impulses. So they may need some emotion management techniques, probably involving a physical release, like hitting a cushion or jumping on a trampoline so that they can see that they're not wrong to have the feeling – it just needs to come out differently.

Of course what you model, as always, counts for a lot. So when you're mad at them make sure you use your words! Take some Cool Down Time if you think you might be tempted to get a bit physical yourself. You're not alone there!

Channelling high energy

Not all children are the same of course but many kids (and parents of boys particularly comment on this) have LOTS of energy. If they're not racing around, high-energy kids are investigating, constantly asking questions or constructing and deconstructing things… and not being able to put them back together!

How can we channel energy positively? We can help our high-octane kids to view their energy as something they can manage safely and enjoy, and not something they need to contain or feel guilty about. We can talk about high energy being a positive thing. When they're racing around outside we can comment "*You have SO much energy.*" With a smile.

We can accommodate it rather than trying to quash it. For example at homework time if your high-energy child is a kinaesthetic learner, i.e. they learn best by doing, touching and moving around, you will battle less and they will be more productive if you incorporate moving into their learning. Instead of trying to stop them from fiddling, as I did initially with my boys, let them squeeze a stress ball while working or move around the room while learning tables or spelling words. They may figure things out better when working to a large scale – try using a flipchart or white board to do their work on. They can take a photo to hand in or copy it out.[54]

Provide MANY opportunities for releasing energy
We may know our active children need lots of exercise, but it's not always easy to make it happen. Try to think of as many ways as possible to get them moving in everyday life. It's worth the time invested and it may keep you fit too.

Encourage more active play, so even if indoors get them to do something that involves their brains and imaginations:

☺ Walk, scoot or cycle to and from school – if you cross a park, take a ball

☺ Go swimming, play tennis and other sports at the weekend

☺ Join local or school sports or fitness clubs

☺ Get a rebounder, football net, trampoline, basketball hoop or space-hopper for home

☺ Get them helping at home, sweeping leaves, washing cars, emptying bins…

Juliet stopped parking outside school and parked the other side of the common when her children were young to get them walking and kicking a ball across the common to and from school.

A high-energy child is not necessarily an aggressive one.

---

[54] Ideas adapted from Alicia Eaton, *Words That Work: How to Get Kids to do Almost Anything*, 2015

Physical aggression

When girls are aggressive it tends to take a verbal form. Boys are generally more physical. These are generalisations but true often enough to make a starting point for discussion. Don't get sucked into stereotypes but know your own child individually.

Boys often charge up and down and turn pencils, sticks or fingers into guns with which they 'kill' each other, repeatedly. Their fantasy games usually involve goodies and baddies and the goodies win. But this kind of play is not an indicator of a violent future. A boy's fantasies about killing bad guys and saving the world don't indicate that anything is wrong unless he repeatedly hurts his playmates. And sometimes an act that feels aggressive to one child was actually intended to be a playful action by the child who did it. Then he needs adult support to help him understand that another child's experience may be different from his own. And so empathy develops.

Boys are more concerned than girls with rank, hierarchy and competition; they need order and will seek it out. If there is not enough order at home or at school boys may seek it in gangs or get into power scuffles. When there is an absence of structure or consistency boys feel uncertain and may respond violently. Games of power and dominance are not necessarily aggressive unless they are intended to hurt.

What do we mean when we talk about aggressive behaviour? According to Webster's Dictionary, aggression is "*a forceful action... the process of making attacks... hostile, injurious, behaviour*". To be aggressive is to take action with intent to hurt. We can teach our children to be assertive without hurting (see chapter 8).

Sometimes kids act aggressively because their feeling of frustration or their desire to win takes precedence. Sometimes they are angry and can't find another way to express that feeling. That physical expression may hurt another. Emotion Coaching helps them learn to control those impulses.

As I write this we have just acknowledged in White Ribbon Day the need to end violence by men against women. Most men are not violent towards women but about one in five women have experienced violence from their intimate partner. Two women a week in the UK die at the hands of their partner or ex-partner.[55] Attitudes toward domestic violence are changing but it is often still seen as 'just how men are'. We have a responsibility to women to educate our sons to get what they want and express their feelings in ways that don't involve violence or bullying tactics.

Teach children boundaries around their physicality
Make sure they get some rough and tumble and don't forget the classic games of Musical Bumps/Statues, Grandmother's Footsteps or What's the Time Mr Wolf?

When a thoughtful adult is involved in these activities children learn:

☺ How to stop – from foot flat on the throttle to flat on the brake (you may need a code word or just 'STOP' – one family found 'coconut' seemed to be very effective!)

☺ How not to take things too personally

☺ How to follow rules

☺ How to handle hurt and upset

Limit screens Spending a lot of time in front of a screen can lead to aggressive behaviour. This may be because of pent-up energy or because of violent content. Check out computer game ratings and lots of other useful information

---

[55] Office for National Statistics, 2015

about games at www.pegi.info or www.commonsensemedia. org (see our website – www.theparentpractice.com/book-resources#chapter-10). You'll find more on this in Chapter 11.

Juliet instigated a general family rule that when friends come around they do one physical activity first, then screens.

Healthy bodies

The World Health Organisation regards childhood obesity as one of the most serious global public health challenges for the 21st century. You're probably aware that obese children and adolescents are at an increased risk of developing various health problems, and are also more likely to become obese adults. Obesity is increasing rapidly across the world and many low- and middle-income countries are now significantly affected as well as wealthier nations. The United States is widely recognised as having the highest prevalence of childhood obesity, although the UK and Australia are not far behind. The UK has one of the highest rates among European countries.

In case you thought this couldn't apply to you…

In 2013/14, 19.1% of 10–11 year olds in the UK were obese and a further 14.4% were overweight, 9.5% of 4–5 year olds were obese and another 13.1% were overweight. This means **a third of 10–11 year olds and over a fifth of 4–5 year olds were overweight or obese.**[56]

---

[56] National Child Measurement Programme UK, http://www.noo.org.uk/NOO_about_obesity/child_obesity

Risks of being overweight

When children are overweight or obese they are clearly at risk for medical problems but the psychological difficulties that go with being overweight may not be as immediately obvious. The emotional and psychological effects are often seen as the most immediate and serious by children themselves. Overweight children clearly have a harder time taking part in active games and sport and may therefore miss opportunities for inclusion in their peer group. They may also suffer disturbed sleep and fatigue affecting performance and mood. They may experience teasing and discrimination by peers, low self-esteem, anxiety and depression. In one study, severely obese children rated their quality of life as low as children with cancer on chemotherapy.[57]

Overweight and obese children are more likely to become obese adults. Some obesity-related conditions start developing during childhood although the symptoms may not show up until adulthood.

Causes

Some causes are more obvious than others.

Children can become overweight because of genetic factors, lack of physical activity, unhealthy eating patterns or a combination of these factors, and occasionally because of a hormonal problem. So far, so obvious. We know some of the reasons why children are getting less exercise these days but why does overeating happen? Sometimes it's because of underlying emotional problems or habits passed down generations.

Some intriguing research from McGill University, conducted by Dr Lisa Kakinami, compared BMIs of children whose guardians were generally affectionate, had open discussions about behaviour and set healthy boundaries

---

[57] http://www.webmd.com/children/guide/obesity-children

with those whose parents had inflexible limits and had little dialogue or affection. Children whose guardians adopted the latter parenting style had a 30% increase of obesity.[58] The study's authors were careful to say that this proved an association, not cause and effect.

Prevention

Clearly we have a responsibility for preventing our children from becoming overweight. Schools and government play a role too and your child will learn about healthy eating practices at school. But it's up to us to make sure our kids get enough exercise and to become informed about what's in the food they eat as sugar and fats and sodium lurk in unsuspecting places. (I know that means shopping takes longer as you have to read all the labels! Maybe you could find out that information online before you go to the supermarket.) And it can be difficult to get our children into good habits when family life is so busy.

Helping kids develop healthy habits

Actually we need to focus on the lifestyle habits of the *whole* family.

Healthy eating

It may be that you are all over the healthy eating thing. Or you may be well aware of what you *should* be doing but struggle to do it for all sorts of reasons.

Clearly our goal is to balance the number of calories we consume with those expended through physical activity. But don't put your child on a diet without talking to your health care provider.

One of the biggest hazards for us is serving reasonably sized portions as portion sizes in restaurants and supermarkets

---

[58] The study was presented to the American Heart Association, March 2014

have grown over the years. Inform yourself about portion sizes. For instance did you know that some larger apples amount to 2 serving sizes? If your child is eating a similar amount to you it's probably too much.

We used to put a serving dish on the table and help ourselves from that but we found that if we left it on the table there was a strong temptation to go back for seconds! Now we serve up at the kitchen counter and keep the rest for lunch the next day.

You may be familiar with what constitutes a healthy diet but are you aware of behaviours around food that can assist healthy eating:

☐ **Eat mindfully.** This means not eating while doing something else such as watching TV. It is easy to form a habit of reaching for food whenever you sit down to watch but if we eat in a distracted way we don't have as much control over how much we eat – we tend not to notice when we are satiated. If we're not consciously looking at our food we don't feel like we're eating it. Have you ever noticed how popcorn just seems to disappear when you're at the movies? Alicia Eaton recommends not eating in front of the TV, in the car or standing up.[59]

☐ **Avoid shopping when you're hungry and only buy what's on your list** to stop impulse purchases. Tell your kids what you're doing, as you'll be passing on these good habits.

☐ **Carve out time to prepare healthy meals.** Fitting cooking into a busy schedule can be really tricky and planning is usually part of the answer. You may not have time to prepare a meal at 6pm but may be able

---

[59] Alicia Eaton, *Words That Work: How to Get Kids to do Almost Anything*, 2015

to find time later in the evening to make the meal for the following day. Many busy parents recommend batch-cooking and freezing. Some recommend slow-cooking and getting to know the auto-timer on your oven.

Talk to your children about the nutritional benefits of what they're eating, but not in a lecturing way. Descriptively praise them for making good food choices or for being nutritionally aware. If you're making changes in your family's eating habits empathise if there's some resistance at first. Do you need to change habits around buying food? When you eat? Where you eat? If you've been in the habit of picking up a chocolate bar for the kids when you purchase petrol maybe you could buy petrol when they're not with you for a while to break the habit. Then tell them about the changes you're going to make in the ways discussed in Chapter 4.

Being active

Talk to your children about the benefits of being physically active, too. Teach them that physical activity has great health benefits apart from helping with weight management, such as:

☺ Strengthening bones

☺ Decreasing blood pressure

☺ Reducing stress and anxiety

☺ Increasing self-esteem

☺ Developing gross and fine motor skills

☺ Encouraging connectivity between nerve cells and the brain

☺ Releasing feel-good endorphins which improve your mood

☺   And it's fun!

Focus on the benefits they can see now, rather than 30 years in the future, which they can't contemplate.

Outdoor play has the advantage of lots of space and fresh air but even indoor play can be physical. Try French skipping (elastics) or dancing. Even playing on a computer game like the Wii is better than sitting still.

Taking part in sport after school or on the weekends not only satisfies kids' physical needs but gives them the benefit of being part of a team. Let them choose which activities they want to take part in and if they don't like conventional sports search around for something that allows them to see themselves as a physical person. Sometimes kids will pigeon hole themselves – I thought of myself as academic or arty but not sporty even though I climbed trees and rode bikes.

Doing physical activities like cycling or rollerblading, bushwalking or playing cricket or baseball as a family allows parents to model healthy habits as well as spending fun time together. There is much evidence that when parents are involved in making changes to diet and activity levels children are more successful in maintaining healthy lifestyle habits.[60] *I didn't do this as much as I could have when my children were young because I was feeble and didn't like being cold – if you live in a place that gets cold invest in a warm jacket!*

If you limit sedentary activities, whether it's time in front of a screen or colouring or even reading, your child will know you're not just anti-screens but genuinely pro-moving.

If you have an overweight child, it is very important that you don't judge but let him know that you are there to support. Since children's feelings about themselves are often based on their perception of their parents' judgment of them, we need to let them know that we accept them and love them

---

[60] www.heart.org

at any weight. It is also important to talk to them about their weight, allowing them to share their concerns with you. If you involve the entire family in healthy activities and eating habits the overweight child will not feel singled out.

Finding the words often isn't easy but try not to criticise or nag eating choices or sedentary behaviours. College student Elisa Maria Torres was overweight as a child. She says *"Criticising kids about their weight is one of the worst things an adult can do."* Torres says she was self-conscious about her weight in middle school – especially when her grandmother compared her unfavourably to slimmer friends. *"She'd say things about my weight during meals and I'd feel awful, I couldn't eat around her without worrying that I was eating too much… Kids need to know that what you feel about them has nothing to do with their weight,"* Torres says. *"Part of loving yourself means taking care of your body and keeping it healthy. If your child knows she's loved and learns to love herself, she's far more apt to make healthy choices."*[61]

---

[61] http://www.webmd.com/parenting/raising-fit-kids/mood/talking-kids-about-weight?page=3

Calling a 10-year-old girl fat means she is almost twice as likely to be obese by the age of 19, new research suggests. A 2014 study revealed that commenting adversely on a girl's weight at an early age is actually counterproductive in terms of weight loss, quite apart from what it might do to her self-esteem. [62]

My mum called me fat and put me on a diet aged 8! Hence a life time of yo-yo weight issues!

– Elaine

See below for some ideas on how to talk to kids about their bodies generally.

If your child is concerned about her weight tell her you want to help, and make getting healthy a project you work on together. Example: *"I know you're worried about your weight and I'm glad you're thinking about ways to get healthier. Maybe I can help. I'd like to improve my strength and heart condition too. I was also concerned about what the WHO has said recently about red meat so maybe we can look at our family's eating habits too. Can you help me?"*

Fussy eaters

You may feel that none of the above is relevant to you because your child hardly eats anything at all. That's not uncommon for small children but if your child is still very restricted in their palate at this age things can get very tense around meal times. And that's the problem. The best thing you can do about fussy eating is back off and know that very few children in the developed world are malnourished. Model good eating (and smile while you're eating), provide good food and don't have less healthy alternatives around, and don't comment on

---

[62] Dr Janet Tomiyama, University of California, published in the journal *JAMA Pediatrics*

what they eat. Don't require them to finish their plates or even just one more mouthful. Descriptively praise them for other things. Most kids grow out of fussy eating.

Body confidence

Body image, or how you feel about the way you look, is a big issue for adults, adolescents and children. Appearance dissatisfaction reaches a peak in the teens but it starts much earlier: 5 year olds have been known to ask, *"Mummy, am I fat?"*[63] Children use the word 'fat' as an insult. Surveys in the UK have found that 50% of 5–8 year olds want to be slimmer. By the time they get to their teens children think being slim is essential for being happy, popular and attractive to the opposite sex. When children and teens don't feel good about their appearance they may not take part in fun activities such as swimming or other sports or go to parties.

More and more these issues affect boys too.

Global studies[64] have found that women and girls across the world had low appearance satisfaction and self-esteem. Findings were that:

☐ Girls and young women feel pressure to conform to body image ideals and this affects their behaviour and well-being. They feel pressure to be thin and to look more like celebrities. This results in almost half (45%) feeling ashamed about the way they look.

☐ There is a significant relationship between a woman's body image and her sense of self-worth.

☐ There are strong links between self-esteem and engagement in activities.

---

[63] Magazine of the Professional Association For Childcare and Early Years
[64] Dove *Beyond Stereotypes* reports 2009 and *Reflections on Body Image* report from the UK All-Party Parliamentary Group for Body Image

☐ When feeling badly about their appearance, women not only withdraw from activities that reveal or showcase their looks such as going to the beach, a party, clothes shopping or doing a physical activity but they also refrain from giving an opinion, going for a job interview, attending school or work and going to the doctor.

"A woman's self-esteem impacts on her willingness to engage in life"[65]

Poor body image is a contributory factor in poor mental wellbeing, eating disorders and self-harming, obesity, low aspirations and a range of risky behaviours including drug and alcohol abuse and unsafe sex, especially among women and girls. It can lead to lack of engagement in study or work and participation in public life. Phew! So this is a big issue for parents.

We need to take the question of body image seriously and do what we can to counteract the negative messages our children, particularly our daughters, will receive on a daily basis. We need to help our kids relate in a more healthy way to their bodies.

In the UK 83% of adults do not feel confident about the way they look.[66] And half of adults believe what they can achieve in life is affected by their looks.[67]

What causes this epidemic of appearance anxiety?

☐ Exposure to the 'thin ideal' in the media

☐ The way parents talk to children about bodies (their own and their children's)

---

[65] Dove *Beyond Stereotypes* report
[66] Be Real campaign http://www.berealcampaign.co.uk/
[67] UK government Body Confidence campaign

☐ Toys can reinforce unrealistic expectations about appearance

☐ Performances which focus on appearance

The thin ideal

In the print and digital media there is widespread dissemination of the attitude that there is only one model of beauty perfection and striving for it is the duty of a woman. The L'Oréal campaign tells us to buy their beauty products 'because you're worth it' with the implication that if we don't we're not worth it. Overwhelmingly the message to girls is that beauty is the most important female quality.

There are cosmetic surgery makeover programmes and programmes ridiculing bodies on TV, ads for cosmetic surgery, fashion and beauty products on posters and in magazines and online. Magazines analyse celebrities' figures and are VERY critical. There are close-up pictures which are very judgmental. Teens say that this shaming of celebrities contributes to their own body dissatisfaction.

Research by Dr Sophie Tomlin in 2014[68] about the amount of exposure to the thin ideal in magazines showed high numbers of articles in women's magazines about dieting, cosmetic surgery or images of the thin ideal. Findings were that while teen magazines were trying to promote more healthy ideals, girls often read magazines pitched at an older age group and can access material online. Dr Tomlin's findings confirmed widespread concerns that the frequency of exposure to the thin ideal can lead to a distorted body image and disordered eating. For a YouTube video from Dove showing examples of what girls are bombarded with in the media see https://www.youtube.com/watch?v=Ei6JvK0W60I (the link is also on our website – www.theparentpractice.com/book-resources#chapter-10).

---

[68] Body Image and Media: A Snapshot of Exposure https://www.rcpsych.ac.uk/pdf/ED%20Poster2014.pdf

This exposure has increased over time. It has been estimated that young women now see more images of outstandingly beautiful women in one day than our mothers saw throughout their entire adolescence.[69] There has also been widespread public concern about the effects of the ways women are portrayed in the media – in particular, about the limited range of ways in which women are portrayed, about sexualisation and about the invisibility of women who are not young, white, heterosexual and conventionally beautiful.[70]

The things we say

Our children form views about their own bodies by the way we talk to them about their bodies and about our own. (The video One Beautiful Thought by Dove shows the things we say to ourselves about our bodies that we would never say to someone else, https://www.youtube.com/watch?v=AzqSZdYHyRI – also on our website – www.theparentpractice.com/book-resources#chapter-10.)

A friend of mine jokingly called her daughter a 'heifer' but even if the intention is not cruel the words still smart. And even if we are never critical of our children's bodies we are often critical of our own. Nine out of ten girls who claim to be 'unhappy' with their body say their mothers are insecure about their weight.[71] (See our website – www.theparentpractice.com/book-resources#chapter-10 – for a link to a very instructive video, Legacy: https://www.youtube.com/watch?v=Pqknd1ohhT4.)

Dr Helen Sharpe from the Institute of Psychiatry at King's College London says, *"it is a kind of humble bragging – one says 'I am so fat' and then the other says 'no you aren't, look at me.' It then becomes a comparison and a competition. We are*

---

[69] http://www.sirc.org/publik/mirror.html
[70] Body confidence campaign Progress report 2015
[71] Study by *Bliss* magazine, 2004

not blaming mums but we need to be aware that as the same gender parent girls model themselves on and derive values and attitudes from their mothers – mothers can pass on to daughters their own body anxieties.[72]

It is difficult for parents to know how to talk to girls about their bodies. We need to find a balance between encouraging healthy eating and exercise and not making girls (or boys) feel pressured or ashamed about their bodies. We don't want them to feel they have to conform to one particular model of beauty to be valuable.

Mothers can be unaware of the impact their comments have on their daughters. Throwaway comments such as *"does my bum look big in this?"* are heard and experienced by them as *"why would my mum think there is anything wrong with her bum? It's normal for women talk about what's wrong with their bodies. I wonder what's wrong with my body?"*

Toys

There is some research which suggests that exposure to unrealistically thin dolls like Barbie can also contribute to body dissatisfaction. A University of Sussex study found that early exposure to dolls epitomizing an unrealistically thin body ideal can damage girls' body image, which could contribute to an increased risk of disordered eating and weight cycling.[73]

Performances

Beauty pageants for children aren't very common in the UK but are big business in the US and becoming increasingly popular in Australia. These obviously make a big feature of how a child looks but so do dance exhibitions which

---

[72] Dr Helen Sharpe, 'Is fat talking a causal risk factor for body dissatisfaction? A systematic review and meta-analysis', in *International Journal of Eating Disorders*, July 2013

[73] Helga Dittmar, Emma Halliwell, Suzanne Ive; University of Sussex 2006.

encourage the application of a lot of makeup and sophisticated hairstyling and quite adult costumes. Some modern dance classes for very young children encourage the girls to make vey provocative and preening movements which are overly sexualised and focus on appearance.

What parents can do

Build strong self-esteem and body confidence

You can help your children have body confidence. You can give them two key messages: that there is more to a person than how they look and that beauty comes in all shapes and sizes. If your child comments on how pretty someone is, say, "*She is, but what else do we know about her? What sort of person is she?*" I once read about a mother who coached her young daughter to respond when people told her she was pretty with "*Thank you. I like books too.*" You might ask your child, "*When you die what do you want on your gravestone – she had lovely hair? She was a size 8?*"

Praise kids descriptively for many things other than their appearance. You are fighting against huge influences so you will have to be really persuasive. Parents say things like 'beauty comes from within' – this is an undeniable piece of wisdom but when your daughter gets to her teens she will look at you and roll her eyes like you just don't understand so it's important to embed positive attitudes before adolescence if you can. What you say will need to be backed up by concrete evidence that you value her for many other things such as being a good friend, consideration, assertiveness (even when she stands up to you!), courage, persistence, being funny, pitching in, making sensible choices, curiosity, thinking ahead, problem-solving, hard work on studies or sports or music practice etc, etc.

Descriptive Praise will be your strongest tool in building up self-esteem, which is the best buffer against appearance anxiety and self-harm.

"That was so kind of you to ring Nana for her birthday. I'll bet she feels really cherished today." "I know you've been finding Laura's interruptions very irritating when we're trying to do your project together but you've shown great understanding of her being too little to be able to wait long for what she wants." "I love how doggedly you've persevered with practising your netball goal shooting. You're not only doing it again and again but I can tell you're thinking about how to improve on each shot. That's purposeful practice." "I was pleased to see you stand up for yourself with Mrs Hunter when she accused you of leaving the school gate open. You explained your position without being rude."

Listening to and asking kids for their thoughts and ideas will also give them the message that they have something worthwhile to contribute.

Create family activities

US research of a sample of 200 families over 7 years found that those who spent the most time with their parents reported highest self-esteem and confidence. Eating together as a family is hugely important as it allows time to discuss the day, parents model sitting and enjoying food together (warding off eating disordered behaviour), and just chatting. By eating together you are conveying the messages *"I want to spend time with you. I want to hear about what you are learning, thinking and doing."* Make the dinner table a 'good news' place only to reduce stress around meals.

Playing games, doing physical activities and telling stories of shared experiences are also very bonding activities which result in higher self-esteem and a sense of belonging and also give children more of a reason to cooperate.

Discuss what they see in the media

Set limits on the amount of exposure your children get to programmes and advertising that have limited portrayals of women. Seek out books and films that show women and girls in powerful roles that emphasise attributes other than appearance. As they get older limit access to social media as too much time on social networking sites has been related to low self-esteem. (More on this in Chapter 11.)

Develop media literacy in your children (discuss beauty ideals, analyse pictures, learn about airbrushing and Photoshop techniques). Be aware of what they see on TV and what messages they are getting. Discuss with them and offer a moderating commentary when looking at images in magazines and on TV. Tell them that the beauty/diet industry want women to feel insecure so that they will buy their products and encourage them not to be conned. *Jenny did this with her daughters and now her 9 year old plays 'spot the airbrushing' – every time she sees an advert on a bus or at a mall she says 'Mummy, that's been Photoshopped.'* Research shows that the best way to get young people not to smoke is not to scare them with health stories but to show a corporation building huge profits on the back of them buying cigarettes... so use the same approach with beauty advertising.

Caring rituals

Encourage them to cherish their bodies by taking part in caring rituals from an early age. *"In the west we aspire to an image of beauty set by someone else, but in India it's about making the most of what's God-given as opposed to chasing unrealistic ideals. Make [caring] rituals a part of daily life rather than a treat. By taking pride in your... body you will enhance your... self-esteem."*[74] *"Improve your relationship with your body by massaging aromatherapy oil into your skin."*[75]

---

[74] Monisha Bharadwa, author of *India's Beauty Secrets*, 2008
[75] Aromatherapist Michelle Roques-O'Neil

Touch is a great way to develop respect for one's body. Give your children a massage or just stroke their arms or shoulders or hair. It gives a lovely message of caring by you and encourages them to care for themselves. It is a nice thing to do for a girl who's beginning to be critical of her own body. Therapist Penny Marr advises it can help an eating disordered person to reconnect positively with their body.

Go naked

Up to whatever age you think appropriate don't hide your naked body from your children. Let your children know this is what normal bodies look like and be proud. Otherwise they'll get their information about bodies online.

Talking to children about their bodies

☺ Don't talk about bodily characteristics as deficiencies – either your own or your child's. Avoid *"I hate my nose"* or *"My thighs are huge"*

☺ Don't talk about dieting in front of children

☺ Instead of talking about anyone being fat or praising anyone for being thin admire other qualities – being strong, resilient, fast, agile, flexible, having stamina

☺ Talk about taking exercise to build healthy, strong bodies, not to avoid looking bad

☺ Celebrate curves/differences in body shapes/appearance. For example: *"In this family freckles are fun." "Your glasses are really cool."*

☺ If you praise appearance make it be about her input. For example: *"I love the way you've put that stripy top with those polka dotted leggings – that looks fun"* or *"You've taken trouble to brush your hair well – it looks really shiny."*

Talking to children about food

Preparing a positive environment at mealtimes is important to invite good associations with food. Make it look and feel pleasant and have conversations about many different things, not just food. If anything negative needs to be discussed, don't do it at the dinner table as otherwise food develops negative associations.

Discouraging words

☺ Talking about 'good' or 'bad', 'fattening' or 'slimming' food.

☺ Talking about yourself as being 'good' or 'naughty' by eating or not eating food.

☺ Requiring children to finish what's on their plates – instead let them stop when they are full and help them to recognise what that feels like. This teaches them to listen to their appetites. Susie Orbach equates it to knowing when you need to go for a pee, then you go. It is a physiological need. Ellyn Satter, nutritionist, says it is a parent's job to provide healthy food and the child's job to choose what and how much to eat. Forcing isn't constructive.[76]

☺ Describing food as 'treats'. Try not to associate food with comfort so don't use food as rewards or as commiseration. This includes using dessert as a reward for finishing their main course. We know that many adults use food 'treats' to cheer themselves up. Let's teach our children other ways to deal with sadness or upset. Give gifts of non-food items to avoid the association with treats – next time you go to a dinner party take flowers instead of chocolates.

---

[76] Ellyn Satter, *How to Get Your Kid to Eat... But Not Too Much*, 1987

Positive words

- ☺ Talk about some foods needing to be taken in moderation as 'sometimes' food and 'everyday' food which we can eat lots of, and why. Talk about balance.
- ☺ Talk about tastes – sweet, sour, salty, bitter – and textures. Discuss what we like about foods.
- ☺ Talk about how a particular food contributes to our nutrition or works in our bodies, e.g. chicken has protein which is good for building muscle, milk has calcium which is good for bones, the effect of salt, sugar and fat etc

Have social gatherings which are not just focused on food but other activities like music and games.

Encourage involvement in sport

Involvement in sport:

- ☺ leads to increased self-esteem
- ☺ teaches many important lessons and rules for getting on in life
- ☺ is an antidote for a culture which is so obsessed with beauty and size. The girl is using her body for something positive which makes her feel good about it. A London University study found that women who participate in sport have a more positive body image than those who don't[77]
- ☺ raises endorphins and consequently mood
- ☺ builds resilience
- ☺ has social advantages too. Taking part in team games gives children a sense of belonging.

---

[77] http://www.sirc.org/publik/mirror.html

For more on encouraging involvement in sport see below.

Helping your child at sport

We're not all destined to become great athletes but all our children should have the opportunity to play and enjoy sports because of the advantages to their health, the sense of belonging that being in a team conveys, the essential social skills learnt while operating as a team and for the awareness of what your body can do when used for sport. This counteracts the idea that your body is just something to look at and that it should look a particular way. Sports psychologist and author Jim Taylor PhD, believes that team sports are good for encouraging respect for others, cohesiveness, fostering the ability to lead, and helping in dealing with disappointment and building self-esteem.[78]

So how do we get kids involved in sport? Well for some there's no holding them back. Chances are they are the ones born early in the school year. Research shows that the month of your birth determines the likelihood of you becoming a successful sports person and your enjoyment of sport.[79] Children who are born early in the school year have physical maturity which gives them an advantage in sport over their smaller and less coordinated peers. If smaller children get disheartened they may lose interest in playing sport and even if they catch up physically they are behind in the acquisition of skills. Sport is often conducted in a very competitive environment and if children are competing against others who have greater physical advantages they will often lose.

---

[78] http://www.sheknows.com/parenting/articles/818473/Team-sports-How-kids-benefit-from-organized-athletics
[79] Dr Adrian Barnett, Queensland University of Technology's Institute of Health and Biomedical Innovation, Feb 2010, http://www.sciencedaily.com/releases/2010/02/100202101251.htm

You clearly can't go back and change your child's birth date so what *can* you do?

☺ **Involve your child in sport outside school** where you have more choice about the environment and the coaches. Check them out carefully before enrolling your child. Are the kids waiting around on the side lines a lot? *6-year-old Lily messes around a lot in her gymnastics class, partly because there's too much waiting around, but also because she can get away with it.* Check out the teacher before signing up. Do they seem to have authority? Do the coaches talk too much rather than getting the children to do? Are they encouraging? Do they break down the skills into manageable chunks? Do they include all the children? Do the kids seem to be having fun? If it's fun the kids will learn: It is generally accepted that about 70% of progress is made by getting stuck in and figuring things out and about 20% of learning comes about through good relationships with the coach. Only 10% of learning happens through direct teaching.

☺ If our children are not the ones who are always getting the cups we need to work harder on motivating them. We can give the speech about taking part but that will ring hollow if we focus on the scores and the results of the matches in which they play or in other games we watch. They need to hear us talking about the way in which the game was conducted. Make sure the emphasis is on having fun more than winning. **Only a few will win but everyone can enjoy it.**

☺ **Point to sporting role models who behave well** in defeat as well as in victory. Kids will emulate their sports idols' behaviour on and off the pitch, be it positive or negative. So let's make sure we're drawing attention to those positive character traits such as humility, respect and kindness as well as sporting prowess.

☺ Use Descriptive Praise to **focus on the small things they're getting right** on the sports field such as following the coach's directions, passing and catching the ball well, setting up goals, following the rules and good sporting behaviour. Point out improvements and attitudes. (See the story below for some great examples.)

☺ **Commiserate with them when things don't go so well** using Emotion Coaching. Don't tell them to "*get over it – life's like that*" but let them vent before trying to explore what they might have learnt from what didn't go so well.

☺ **Model taking part in sports yourself** and enjoying the game even when you don't win. Play with them if you can. Tennis, golf, swimming and cycling are all good activities for families to do together.

In his book *Bounce*, Matthew Syed[80] looks at what makes a great sports champion. Syed persuasively argues (with reference to a lot of evidence) that anybody CAN be great with hard work and the right attitude. He refutes the idea that some are born great or with special talent but instead looks at the greats in many fields – sports, music and chess in particular – and sees that the only common ground between them is application. (Occasionally specific physical characteristics, like height for a basketballer, are useful.) He looks at long distance and sprint runners from Kenya and from the Caribbean and finds fewer similarities in their genetic make-up than you might expect given those places' reputation for producing great runners. He does find

---

[80] Matthew Syed, *Bounce: The Myth of Talent and the Power of Practice*, 2011

instead a culture of enthusiasm for those sports and plenty of opportunities for practising running. He talks about 'purposeful practice' and stresses that 'failure' is actually the route to achievement, not an excuse for quitting. He cites Carol Dweck's mindset research.

Your turn

You're concerned that your 10-year-old daughter is putting on a bit of weight. When you were that age you got teased for being a bit plump and you're worried.

Check: how do you talk about your body in front of her? What about your partner?

....

....

Check: how do you talk to her about her weight? What can you say to her to build her self-esteem/how can you praise her for non-appearance related things?

....

....

....

What changes to diet or physical activities can you make as a family?

....

....

How can you encourage her to enjoy sport?

....

....

Your son is like the Duracell rabbit – he just keeps going and going. How can you talk to him about his high energy?

....

....

Do you need to provide some opportunities to release energy? What could they be? When do they need to happen?

....

....

Sometimes he gets a bit carried away and his brother or sister gets hurt. What can you do to teach him without making him wrong?

....

....

Sometimes he gets frustrated and lashes out. What do you need to do in the moment? What can you say to him once he's calmed down?

....

....

....

....

"Once again I did so badly...."

My daughter Maia is 10 years old and was born very premature. One of the consequences has been serious breathing difficulties which has made her a very bad long distance runner.

Recently the day came for her school's annual Cross Country Run. As usual she didn't get selected to run the 'actual run' but she was meant to run the 'fun run' along with other slower runners. In the morning before the race she was very determined that this time she was going to try to be one of the first ones in the 'fun run'. Unfortunately this didn't happen at all. She came the second last out of about twenty girls.

When she came home that afternoon she was very disappointed in herself and started to talk about how hopeless she is at running and other things at school.

My usual response would be "No, you didn't do so badly," "Well, you did your best and that's what matters," "You are good at other things," "Maybe we have to train harder for next time," or "Next time I'm sure you will do better." Instead I paused and thought of what I had learnt in my Parent Practice lessons.

I started by listening to her without making any comment, which I am normally not so good at. I think that was really important for her to be able to hear what came next. After that I told her how well I understood that she was disappointed as she had wanted so much to do better but I also told her that I disagreed with her. She looked at me a bit surprised, then I continued: "I actually think you did really, really well today and I am going to tell you why...

- *This time you ran the whole race without stopping at all, which you have always found difficult.*
- *I think you ran very smartly today because you made sure you would have the energy to run the whole time and you really gave it your all when you sprinted at the end of the run.*
- *You had a very determined look on your face when you came to the finish line, which tells me you were really doing your best.*
- *You had a smile on your face shortly after the run even though you were disappointed with not being in front.*
- *You didn't allow yourself to start crying.*
- *You encouraged all the girls in your House, which is so important and by doing that you showed how great a team player you are.*
- *I saw how much the younger girls looked up to you, especially those two from your House who followed you the whole time.*
- *You made such an effort by bringing your yellow teddy to bring your team some luck and you made a nice poster to cheer your House.*
- *Not once did you think of not taking part in the 'fun run' even knowing how hard it is for you to run long distances. Some people in your place would have made all kind of excuses not to take part."*

After what I said she looked much happier and she didn't mention the run or not being worthy of anything again that day. She went happy to her room to play and

I honestly think she thought to herself, "Well, I didn't do so badly after all."

Toni, mother of one

Their Physical World in a nutshell

☺ Don't mistake high energy for aggression but find outlets for releasing energy. Teach boundaries around physical behaviour and use Emotion Coaching to help children control aggressive impulses.

☺ Limit screens and make sure the content is appropriate for your child, especially the levels of violence or other values expressed therein.

☺ To guard against obesity take action as a whole family to adopt healthy eating habits and a more active lifestyle.

☺ Body image is a big concern for girls and increasingly an issue for boys too. Body dissatisfaction can result in decreased self-esteem and willingness to engage in life.

☺ Appearance anxiety can arise because of the prevalence of the 'thin ideal' in the media and because of the way parents unwittingly pass on their own body concerns. Toys portraying unrealistic body types may also play a role in reinforcing unrealistic expectations.

☺ Parents can help children develop body confidence and self-esteem by:

- ○ Using Descriptive Praise for many things other than appearance, celebrating difference in body shapes and paying attention to their feelings, thoughts and opinions
- ○ Engaging in whole family activities
- ○ Teaching media literacy
- ○ Encouraging them to take part in sport
- ○ Talking positively about food and bodies – no 'fat talk'
- ○ Going naked
- ☺ Help children to enjoy sports by choosing positive environments and coaches, by encouraging with Descriptive Praise for effort, not outcomes, by teaching children to have growth mindsets and by using Emotion Coaching to develop resilience and good sportsmanship. Model it!

Further reading:

Steve Biddulph, *Raising Boys: Why Boys are Different – and How to Help Them Become Happy and Well-Balanced Men*, 2013

Steve Biddulph, *Raising Girls*, 2013

Celia Lashlie, *He'll Be OK: Helping Adolescent Boys Become Good Men*, 2011

Matthew Syed, *Bounce: The Myth of Talent and the Power of Practice*, 2011

Alicia Eaton, *Words that Work: How to Get Kids to do Almost Anything*, 2015

11

Their digital world

"Good people do good things with their access to the internet and social media... Bad people do bad things... The internet grants power to the individual according to that individual's wisdom and moral stance."

– Martin D. Owens[81]

When reading with her mum one evening 8-year-old Alisha told her she was so pleased her mum was reading to her that evening because she said "I want to get the zombie girl images out of my head mummy." She was clearly a bit disturbed, and they talked about where she had seen these images and how. Until Misha went to check her iPad she thought it was perhaps the Michael Jackson thriller video, because they had been listening to his music that weekend. When she checked she was alarmed to see hard-core porn on the iPad. Alisha had typed in the questions 'sex with a boy' and 'snogging'. Misha thought they were all protected and filtered and that a young girl of 8 years old wouldn't be asking those kinds of questions. She realised that was naive when she thought about the bombardment of messages they receive weekly from media, magazines, pop videos, songs, radio, billboards, shops, cinemas, etc.

After a very bad day with the boys, we all agreed we would write down the top 5 most horrible things and both boys, independently, wrote down that me being on my computer made them sad. Gulp... This was when they were about 6–8 years old.

Jane, mum of 2

---

[81] Lawyer and author of Pew Research Centre Report on the internet, 2012

Life in a digital world

The main things to remember about keeping children healthy and safe in a digital world are:

☺ Access to a digital world is a fact of life for our children's generation and there are many great benefits to it, just as the motorcar significantly improved life when it came into common usage. And as with vehicles there are some things to be cautious about.

☺ It is a parent's job to teach a child to be safe online and to provide boundaries around use of gadgets. Digital protections are not enough – we need human protections.

☺ We will not be effective if we rely on coercion and control. Instead we need to communicate and educate.

☺ We pass on our values through what we model and what we require in rules.

We are first-generation immigrants in a digital world and experience some of the upheaval and discomfort that migrants do in adapting to the way of life brought about by each new technological innovation. If you are under 35 you will have had technology as a big part of your life since your teens and even if you are a teeny bit older you probably couldn't imagine your life without the internet and smartphones. But our children were born into a world of touch screens, instant access to information and entertainment, a world where you can connect with people and facts (and delete them) with the swipe of a finger. The possibilities brought about by existing and emerging technologies can't even be imagined and we are all too aware that there are some risks associated with them. There has been much divided opinion and some scaremongering about those risks. As ever the challenge for us as parents is to find a balance: helping our children take advantage of the opportunities provided by technology while keeping them safe and healthy in the digital sphere.

There are many opportunities provided by the gadgets with which we are surrounded for education and entertainment, for creativity and connection. Our children definitely need to know how to use the technology and generally embrace it. Many of us do too. And yet we are reminded all the time by articles in the media about the downsides of this all-embracing world. Research in this area is in its infancy of course; new studies are being done all the time and there are conflicting views about the effect on our children of living in the digital world. And your own gut may experience some disquiet about balance in this area.

What do you worry about?

☺ **How much?** – Many of us worry that our children's cognitive, emotional and social development may be impaired by too much time in front of a screen. We worry that they turn into zombies and become irritable after hours on games, that they neglect other activities and don't connect with people. We stress that their attention spans and memories are reducing and that they develop a very high expectation for stimulation and fast-paced entertainment. We may be concerned that they are losing vital social skills and depth of connection with real human beings. We may have real fears that our children's digital habit (and perhaps our own) is becoming an addiction.

☺ **Content** – We are concerned that our children can easily be connected to a world we can't control and so they may access, inadvertently or intentionally, content that is not healthy for them. We may fear that the content of the games they play will have negative effects on their behaviour or their thinking. We may worry about the effect of a steady diet of social media – what happens to self-esteem, what about opportunities for bullying, will it turn her into a shallow, selfie-taking narcissist?

These are all legitimate concerns. The downsides of the electronic world are well documented although maybe some aspects have been a bit exaggerated. Nancy Willard at the Centre of Safe and Responsible Internet Use says: *"Fears in the media are disproportionate to the data or the actual degree of risk."*[82] Although there were figures being bandied about citing the average age of access to internet porn being 11 years old this statistic has been shown to be without foundation.[83] Serious studies show that the average age of seeking out sexually explicit content is in fact 14, when children are naturally sexually curious.[84] But as our opening story indicates, children can access explicit material without understanding what they are doing or by accident so parents clearly need to do something to keep children safe.

Maybe for some parents it's not the technology that we fear, so much as our lack of knowledge and our lack of confidence with it. Even if you've really embraced all forms of technology your children will always be a step ahead of you. If we don't know WHAT we're dealing with, or HOW to deal with it that's scary – we make technology the bad guy and our children wrong for wanting to be involved. Fear is never a good place from which to be operating as a parent, so let's get informed.

---

[82] Bex Lewis, *Raising Children in a Digital Age: Enjoying the best, avoiding the worst,* 2014

[83] 'Sex, Lies and Statistics' by Seth Lubove, http://www.forbes.com/2005/11/22/internet-pornography-children-cz_sl_1123internet.html

[84] University of New Hampshire, http://www.unh.edu/ccrc/pdf/jvq/CV76.pdf

What are the benefits?

All our fears can make us forget that there are upsides too. The internet of course provides access to information at a click, way beyond the capacity of what I had as a child with my local library. The possibilities for connection with others provided by social media and Skype far eclipse the ability to communicate when all you had were expensive long distance phone calls or letters (you know – writing on paper and putting it in an envelope – you remember them). The anxieties of dyslexics and poor spellers everywhere have been soothed by voice-activated software and spell checks, although of course nobody learns to spell anymore, and auto correct is definitely a mixed blessing! You can take all your summer reading away with you on one device rather than lugging loads of books.

The opportunities for science, medicine and other scholarly endeavours are huge as researchers connect with each other and doctors connect with their patients remotely. Time can be saved. (Yes, we know it can be wasted too – more on that below.) Learning can be undertaken remotely and therefore opened up to many more people. Programmes have been developed to promote brain development for sufferers of neurological disorders, dyslexia, autism and Alzheimer's. And much, much more...

Apart from these high-brow benefits even the much maligned games that our children love (the ones that parents say will addle your brain) can have some advantages for their cognitive development. Not all games were made equal. Some games teach cognitive flexibility, problem solving, executive functions such as planning, organisation, patience, working memory, focus and many other skills that improve selective attention and processing speed. Some games can connect children to their peer group either because they are multi-player games or because children spend hours together discussing these games. Some games encourage real creativity and allow children to make mistakes and learn from them in a private, non-judgmental atmosphere. Social media, used judiciously, can be a great connector, to people and to ideas. Now you can sign with a click a petition that helps you to engage with issues, you can stay in touch with friends and family wherever they are in the world and share photos, stories and music with others. *When I lived in London and my family were in Sydney rare phone calls were a bit forced because of awareness of expense and because we hadn't spoken for a while. It felt like we had to say something significant, which was a bit pressurising. Now I know what my family abroad are up to (well, some of it) and can chat more easily when we talk.*

What do the kids say?[85]

I get to control what's happening – I have to do what everyone tells me all day, it's good to be able to make other people do stuff for a change.

I get to be a gangster; I don't really want to be a gangster in real life, don't worry, but it's quite fun – the baddies have really exciting things to do and I can be one for a while.

I have nothing else to do. You won't let me go out, or make a noise or a mess... It's always raining and I have no-one else to play with.

The only other thing I am allowed to do is homework.

Sometimes I just want to hit my brother, so I play Assassin's Creed instead. I feel better afterwards. And he's not got hit. You should be happy.

---

[85] We asked several parents in our current classes to ask their children what they loved about games

I lose track of time – I just get lost in it...

I prefer playing to watching TV because I get to be in charge, whereas the stuff on TV I just have to watch and not be involved.

I would rather play real football. But FIFA is the next best thing...

I love being good at stuff. And I am getting really good at this...

I love fighting – it's not real, everyone knows that, not like the actual news that you and Daddy watch with real blood and stuff. With that, you know they are real people...

What can parents do?

The electronic world is a vital part of children's lives today and will continue to be, so **opting out is not an option**. Our goal is to produce digitally responsible adults with healthy online practices. We also want them to have a life and friends, study hard, pick their stuff up and walk the dog... To get there, they need to listen to us and be willing to do what we ask. Our aim is to encourage self-regulation but that begins with some parental regulation.

We need to think this complex issue through, and decide on what we feel is right for our own families. And we have to take our children's temperaments into account – there isn't a one-size-fits-all solution. Intense, persistent, slow-to-adapt or ADHD children are highly impulsive and/or have low transitional ability, so it's always going to be really hard to turn off, however you approach it.

Technological protections

Do use parental controls, timers, content filters and passwords and understand and use privacy settings on social media platforms. But the answer is not just about technological protections. Although these play a part in helping families stay safe online and develop healthy internet habits electronic protections only go so far – we need human protections too. And, even if we were to get on top of these ever-changing strategies, our children are likely to be more on top of them and very adept at finding their way around them. Many's the time we've heard of a child breaking mum or dad's 'secure' password. Perhaps you've had this experience?

The National Research Council's report *Youth, Pornography and the Internet* likens it to a swimming pool – pools can be dangerous for children, and so we protect them from falling in by putting up fences, setting alarms and using padlocks and banning them from going near unsupervised. But the most important thing we can do is teach them how to swim.[86]

Do try to get familiar with the technology as much as possible, not so much to keep ahead of your kids (because you can't) but because if you seem like a digital dinosaur they won't respect what you say. They will just think you don't understand, especially if you're criticising their digital activities. By the way, don't (criticise them). More on that later.

There are guides for clueless parents like me such as Google tips https://get.google.com/tips/ and others (Parents' Guide to Facebook; Parents Guide to Ask.fm; Parents Guide to Snapchat; Parents Guide to Instagram http://www.connectsafely.org/; https://www.fosi.org/good-digital-parenting/seven-steps-good-digital-parenting/) – see our website (www.theparentpractice.com/book-resources#chapter-11) for more.

---

86 http://www.nap.edu/read/10261/chapter/1

Useful sites for deciding on the appropriateness of computer games and films are www.PEGI.info and www.commonsensemedia.org (see our website – www.theparentpractice.com/book-resources#chapter-11) which offers information to parents about the film, game, app or website as well as discussion points for family conversations about the content. They include details such as whether content is violent, appropriateness of language, quality of role models and level of consumerism. Kids rate the games too.

What is YOUR view? What do you feel is the right amount for YOUR child? Is there a problem with your family's current levels or type of consumption?

There is no one-size-fits-all formula. We recommend that each family decide what works best for them. Changing the level or the kind of electronic consumption is likely to be helpful to family life if you find that:

☺ Screens interfere with other activities or create pressure around things you want to do with your child, or that he needs to do, including being physically active

☺ Your child prefers to be in front of a screen than doing things with family and friends or being outdoors

☺ Your child seems angry/depressed, or simply at a loss, when she is not using screens

☺ Your child's performance at school is below par, particularly in areas such as literacy or creativity

☺ Your child wants to use the TV/computer first and last thing each day

☺ You're worried that your child is addicted. That means that not only is his use compulsive, involving arguments every time you ask him to turn off, but it also involves secrecy, deceitful behaviour, going undercover, lying about what he is doing, perhaps even cheating and stealing to do it.

☺ Your child is behaving aggressively and you're concerned that it may be linked to the type of content he is being exposed to.

One 12-year-old boy would be playing a computer game and when his mum asked him politely to stop he would literally SCREAM at her "you can't make me, I HATE you, I wish you weren't my mum." He would also use his height and strength in an aggressive manner.

What won't work

Imagine you're the child in the following scenario and consider how you'd feel and how you'd react if your parent spoke to you like this:

What are you doing? I thought I said no computer until your homework is done and you haven't put your games kit in the wash either – it won't be clean when you need it next. You're so sneaky coming in here to your bedroom to play games behind my back. Your brain will rot with all the nonsense you get up to on these games. I seriously worry that you're becoming really shallow with all the triviality you fill your head with. When was the last time you even opened a book... or went outside? You're really going to ace these exams at the rate you're going aren't you?

Oh Greg you've left a dirty plate on your chest of drawers – honestly you're such a mess! And look at the state of your room – it's a floordrobe again!

Don't give me any lip young man or you can say good-bye to the laptop – which would probably be a good thing with all the time you spend on it instead of getting some exercise. You used to play so much sport when you were little – now look at you!

Did you feel like running away, ignoring your parent, shouting back? Did you feel undeterred about your computer use but determined to not get found out? The more we nag, criticise, shout, blame, catastrophise, push, ban, forbid, threaten and take away, the more they push back and try to regain control from us. This approach may work to get them off the gadget in the moment, but it does nothing in the long-term to help them to develop a good relationship with technology or with us.

What does work

Back to us (of course)

Have you thought about your own digital footprint? Practising what we preach is always important but nowhere is this more important than in our own use of electronics. Many children say that they have to vie for our attention with our gadgets and devices. We may be engaged in different digital activities than our children but it can be no less time-consuming. We're just as susceptible to the dopamine hits that come from being online. We get a kick every time something wings into our inboxes or onto our newsfeeds. If you've got an audible alert on your emails or it pings onto your screen it can be almost impossible to ignore this. Our children are not the only ones who suffer from FOMO (fear of missing out). Incoming emails or texts definitely fall into the *urgent* category discussed in Chapter 7 but are not necessarily important to us when we re-examine our priorities. Every Facebook user knows that 5 minutes easily morphs into an hour.

> *We are a high digital usage family and all have PCs and iPads and iPhones and the scary bit for me was when, after reading Frances Booth's* The Distraction Trap, *I got the whole family to do the questionnaire on how digitally toxic you are. The results were truly shocking as I realised that I was the one most digitally distracted!*
>
> **Elaine, mum of two**

One of our concerns for our children is that their electronic activities are sapping their ability to focus and yet we model these behaviours ourselves if we convince ourselves that we are multi-tasking when we are writing emails and surfing the web and posting on Facebook and supervising homework all at the same time. Multi-tasking has been exposed as a fallacy and task-switching (which is what it is really) robs us of our precious time. Each and every time we switch from one task to another, it takes 5–10 minutes to get engaged with each task. So either we never get engaged OR we're taking way too long to do each task. Multi-tasking is distracting and leads to less satisfaction. Multi-taskers experience more stress because of their self-imposed constant interruptions, which reduce their short-term memory.[87]

We are losing connection with our children if, when we are ostensibly spending time with them, our phones are on the table and we respond to texts or calls. We give them the message that they are less important than the sender of that text or that caller. Let's turn it off and be present. Let our behaviour tell our kids that they matter. One little boy was overheard telling a friend that *"my mummy loves me so much she puts her phone away for me."*

---

[87] Alan Brown, ADHD coach, Screen Time Sanity Telesummit 2015, http://habyts.com/screen-time-tips/

The best way to encourage a healthy digital life in our children is to adopt a **whole family approach**.

1. Work out what your values are around electronic use
2. Model the behaviours you want to see and
3. Require them of your children

What are your values here? Parents tend to be unclear about what they want – and then they vary it from day to day anyway! It's hard enough for children to turn off, without having the rules change every day.

Sometimes you will give your child the tablet to occupy him while you need to do something else. Don't beat yourself up as a bad parent but be aware of how often it happens. Awareness is the first step towards changing habits.

If you find you are deferring doing the things that matter to you in favour of the things that pop up and distract you then it would help to remind yourself here of the things that you want to be doing. In addition we can't just ban our children from their electronic lives – we need to offer valued replacement activities.

Asking your child questions to work out what she gets out of being on a game or online means you may be able to help her get that buzz elsewhere in life. If children are doing what they do to show their skills or be competitive or to feel good then parents can find other areas where kids can satisfy their needs. Don't just ban electronics but find satisfying alternatives. Rather than telling our children NOT to play on the computer, help them do other things and make them a very appealing alternative to solitary electronic usage. Why not start with a Detox Weekend and let everyone choose a favourite non-digital activity?

Just as we talk to them about finding a balance between 'everyday' foods and 'sometimes' foods, so we need to find space in our lives for work, time alone and with friends and family, play inside and outside, creative time and active time, structured time and unstructured time. And we need to provide and plan for this balance and model it too.

Your turn

What's important to you? List five activities that you want to do as a family. Some families have suggested making movies or photo albums, going bike riding, getting involved in animal welfare projects, planting a garden, cooking up a storm, a construction or sewing project, take classes in surfing/watercolours/fencing/cake decorating/Japanese...

....

....

....

Family planning

Sit down with the whole family and talk. It's important to include the children for the general atmosphere, for the success of the plan, and for their self-esteem. When a child is involved in setting the limits it's much more effective because (a) the child knows and has a greater commitment to the limits and (b) the child feels respected and trusted. Limits only work when you've listened. Then you can help them develop really key skills to self-regulate, balance, understand and satisfy their needs. They can't learn self-regulation if limits are imposed on them without discussion.

> *I think the Parent Practice skills have been vital in negotiating our way through this – so tons of EMOTION COACHING because of course, EVERYONE else has the game they want to play, watches the programmes they're not allowed to watch etc; FAMILY MEETINGS regularly to look at the RULES and listening to what both boys say, being prepared to compromise on some things but being very clear beforehand about what is a no-go for negotiation; the RULES on screens are written up, signed by all, laminated and displayed on our kitchen wall! And obviously, lots of DESCRIPTIVE PRAISE when they adhere to the Rules, come off when asked without meltdowns, etc.*
>
> Vicky, mum of two

Communication and connection, not coercion and control

Don't demonise

It's really important that we don't demonise technology. If we do that we alienate ourselves from something that is integral to our children's lives. If we rubbish what is important to them they may hear that they are not important/worthwhile, that they are silly or not valued. We need to enjoy the technology, celebrate it, join in and appreciate the skills involved while educating them about potential risks. When we do this, we connect with our children.

When my youngest was little he was a Star Wars boffin – something I had limited interest in – but his eyes would light up when I engaged with him about it. Even now he has interests that I don't share – he is fascinated with the mechanics of vintage weaponry. He knows other people are not only not interested, but think his interest is a bit 'off'.

When he said to me *"I know you're not interested in this"* I could respond, *"No, but you are, and I'm interested in you and I love your passion for it and your detailed knowledge about it and actually I've become interested in it because of your enthusiasm and expertise."*

We need to inform ourselves about our children's digital practices. Far from something to be feared some games actually assist cognitive development and connection to peers. But overuse may be something that needs to be addressed as it can lead to poor psychological functioning and reduction in other healthy activities.[88] In fact research undertaken at Oxford University[89] found that of the 4,500 children studied, those who played 1 hour a day were the most psychologically well adjusted. Those who played 3 hours a day were the least psychologically well adjusted, which means that a Goldilocks approach is warranted and a moderate amount of play is better than none!

So when our kids want to show us something on screen we need to avoid the temptation to belittle it to show that we believe it is not important in the hope this puts them off – it doesn't, it only disconnects and alienates. The way social media is used does need training and overseeing but the child should not be denigrated for their use.

Do it with them

When we play games with our children we sometimes learn that the games that our kids enjoy most are the ones that really stretch them and test executive functions like organising, planning and remembering. Now it's up to us to help them see that they can use those skills in real life!

Children have always learnt through play – this is just a new medium. Some games really encourage creativity, much

---

88 Randy Kulman, Screen Sanity seminar, 2015
89 Andrew Shibelsky, referred to in Randy Kulman's interview, Screen Sanity seminar, 2015

more than passive TV viewing, so it depends on the game. You can find out more about the games by reading reviews on games rating sites or by playing with them. The Common Sense Media rating site[90] has a section on what learning outcomes are possible from the game. Some games have characters that experience different emotions depending on what happens in the play so children can learn the impact of their character's actions on others in a simulated setting.

Our children absolutely love it when we engage in their world. When we play with them or even just observe their play we get a sense of what's involved and how much it means to them. *Jane's son Fred was completely devastated when he accidentally auctioned off one of his players on a FIFA game for a lot less than he was worth. He felt 'such a plonker' and was really anxious to earn the coins he needed to buy him back as quickly as possible. Jane could understand how much it mattered to him and why he wanted to spend more time on the game earning the coins. This allowed her to be understanding and find some compromises without abandoning her values about time on screens.*

We recommend that parents of older children use some form of social media themselves so that they get familiar with its use and so that they can be friends (in the digital sense) with their child. Follow, but don't comment (online) on your child's posts. (Some families have godparents or other family members as friends too as a condition of Facebook use.)

Talk to them and listen to them

Obviously you will need electronic protections but the best form of protection is to talk to your kids (and have some rules) to help them navigate the digital word and be safe. Our children are more likely to listen to us if we are speaking without judgment or criticism and we're not belittling their

---

[90] www.commonsensemedia.org

interests or making them wrong for wanting more screen time than we think is healthy.

Our children want to please us. They don't want to annoy us. So if they're breaking the rules around screen use it's because the compulsion of the screen is outweighing the competing desire to please us in the moment. So ramp up their natural urge to win your approval by making clear how they can get it – in other words give lots of Descriptive Praise, especially for sensible use of their time and appropriate choices of content or for following your screen rules and for not making a fuss when it's time to end a screen session. You are helping your children by providing an extrinsic motivator until they develop the more adult kind of motivation that feels good when they get done the things they need to do.

Ask them what they love about their screen use. You may find that what they like about games are perfectly healthy things such as their ability to control the game, its adaptability, the fact that they get instant feedback and can learn and progress quickly and without an audience. They may love the fact that it is challenging and that they are good at it. You may find that the skills they are acquiring can be applied to different areas of their lives. Randy Kulman[91] suggests that parents:

☐ DETECT – identify a skill in a game

☐ REFLECT – interpret how that skill can be used in the real world

☐ CONNECT – practise it with them

Knowing the game can also help you get your child off it! For example Minecraft is a sandbox game which is based on projects that take varying lengths of time to complete. So it

[91] Screen Sanity seminar, 2015

may be hopeless to say to your child that he can have half an hour's time on the game and rigidly enforce that. It would be better to talk in terms of what project could be completed in the time he has available.

Acknowledge how they feel about:

☺ the game, being connected to their friends through social media, their YouTube viewing habits, their access to music, etc

☺ having to turn off

☺ preferring their digital activities to things they have to do. Maybe ask them why they think it matters to fulfil their responsibilities. Descriptively praise any sensible answer and acknowledge that even when you know it's a good idea to do something, like revise for your test, you still may prefer to do something else that's more fun or compelling. Admit that sometimes you've neglected things that are worthwhile, like getting more sleep, in favour of watching TV.

☺ your silly rules, your unfairness and total unreasonableness, etc

I know you think I'm being really mean not letting you have Grand Theft Auto when many of your friends have it. I take your enthusiasms very seriously so I looked into the content on that ratings site I told you about and I have real concerns about it. Because I really respect you I'm not going to just ban it without telling you why...

I get that you are very involved in that game and would love to do just one more level. It's really compelling isn't it? And the time we agreed is up so it's time to turn off. I know how hard that is. It might help to remember that turning off promptly means you earn your play for tomorrow.

I think earlier I was very dismissive of your wanting to be on Facebook with your friends. When I said you'd just seen them at school today my words didn't appreciate how much that connection means to you. I'm sorry that I made light of your feelings.

I know you love playing on Mummy's tablet, don't you? It's hard to stop when it's time to do other things.

What else are they doing on screens? It's not all games. Some children will be researching the things they're interested in. Jane's son is always looking up random facts. When learning happens spontaneously it's the best kind and it counteracts the curriculum at school where they don't have any say.

What are we worried about here? Fred challenged Jane that if he were spending as long looking up facts in books she wouldn't have a problem with it and she concedes this point. If the information is digitally sourced it doesn't necessarily make it less accurate or valid than if it were found in print. We need to teach our children to query what they hear/read and test the source wherever it occurs.

Social media

Although this book is aimed at parents of children under 12 the age restrictions of most social media sites are not enforced and parents often allow their children access earlier than those age guidelines. A car is a great resource but you wouldn't give your kids the keys without first teaching them how to be safe behind the wheel. There are reasons why you have to be a certain age before you can operate a potentially dangerous machine, and it's the same with social media.

Your children will probably be aware of the various social media platforms and may be clamouring for access now.

Alex (aged 10) is obsessed with getting some kind of social media account (and knows the names of all of them!) and we have always said when he is 13 we will set up a Facebook account with him but I imagine by then Facebook will probably be very passé and he'll want the next thing.

We have had lots of conversations about being aware that people are not always who they claim to be online (indeed, he sadly learnt this when he was 7½ following his joining a Clash of Clans group (completely unbeknown to us) and finding himself being potentially groomed...).

Vicky, mum of two

When Imogen was 12 she was allowed a Facebook account and quickly she encountered problems as someone FRAPED her account – she left her Facebook page open and a so-called friend then posted obscene comments under her identity. Because I insisted on other family members befriending her this was picked up within the hour and deleted but resulted in quite a discussion with Immy and her friends about the implications of this.

Ellen, mum of two

Some older children will spend time on social media and some will watch cat videos on YouTube. Social media use will obviously be about connecting to others – not a bad thing in itself. Social networks are a great way to build up friendships, yet they can also be great time-wasters and are no substitute for real relationships. Social media can also be very destructive of friendships.

Clearly we need to talk to our children about appropriate behaviour online for their protection and to encourage kindness toward others. We need to be aware of what is online and how we can control and monitor access, and then we need to teach our children how to be aware of possible dangers for themselves and how to manage their online life. There are clear risks connected with sharing inappropriate information and bullying is an increasingly prevalent problem. Talk with your children about what material is appropriate, and how they can monitor their own screen presence and what they can do if they wish to remove something. Make sure the tone of your conversation is not nagging or blaming but instead about skill-building to keep them safe, the same as crossing the road.

Be aware that social media can affect friendships. Technology can:

☺ Increase the speed and intensity of gossip, humiliation and drama

☺ Enable fighting/meanness in ways that wouldn't happen face to face

☺ Mean that home is no longer a safe haven, out of reach of bullying

> *In year 6 Imogen was the recipient of some nasty cyber bullying via vile text messages sent to her phone. It was incredibly upsetting and the perpetrators had little comprehension of the upset it could cause and were counselled by the school – some education resulted.*
>
> **Ellen, mum of two**

Cyber bullying is a very real problem which can affect anyone using social media. Even if your children don't have social media accounts yet it's wise to make yourself aware of the issues so you can talk to them about it before they get there. It's not just those directly engaged in the bullying who are affected but those on the side lines, observing, too. They can feel trapped and unwittingly involved as if they are giving tacit approval. They know that if they tell their parents what's going on, they will lose their devices.

Watching the film *Cyber Bully* with older children may be a good way to start a conversation. Check out the trailer on YouTube: https://www.youtube.com/watch?v=fk_YSO0py7s (see our website – www.theparentpractice.com/book-resources#chapter-11).

Rules

Children need limits. They need help to keep to those limits and they need practice keeping to the limits. With your support they will, over time, develop habits of sticking to limits of their own making but we mustn't expect that to happen any time soon. After all, how good are we at sticking to our own limits? We need to use all the tools in Part One repeatedly. THIS IS OUR JOB and to expect to do otherwise is courting disappointment. It's not a problem. It's just the way it is bringing up children. It's not easy for kids to keep to limits when what they want is so enticing. It's just the same as educating children about healthy eating – you wouldn't let your kids choose a diet made up entirely of sweets. So we need to educate them about a healthy digital diet.

I have seen some arguments for allowing children to self-regulate around screen usage and this might be possible for some temperaments. Most parents wouldn't have an issue with self-regulation if their children were turning off and doing the other things they value and their internet usage was sensible. But generally kids have a hard time turning off and they need external limits until they can do it for themselves.

As usual **decide on your values** around this area first, in discussion with your partner or other trusted adult. Decide on how much, what, where and when.

☐ **How much** screen time do you think is reasonable given the other activities you would like your children to take part in as well as what they MUST do? Maybe make a pie chart! Be realistic – 30 minutes of gaming might actually take 45 minutes, including turning on, loading, playing, saving and exiting.

☐ **What sort of use** do you think is ok, what sites can they access, what games can they play, what manner of social media use do you think is healthy – do you need rules for conduct online? (As to being kind in social media I think two useful rules are the 'Golden rule' – treat others as you would have them treat you – and the THINK rule – is it True, Helpful, Important, Necessary or Kind? If not, you can think it but don't write it.)

☐ **Where** can your children access screens? We recommend that children don't have devices, including smartphones, in their bedrooms as this makes it so difficult to monitor and really interferes with sleep. Instead keep and use screens in common areas. Maybe have a drop off/charging zone. Will you have screen-free zones?

☐ **When's** a good time? Mornings? Afternoons? After homework and chores, not too close to bedtimes, not at the dinner table? Will you have screen-free times?

☐ **At what age** should they have their own devices/access to games or programmes online/a social media account? When it comes to games and TV programmes or films online will you be guided by the provider's age guidelines or make your own investigations?

Then **discuss with your kids**. Once you've outlined your values and your objectives ask for their input in how to achieve this. Remember you're helping them develop key skills to *self*-regulate, balance, understand and satisfy their needs. It's important that the rules are relevant and have some application to **all the family** – include everyone in the creation, and the implementation. And write them down... Maybe draw up a digital code of conduct for each member of the family. See examples on our website – www. theparentpractice.com/book-resources#chapter-11.

Make sure the **rules are framed positively** – what they can do, not what they can't do. Rules are easier to understand and accept when they are detailed and positive – there's no room for misunderstanding and they are more motivating than constraining. Make sure some rules are easy for them to follow. We need to make sure that the rule is reasonable and achievable for the child.

Then **follow through**. With empathy. (And Descriptive Praise, of course.)

Remember, the focus will be on acknowledging when the children have followed the rule, rather than immediately worrying about what we have to do when they don't follow the rule.

Set up a system where children 'earn' the right to play games, surf the web, watch YouTube etc by keeping their phone or tablet in the right place, turning off at the scheduled time, or keeping to approved sites/games.

Then if they haven't kept the rules they haven't earnt the privilege of screen time. If you don't behave responsibly with technology, then you can't have it to use for a time. If you go over a time limit, or go to a banned website, then you can't do it again until you've earnt back some trust. But this needs to be explained with understanding and empathy, not judgment.

Choosing games/programmes
There is a bewildering array of choice and at first this has to be our responsibility. Ultimately, we want our children to be able to make their own choices and they will follow where we lead, so being selective in our choices and considering options is a good habit for them to learn. We can read reviews, or even watch programmes in advance. And we can talk to other parents to hear their opinions.

Some things to think about:

☐ What does this programme/game teach my child?

☐ Does this programme/game leave my child motivated, or apathetic? Does it leave him calm, or full of pent-up energy? Does it leave him frightened or disturbed or angry?

☐ Does this programme/game give my child an improved vocabulary and positive tone of voice, or does it teach him bad words? Does it contain positive role models?

☐ Does this programme/game encourage good relationships, or does it encourage sibling/peer conflict, or leave him wanting to withdraw?

☐ Does this game offer my child opportunities to plan, be creative and make decisions, or does it glorify violence?

☐ Does this programme/game expose my child to values/ideas that I think are healthy or that I want my child to know about or does it over-familiarise them with concepts that I think are not healthy or appropriate for them?

> If a child's response to a programme or game is positive, and the content is acceptable, stay switched on; if not, turn off. So much easier to write than to do, I know!

Your turn

What do your kids like to do electronically? What do they enjoy about it?

....

....

Can you see some benefits to them from this activity?

....

....

Is there any downside to their digital activity?

....

....

What about the amount of time in front of a screen? Is it balanced with the other things that are important to you?

....

....

What rules do you need for your family's digital use? Consider what, when, where and how much.

....

....

....

....

If you need to alter your own digital practices what small step will you undertake this week?

....

....

Digitally different

Fred, aged 11, who often had difficulties sleeping, had stayed up half the previous night messaging his friends. His mum had then said that he couldn't have his phone in his room at night anymore but needed to leave it to re-charge in their new 'drop off zone' and she and dad would do the same. Fred wasn't keen on this new plan of course and Jane empathised with how he felt. He said it was really mean and it singled him out because all his friends had their mobile phones in their rooms and messaged him and he wouldn't be able to answer and they would think he was rude. Or they'd assume he was asleep and went to bed really early. He was clearly embarrassed.

Jane said she'd need to think about a solution to this that would meet both their needs and asked Fred to do the same.

Fred was back within 10 minutes with his solution. He said he'd tell his friends he no longer had wi-fi in his room and that he couldn't be bothered to get out of bed and go downstairs as his mum was too mean to put the heating on. Jane was happy to be the fall guy for this one.

Jane, mum of two

Their Digital World in a nutshell

There are lots of good things about use of electronic media and some things to be wary of to keep our children safe. We have to educate ourselves about the continuous advancements in technology so that we can support our children to be safe and so that they don't dismiss our concerns as being out of touch.

While electronic protections will be part of our arsenal the best line of defence is communication and education. Bans and prohibitions won't work – we need to talk to our children respectfully, acknowledging what they love about their digital world.

In order for children to have healthy digital habits, we need to:

☐ MODEL it – be aware of our own digital footprint and don't be hypocritical

☐ REQUIRE it – formulate rules in family meetings. Involve children in creating rules for the whole family.

☐ INVOLVE ourselves – play with them and get to know what the games are like, befriend them on social media

☐ MAKE IT HAPPEN – get books, get outside, get friends, get moving. Provide engaging alternatives to electronics.

Further reading:

Frances Booth, *The Distraction Trap: How to Focus in a Digital World*, 2013

Teresa Orange and Louise O'Flynn, *The Media Diet For Kids: A Parents' Survival Guide to TV and Computer Games,* 2005

Bex Lewis, *Raising Children in a Digital Age: Enjoying the Best and Avoiding the Worst,* 2014

12

Their moral world

Claire had been busy packing all afternoon to go on holiday. The family were visiting a friend whom Claire hadn't seen for years who had a severely disabled daughter. The girl apparently loved dolls so Claire had bought a doll to take with them. Scarlett, her 6 year old, was showing a great interest in it. As Claire was packing the doll in the suitcase Scarlett started whining, "It's not fair, why can't I have that doll." It really pushed Claire's buttons and she barked at her "Look, it is for a little girl who doesn't have much and you have loads of dolls, so let's think about others please…" Her husband piped up from the other side of the room "Emotion Coaching, darling?" At which point Claire realised that it is quite normal for a 6 year old who loves dolls to see a new one in her box and to want it. So she got down to her level and said, "It probably makes you jealous when you see a big doll like that. You just want it so badly for yourself even though you know it is for Lucy..." Scarlett nodded quietly and went happily to bed after that. Claire was grateful for husband prompting her – helps the united front!

Things to remember about teaching children moral sense:

☺ Children develop concepts of morality alongside the development of cognitive ability so our expectations need to be based on what they're capable of understanding given their stage of development.

☺ Parents' responses to children's behaviour can lead to children avoiding or taking responsibility.

☺ Children will lie, steal, cheat and use 'rude' words from time to time so we should expect it and respond calmly with prepared strategies.

☺ While developing sexual interest is a natural part of growing up it can cause parents anxiety or discomfort so it's as well to be prepared before your children reach puberty by thinking about what messages you'd like them to learn about sexuality and sexual relationships.

What is morality?

At its core, morality is understanding the difference between right and wrong, and we have focused on that quite a bit already in this book, especially in the sections on Family Values (Chapter 5) and Positive Discipline (Chapter 6). But since raising children to understand the difference between right and wrong, and to act on what they know to be right, is a clear goal for all parents we take a further look here at how morality actually develops. When our children do something that breaks a moral code we tend to get particularly upset and our reactions aren't always calm or constructive. So understanding what is a normal part of children's development will help us keep our cool. We'll take a closer look at how to deal with some moral hot spots too, such as lying and stealing.

Moral rules are different from social conventions and children learn to distinguish between the two as they get older. A moral issue is something that concerns the concepts of justice, fairness and human rights and we get more worked up about breaches of moral codes (for example, if Jake tries to put the blame on Tasha for something that he himself has done), whereas social conventions are just socially agreed-upon rules such as saying 'please' and 'thank you'.

Children's beliefs about morality are at least partly shaped by the value systems of the society in which they are brought up. For example in Australia traditionally raised indigenous peoples take very seriously family connections and 'sorry business' so when someone dies the whole extended family will drop everything (including work) to attend the funeral, thus meeting familial obligations. White Australians generally don't have quite the same value and would rate attending work as a higher value unless the deceased person was close.

How does morality develop?

I find understanding how morality develops makes it much easier to comprehend and not judge kids' behaviour. Even after all my years' work on these skills I still find I have to remind myself to look behind behaviour which has pushed my buttons!

Morality develops along with understanding so we adults need to make sure we're not imputing to children higher capacity for moral reasoning than is appropriate for their age. For example, no one holds a 9 month old responsible for breaking a vase if he pushes it off the table because he doesn't have the capacity to reason or foresee consequences and understand the 'wrongness' of that action.

Professor Mark de Rosnay, behavioural scientist, argues that children are not morally responsible for their actions until they have the capacity to fully understand the implications of their actions. This develops with cognitive growth and adult guidance.[92]

Babies are focused entirely on their own needs and can only judge 'right' or 'wrong' by reference to those. As a toddler grows he becomes more aware of others and their (different) needs and feelings. He doesn't really have a fully developed sense of right or wrong as yet, just the competing claims of what he wants to do and what others say he must do. When he hurts someone or breaks something he doesn't have much sense of the consequences of his action. During the preschool years he will hopefully absorb the family values in the sense of knowing that 'we do this' or 'we don't do that' as a set of rules even if he doesn't yet understand why.

I was very amused by the way my daughter expressed her absorption of family values, aged 5. She was in the back seat of the car with a friend who was coming over for a play date when the friend used some offensive language. Gemma drew herself up and said rather pompously "Ours is not a rude house." I'm pretty sure I'd never expressed it quite like that, but she got the point.

Jean Piaget explored the development of children's morality. He referred to children up until the age of about 7 as being in a stage of Morality of Constraint; that is, they follow rules because of the risk of getting in trouble if they do not. The child thinks in very black-and-white terms, with no grey areas; there are good people and bad people. Adults' authority isn't questioned. Rules are set in concrete and must

---

[92] Professor de Rosnay, Head of the Early Start centre at the University of Wollongong, in an interview on ABC radio 702, 1 September 2015

not be broken and there is no scope for negotiation... unless they conflict with the child's own wants in which case he may break the rule! In this stage a child will determine whether something is wrong by reference to the outcome of the action. To illustrate Piaget posed this moral dilemma to the children he interviewed: a child accidentally knocks over and breaks 15 cups, another child is reaching for some forbidden treat and knocks over one cup. Children in this age group tend to rate the latter child as less culpable because he broke fewer cups. A young child may have difficulty understanding the idea of an accidental wrong.

As children get older they can better consider other people's needs and feelings and become concerned with the good of the group. They also begin to judge the rightness or wrongness of an action based on the person's intention. So it may be deemed ok that a person breaks into a pharmacy and steals some medicine if it was after hours and the person's child was very ill even though they would normally consider stealing to be wrong.

Feelings such as guilt, sympathy, shame and pity can all play a role in everyday situations involving moral choices. A child's ability to handle these feelings therefore will affect their choices and behaviours. So if your child hurts another child and feels guilty and experiences compassion for the hurt child then he is likely to want to say sorry and make up for it. And the memory of those feelings may play a part in determining future actions.

Empathy is a skill that is learned. A 4 year old may understand that another child is feeling distress but may not yet know what to do about it. Children under 5 won't be able to deal with hypothetical questions such as 'how would you feel if...?' They learn best from observing empathy. Children generally develop empathy as they get older if they are shown empathy.

Yet we all know that even when children know what is the right thing to do their actions may not be aligned with these thoughts. This is because they may be overcome by their impulses. We put this down to immature frontal lobes, but adults can have this problem too. I knew full well the consequences of that piece of cake I ate on Monday but I ate it anyway.

After 7 years of age children may realise that parents and teachers are fallible and begin to question adult authority. Bad luck! After that respect needs to be earnt by fair (consistent) treatment.

How do parents teach children right from wrong?

When teaching right and wrong we need to be aware of the difference between shame and guilt and how those emotions make us behave. Our responses to our children's behaviour may result in them feeling either shame or guilt. Shame is the feeling that I am a bad person, a judgment about myself as a person, whereas guilt is the feeling I get when I've done a bad thing, a judgment about my actions. When children feel shame they can feel worthless and then may lash out or try to avoid the situation.

I realise now that this is what happened to my son Christian when the adults yelled at him and his teachers sometimes humiliated him. He felt such shame to the core of his identity that he could not survive it, so he pushed it away. He made excuses or lied or tried to cover up his actions, most of which were as a result of impulsivity.

When children feel guilty about their actions they tend to experience regret and want to make amends. They think, "I am a good person who made a mistake." (See the Brené Brown TED video on shame on YouTube:

https://www.ted.com/talks/brene_brown_listening_to_
shame?language=en#t-8812 (see our website - www.
theparentpractice.com/book-resources#chapter-12).

In a study conducted by psychologist Karen Caplovitz
Barrett[93] on the effects of feeling shame or guilt over actions,
children were given a doll, and the leg fell off while they
were playing with it alone. It was made to appear as if the
child was responsible for the mishap. Those children who
had previously been identified by their parents as prone
to feelings of shame avoided the researcher and did not
volunteer that they broke the doll. The guilt-prone children
were more likely to fix the doll, approach the experimenter,
and explain what had happened. The ashamed children were
avoiders; the guilty children were amenders.

So our goal as moral educators is to not cause shame. That
means we need to avoid words that amount to criticism, labels,
put downs, name-calling or actions that tend to humiliate or
ridicule or suggest that our children are bad people.

Research[94] shows that shame is more likely to be experienced
when parents express anger and use harsh discipline methods
involving punishment or withdrawal of affection. Of course
if no discipline is used at all children aren't going to develop
a moral code either. So we need to teach our children gently
about right and wrong with compassion and understanding
of their state of development.

Luckily we have the Mistakes Process! (See Chapter 6.)

The Mistakes Process

Remember that a crucial part of The Mistakes Process is first
taking some Cool Down Time. This is particularly important

---

[93] 'Avoiders vs. Amenders: Implications for the investigation of guilt and shame
during Toddlerhood.' in *Journal of Cognition and Emotion*, Volume 7, Issue 6, 1993
[94] Nancy Eisenberg, Department of Psychology, Arizona State University, 'Emotion,
Regulation, and Moral Development' in *Annual Review of Psychology* Volume 51: 665-
697 (February 2000)

when dealing with emotive issues like lying, stealing or cheating because parents are apt to get really steamed up at the thought of their children being dishonest. When everyone is calm you can connect with your child and talk about what happened with the purpose of teaching, not making the child afraid or ashamed.

1. No **anger**
2. Help your child to **admit** what happened. She may need to help to understand why what she did was wrong or hurtful, to understand how the other person felt.
3. Support him to find ways to make **amends**
4. Discuss ways of **alter**ing behaviour for the future
5. **Accept** that you're human and make mistakes. Move on.

Apologies

As discussed in Chapter 8, a hollow 'sorry' is worthless and teaches the child nothing. If a child is not feeling ashamed they will be genuinely remorseful and willing to apologise. When they are really ready to apologise it needs to be more than just 'sorry'. A form of words that shows genuine regret is as follows:

1. I'm sorry for…:
Be specific. Show the person you're apologising to that you really understand what they are upset about. *I'm sorry for saying that nobody wants to be your friend.*

2. This is wrong because…:
This might take some more thinking, but this is one of the most important parts. Until the child understands why it was wrong or how it hurt someone's feelings, it's unlikely they will change. *This is wrong because it hurt your feelings and made you feel bad. And it isn't true.*

3. In the future, I will…:

Use positive language, and say what he **WILL** do, not what he won't do. *In the future, I will keep unkind words in my head. I will try to say how I am feeling instead.*

4. Will you forgive me?

This form of words obviously has a lot of similarities with the Mistakes Process. As well as the sorry, the child who did wrong may need to make amends by doing something kind or friendly for the other person. This, together with the genuineness of the apology, makes it more likely that the relationship will be repaired.

Modelling

You won't be surprised to hear that modelling of course plays a big role in our children's acquisition of morals. Actions speak louder than words and according to some research, words (in the form of preaching) can actually be detrimental. In one experiment, psychologist J. Philippe Rushton gave school-age children tokens for winning a game, which they could keep entirely or donate some to a child in poverty. They first watched a teacher play the game, either keeping the tokens for himself or giving some away, and then the teacher either talked to them on the value of giving or not. The teacher's influence was significant – when the teacher behaved selfishly, so did the children. Children gave fewer tokens after observing the teacher's selfish actions, regardless of whether he verbally advocated selfishness or generosity. When the teacher acted generously, students gave the same amount whether generosity was preached or not. When the teacher preached selfishness, even after he had acted generously, the students still gave generously.

Two months later the children were tested again. Those who gave most generously were the children who had seen the teacher behaving generously but saying nothing. They gave more generously than their counterparts who had seen generous behaviour but were also preached to on the value of generosity.

And the moral of the story is: children learn morals not by listening to what their role models say, but by observing what they do… No pressure, then.

Moral dilemmas

Children's books are a great way to discuss moral dilemmas. You can also pose questions to your children in the form 'what would you do if…?' Your aim is to engage them in thinking, not to fish for information or to judge. Examples:

☺ What would you do if Dad told you to clean up your toys but you were having fun? You don't want to stop playing.

☺ You're practising on your skateboard in the house and break Mum's new ornament. She hears the crash and comes running to see what happened. If you tell the truth, you know you will be in trouble. What will you do?

☺ A boy is hanging out with friends when they start teasing a quiet kid, taking his things and calling him names. If he sticks up for him, the group could turn on him. He starts to slip away, but someone throws him the boy's bag. What should he do?

☺ A girl is playing with two good friends. They both want to be her best friend. She thinks she likes one friend better. That friend says, "Let's go play by ourselves." She knows her other friend's feelings will be hurt if she's left out. What should she do?

☺ You got in trouble, and you're angry. Mum and Dad punished you, but you think your sister deserves to be punished. It doesn't feel fair – she was being annoying.

You feel like hiding or breaking one of her toys. What will you do?

Lying

"What in me was not safe enough for you to tell the truth?"
– Gandhi, when his grandson lied to him

All kids lie

Well, researchers estimate that 96% of children lie. And they lie all the time. They start as young as 2 and lie more and more frequently until the age of 12, when lying begins to decline. Dr Victoria Talwar, an expert on children's lying behaviours, found that 4 year olds lie once every 2 hours and a 6 year old about once an hour! And parents usually can't tell if they're lying.[95] Most of us are uncomfortable with this idea.

Why do they lie?

Generally to cover up a transgression, to avoid getting into trouble or causing hurt, to bond with friends or to gain a sense of control. By about age 6 the reasons for lying can be quite complex. As a child develops empathy they start to consider others when they lie and they may lie to spare a friend's feelings or to keep their secrets. But they may also use this new awareness of others to manipulate them, to brag or make up tall stories and get attention. She may lie to get her brother into trouble. He may enjoy the power and sense of control that he gets from fooling his parents.

You'll have been expecting me to say that kids learn to lie by observing us. Adults admit to lying about once a day. These are often white lies designed to prevent hurt and if a child tells just

---

[95] Dr Talwar, Professor of Developmental Psychology at McGill University, in Montreal, referred to in Po Bronson and Ashley Merryman, *Nurtureshock: Why Everything We Thought About Children is Wrong*, 2011

such a white lie parents are often pleased at their politeness. But if lies designed to make someone feel better are acceptable you can see how a child might decide to lie about his misdeeds in order to make his parent feel happy! If we're honest (!) some of our lies are purely to serve our own purposes as well, such as when we say to the charity collector at the door that we have no cash on us or we tell the parking warden that we've just pulled up whereas we've been sitting in the spot for 10 minutes. We may be able to justify these lies to ourselves but it allows our children to get used to disingenuity.

Professor Angela Crossman recommends that when you have to tell a 'little prosocial untruth' (a white lie) in front of your child, the best strategy is to acknowledge it later and tell her why you did it: *"Explain you've been a little dishonest to avoid hurting someone's feelings. Kids can understand why someone wouldn't want their feelings hurt."*[96]

A sudden spate of lying (in your child) may be a sign of an underlying problem. Adopting a non-judgmental approach and using all your Emotion Coaching skills may help you find out what's going on, and in any case will show your child you are open for a conversation.

What does it mean when your child lies?

It obviously doesn't mean that she is a sociopath. And lying as a child is no indicator that your child will grow up to be a fraudster or other criminal. Parents are often surprised to learn that their child is lying and in fact it is very hard to tell if a child over the age of 7 is lying. Even trained law enforcement personnel are only right half the time. We find the idea of our children's dishonesty very troubling and deem it to be slur on us as parents.

It may be some compensation to know that if your child is

---

a good liar it is a sign of advanced cognitive development as it involves understanding the truth, imagining an alternate reality and convincing someone else of that alternate version. A really adept liar will be able to extend a lie, maintain consistency and offer plausible explanations.

Fred is a magnificent liar. Inspired and very convincing. We first discovered it when he was 3 and he was found cheating at cards. We would not have spotted it other than for a bizarre coincidence. We were horrified... and also proud. And since then we have had many conversations about honesty. The cheating was purely to win and feel happy, but his interest in lying is very much about not wanting to get me cross. I am glad we had that fateful game of cards and I became aware of his ability and I'm careful about getting cross!

Jane

What does it mean to them? Children start out by thinking all lies are bad and gradually learn that some lies are ok. They start out by thinking lies and liars are morally wrong, and intent doesn't matter. The salient fact is that the information is incorrect. Have you had the experience of your young child accusing you of lying to them when you innocently give them false information or when plans change? *Your 5 year old may be furious when you promise to take them to the swimming pool on Saturday not knowing that Mum has arranged to get the car serviced that afternoon.* Accusations of lying are very common for children on the autistic spectrum who are usually very literal.

92% of 5 year olds say lying is always wrong and when asked why would say that it is because you get punished for it.[97] It's

---

[97] Dr Talwar, Professor of Developmental Psychology at McGill University, in Montreal, referred to in Po Bronson and Ashley Merryman, *Nurtureshock: Why Everything We Thought About Children is Wrong*, 2011

only much later that children can identify that lying destroys trust and carries guilt with it.

What to do about it

The biggest mistake parents make according to Dr Talwar is not to deal with lies early on. We don't do anything because when a child first starts lying he is too young to understand that lying is wrong. This is based on the mistaken idea that because the child is not at fault we shouldn't discipline them. It is understandable that you wouldn't want to discipline if your only options were punitive and would make the child wrong – but we have many other teaching strategies.

The main thing is to talk to them about lying and the impact it has on others. Help him see it from his own point of view if the tables were turned. Example: *How would you feel if Daddy said we were going to the cinema and really we were going to the doctor's to get vaccinations? Would you believe Daddy the next time he said we were going somewhere nice?*

Punishing doesn't work.
This just makes them better liars to avoid getting caught. Saying you won't be cross if they tell the truth doesn't work either as it seems children don't trust that promise of immunity. What works is to **tell your child you will be happy with them for telling the truth, and mean it.** They want to make you happy.

Say things like: *"Let's assume we haven't talked about this before. I trust you to tell me the truth."* Or *"Even if you made a mistake before I trust you to tell me the truth now." "I know you don't feel good about telling me something that isn't true – it's no fun being left feeling guilty about what you've said."*

Descriptively praise any signs of honesty and don't try to catch your child out in a lie. *"When you told the truth just now, it was brave,"* or *"That was the right thing to do and it meant there was no argument and we all stayed* *calmer."* *"The fact that you told me the truth means that I can trust you. I really value that."* If you tell your child you won't be angry with them for being honest you've got to be true to your word. It might be safer to say you probably would be cross initially when they tell you about some wrongdoing but that you'll be very happy with them for being honest.

Call a lie a lie (not fibs or porkies, which trivialises it) but **don't call the child a liar.** If you suspect your child is lying to you, the best approach is to be empathetic rather than accusatory or threatening. Using age-appropriate language, try something like *"Telling the truth can be really tough. Perhaps you are worried about what I am going to say. Would you like to have another go to explain what happened?"* Don't expect George Washington honesty straightaway. You have to prove that you do value their honesty.

When you uncover a transgression that your child has sought to hide with a lie **take action** about both the underlying misdeed and the lie. But not punitively. Use the Mistakes Process and express disappointment that you will no longer be able to trust the child. Depending on their age they may lose some privileges that involve trust for a period. Example: not being able to go round to the neighbour's to play on their own. You need to be able to trust that they are where they say they are. In fact your job is to create an atmosphere where your child can trust that you will handle mistakes with calmness and without judgment so that it is easier for your child to 'fess up. Remember you're aiming for guilt, not shame.

Nick used to read well into the night after his light was meant to be out. When I walked upstairs I could hear him turning off the light, pretending he hadn't been breaking the rule. Initially I was angry with him for deceiving me but then I thought better and said to him, "I can tell you know the rule about not reading after lights out." This made it possible to talk to him about how his actions amounted to lying. Because it was said gently he could learn. I held him accountable for his actions but without drama. I could acknowledge that reading was a really good thing but that he also needed his sleep.

Sue, mum of 3

One day whilst in science lab Sam (8) had a spat with his science partner and ended up lashing out, resulting in a Bunsen burner falling over, a flame needing to be extinguished and a glass vial broken! The science lab had to be evacuated. It was a frightening episode for everyone.

By the time Sam arrived home the head teacher had told me everything. Sam was suspended from school for 2 days.

Luckily I had the Mistakes Process to hand and very quickly he had told me the truth and was working out how to make amends. Being suspended from school was significant; he also had to make a cash contribution to replace the vial and that really stung as it came out of his birthday money; then he wrote an apology note to the whole class and spoke his apology out loud to the class on Monday morning.

> *On Monday afternoon I had a call from his class teacher to say what a profound impact Sam had had in the classroom that day. His courage and honesty in standing up and apologising for his mistake was great modelling and later that afternoon she confessed she got cross with the class as for the umpteenth time the rubber from her desk had gone missing! She asked the class who had taken it and no one owned up. At that point Sam stood up and said to everyone it's ok to make mistakes; we all make mistakes in life but the most important thing is having the courage to admit and put things right. She said in all her years of teaching she had never witnessed anything so powerful, and indeed the culprit owned up.*

Elaine, mum of two

Cheating

Has your child ever bent the rules to ensure he won a game? He's not alone. Cheating is also something that begins early, generally at around age 5 or 6. It is similar to lying in that the child first has to be aware of the rules and then pretend that he is complying. He also needs to comprehend that it's wrong to break them. He usually needs to lie to cover up the cheating. And like lying, it's a sign of cognitive progress.

We don't need to panic but we do need to act… calmly.

Children cheat at games and on tests if it is really important to win, to come first, to establish prowess, to feel important. When it's put like that I'm sure you can see how to counteract the imperative to cheat: by putting more emphasis on character than on outcomes and helping them feel important in ways other than by winning.

"Children need to see that we value their character first, their effort second, and then their grades."

– Dr Madeline Levine[98]

If a child's self-esteem is low or is under stress, winning may become even more important to help her feel better. Cheating is very much on the rise within the education system because of pressure to succeed. Children who copy another's work may not see it as a wrong thing to do. They may just be anxious to keep up. As one fifth grader put it, *"your parents tell you not to cheat, and you know you shouldn't cheat, but you feel pressured because you also know that your parents feel that the grade is the most important thing."*[99] The modern emphasis on results connects the child's value to their results. We examined this in Chapter 9 and looked at ways of encouraging children to do their best without making them feel that our love and approval is conditional upon their achievements.

Outside the classroom children may cheat at games. Much of children's learning about right and wrong happens through play. All children find it hard to lose and intense or stressed children may find it even harder, taking the ball or upending the game board and leaving when things don't go their way.

Parents can help by:

☺ **Playing games with their children.** Play games that are within their capability levels. Don't let them win all the time but often enough for them to want to stick

---

[98] Madeline Levine, *The Price of Privilege: How Parental Pressure and Material Advantage Are Creating a Generation of Disconnected and Unhappy Kids*, 2009
[99] Judy Molland, *Straight Talk about Schools Today: Understand the System and Help Your Child Succeed*, 2007

with it. Point out the micro skills within the game that they are mastering. Talk through the strategies that are involved. Example: *when playing a game like Connect Four where you have to get four counters in a row (similar to tic-tac-toe) an important strategy is to keep an eye on what your opponent is doing so that you can block their attempts to make a line of four.* They need to have some experience at winning in order to feel it is ok to lose. Practice also means they get good enough at the game to be able to win by their own skills.

☺ **Holding them accountable.** If you see that your child has cheated, say by only picking up two cards when he had to draw four (in a game that depends on getting rid of all your cards) then don't just turn a blind eye. Empathise: *"You really want to win, I know. Winning is great. Everyone likes to win. You can't play this game on your own. If you are the only one who wins I don't think anyone else will want to play. You probably wouldn't want to play if I won all the time."*

☺ **Descriptively praising honesty** and integrity everywhere, not just in games. Show that you value that more than winning.

☺ And, of course, **modelling it!** Maybe dial down your own competitive spirit when playing with your younger children. So if you're playing 'killer croquet' (!) maybe don't bash your opponent's ball into the next neighbourhood but just knock it out of line of the next hoop… (Yes, there's a story there.)

As your child gets older he will probably realise that cheating taints his victory.

Georgie (8) was being really grumpy one Monday afternoon. Her mum did some Emotion Coaching and eventually found out that Georgie had really wanted a Headmistress's certificate for ages. They were earnt through good behaviour or good work. Georgie's teacher had asked her to take the list of those students who had earnt certificates during the week to the Head's office on Friday so that they could be typed up on certificates to be given out the following Monday. Georgie had added her name to the list.

On Monday she had gone up with the other students to collect her certificate and shaken the Head's hand and heard the applause. But Georgie found she couldn't enjoy her moment because she felt guilty. She knew that the accolades were not for her really. Her victory was hollow.

Valerie helped her daughter write a really difficult letter to her teacher and to the Head to admit what she had done and to apologise. The school commended her for her honesty and Georgie learnt an important lesson.

Stealing

Very young children don't understand the concept of personal property and so help themselves to what they want when they see it. There is no moral culpability here. Similarly families or cultures which don't recognise private ownership wouldn't have a concept of stealing. Assuming this is not the case in your family let's see how to address it as stealing's not uncommon.

If preschool children take something that doesn't belong to them instead of making them wrong for it we can point out that *"that toy belongs to Jake. He will be sad if you take it away. Let's give it back to him and find something for you to play with."* We can teach them that some things belong to individuals and some belong to everyone in the family without making a drama out of it.

We know that young children are impulsive so even when they know they shouldn't take something that doesn't belong to them they may not be able to help themselves if it looks fascinating, fun or delicious. They might be able to see it from the other person's perspective if you approach it gently. *"You really love Gemma's new gel pens don't you? I'm guessing you wish you had some in those lovely glittery colours. I bet you'd do a great picture with them. Gemma loves them too and they belong to her so you need to ask her if you want to borrow them. If she wants to play with your Digimon cards she needs to ask you because they're yours. You wouldn't like it if she came into your room and took them without asking."*

As usual when children are older the reasons for stealing become more complex.

They include:

- ☺ For the thrill of it
- ☺ Because their friends are doing it or because they want to impress friends or buy their friendship with things. Their friends may dare them to do it.
- ☺ They're rebelling or exerting control
- ☺ They may feel they don't get their fair share
- ☺ They're angry and want to get back at someone
- ☺ They need attention – psychologists suggest that the child may be searching for something they need that they can't identify. It could be attention or love or stability.
- ☺ Stress or unhappiness
- ☺ It's a cry for help.

A mum who had recently separated from her husband told us that her son was using her log in and account details to buy things on eBay without her authorisation and she thought it was because he was so unhappy about the family situation.

If you think your child understands that it is wrong to steal then consider if one of these reasons fits her. That will dictate your response. You do need to take steps to address the underlying causes. But even if you don't know exactly why she's done it there are helpful ways to respond. The chances are she won't know why she has stolen so it probably won't be helpful to ask her why. *I couldn't have told my mother at the age of eight that my recent kleptomaniac spree was because I was unhappy at my new school and needing more attention than she was able to give me just then (three other kids, one of whom was a baby and she was working). I didn't want her to know I was unhappy at school because I knew she thought this school would be really good for me and I didn't want to make her unhappy.*

What to do

Don't call your child a thief, shout at him, punish or shame him but do hold him accountable. Support him to return the pilfered goods to the shop or their owner, apologise and make amends.

The essential requirement of modelling may be a bit easier here, but remember that stealing includes manipulating systems to pay less or evading fares or fees!

Talk to your child about respecting others' belongings by taking care of them as well as asking to borrow them.

If you suspect your child has stolen money from you but can't be sure don't accuse but monitor carefully while keeping money safe. I don't always have an exact knowledge of how much is in my wallet so I'd give the benefit of the doubt until I was sure that some had gone missing. You might say that money has gone missing from your purse if you're sure but without pointing the finger unless there's no one else who could be responsible. Say how uncomfortable it makes you feel that someone (or your child if it could only be him) has breached your trust. Telling your child of the reasons for your suspicions makes it clear to him that he is likely to get caught and may deter him from stealing again. (Although the prospect of getting caught isn't much of a deterrent, as criminologists know.)

A better approach, as with lying, is to let your child know you would be very happy if they respected other people's belongings. Back this up with Descriptive Praise when you see them being tempted but keeping hands to themselves. You have to be on the ball to spot that! Descriptively praise honesty generally.

If the stealing is frequent or of substantial items or your child appears indifferent when the matter is discussed you may need to delve further. Revisit Chapter 6.

Swearing and rudeness

I work with a group of troubled adolescents for some of whom very colourful and sometimes downright offensive language is the norm. For them, and their community, it is a standard way of speaking and has become quite habitual (although of course swearing is not confined to families who are down on their luck). We are working on developing a relationship of trust and respect with these teens and hope that they will learn to modify their language when at the centre, not because it matters to them but because they know the mentors, for whom they have affection, are offended by it. We want them to *want* to change their behaviour... It's early days.

Assuming that is not the case for you, you may have been quite shocked to hear your beloved utter an expletive or two. Even a hardened expert like me with my level of exposure was quite taken aback to hear my 6-year-old niece (I'm not identifying her – I've got many of them) call her brother p------breath (insert biological term for the male member). You may have wondered where she heard that kind of language or whether she has any idea what it means.

Kids pick up language at home of course (many parents admit that they use language they don't want to hear from the kids when angry or frustrated or hurt) and they'll also hear it at school and in the media.

So why do kids swear or use offensive language?

☺ They're exploring language – trying out this new word. They may not know what it means but they've heard other (maybe older) kids use it and maybe saw it get a laugh.

☺ They're doing it to be like the other kids, to fit in

☺ To shock, provoke or get attention. It's a pretty sure fire way to get a reaction from a parent.

By the age of 5 or 6 children know that words can hurt. You'd think therefore that if you pointed out that the words are offensive they'd stop using them. Right? Well, it depends how you go about it. If we have a big dramatic reaction and make them feel shame we may get exactly the opposite response. The child may learn that all he has to do to get a big reaction from the parent is to use his 'magic' words. If he feels badly about himself or angry with you he may not care to do what you want.

So what's the solution?

☺ The most important thing is also the hardest – **stay calm**. This is a bit easier if you expect that at some point your child will trot out something you don't want to hear. Nonetheless it can be a bit shocking. Try not to overreact.

☺ **Explain that the word used is unacceptable**. Set up some rules around the words used in your family. They may be different from what another family will find acceptable.

☺ If you hear other people swearing explain that **other families have different rules**.

☺ Teach them that what is acceptable in one environment may not be in another. They will know that **different rules apply in different situations** already. So an older child may want to use language you don't like when he's with his friends to appear cool but not at home, and definitely not in front of granny. If you address this potentially emotive issue without anger and judgment your child is more likely to listen to your advice about how to fit in socially without gutter language or in what other ways he can express himself strongly.

☺ You may need to **explain what the word means** and why it's not appropriate and state that *in this family we don't use that word in that way*. It helps if you do use proper anatomical names for body parts and say that they are used to refer to parts of the body not for name-calling. Even if you're not offended by the words your children use toward others, name-calling shouldn't be tolerated since it is so hurtful. *When my mother was teaching she used to adopt the approach of saying the offensive word several times and writing it on the board to take the shock value out of it while explaining what it meant... That took some explaining when the head popped in!*

☺ If your child is old enough to understand what is right and wrong about language and he does it anyway it may still be age related in that he doesn't yet have very good **impulse control.** If he is 9+ then the chances are there is some other reason underlying the language.

☺ **Emotion Coaching** teaches children that it's ok to be angry or frustrated or feel really jealous of a sibling and gives them acceptable words to use and alternative strategies for dealing with the underlying anger or annoyance. It opens up the way for problem-solving to tackle any underlying issue. *"Wow, for you to speak to me/your brother like that tells me that you're really upset! I'm wondering if something happened at school today..."* then, when calmer, *"What words can you use to tell me how you're feeling?"*

☺ **Watch your mouth!** We all get provoked of course but try to substitute less offensive words or voice your frustration *"Oh I'm so annoyed!"* When my daughter was about 10 when she was frustrated she used to say *"Oh... rude words!"* If something regrettable escapes then apologise and explain why it happened.

☺ **Descriptively praise** for not swearing, for using alternative language or strategies to vent.

Sex

Sex and how kids think about it and ultimately engage in it is perhaps not really a moral issue. I could have included it under Their Physical World but frankly there was enough in that chapter already. Also parents can get very worked up about it so I thought we'd look at it here amongst the other emotive issues.

Is there a right and wrong about sex? No doubt you will have views about what is a healthy approach to sex and when is the right time for your children to experiment with sex. You may be thinking that's a long way in the future but actually you need to prepare your children while they're young because the conversations get too awkward when they're older and because the scope for getting a lot of misinformation in the playground or skewed information via the internet is so great.

When your children are little they often ask questions about where they came from and that is the opportunity to tell them about how babies are made. Two of my three children asked me this question, years apart but both in a crowded lift in a department store! While you can ask them to wait until you get out of the lift you need to answer their questions honestly (no stork stories) and clearly, with only as much information as they want. There are many great books on the market to make this process easier. See our website for some recommendations.

We will also have conversations with our children as the question arises, often in parallel with what they're learning at school (in the classroom) about safety, privacy, modesty and the right to say 'no'.

But there's a whole lot more to sex than making babies and protecting against abuse. While your children may not be anywhere near puberty yet and the thought of them becoming sexual beings feels very alien we sow the seeds when children are very young for healthy attitudes towards sex. Clearly children model themselves on the intimate relationships they see most – that between the adults they live with. If they see affection expressed through kisses and cuddles they will regard that as normal, even if they say it's gross. If they see you being comfortable with your body by walking around the house naked they are likely to be comfortable with their own bodies. If you use the biological terms for body parts instead of euphemisms they will feel no shame about those bits – after all we don't feel such shame in talking about knees that we need to use a different word.

What won't work is to talk about sex in an atmosphere of shame, squeamishness or titillation, prohibition or wrongdoing. Before your children get to their teens, while you still have their ear, you may want to convey some of the following ideas:

- ☺ that sex is best in the context of a caring relationship
- ☺ that sex is meant to be pleasurable, for both partners, and if you're not enjoying it that doesn't mean you're deficient in any way and you don't have to carry on
- ☺ that sex is best when the partners talk to each other about what they like
- ☺ that what you see on the internet is not real life

Your turn

If you find your child has done or you suspect he has done one of the following, bearing in mind his stage of

development, what will you say to him? What will you do?

Lying

What can you say?

. . . .

. . . .

Do you need to do anything further?

. . . .

. . . .

Stealing

What can you say?

. . . .

. . . .

Do you need to do anything further?

. . . .

. . . .

Cheating

What can you say?

. . . .

. . . .

Do you need to do anything further?

. . . .

. . . .

Rude words

What can you say?

....

....

Do you need to do anything further?

....

....

Sandy fibs

Towards the end of our holiday Charlie was getting restless. He asked if he could go back to our room which wasn't far away to get his yo-yo. I agreed that he could but asked him to come straight back afterwards. On the way, I noticed he stopped and played football (his current obsession!) with some of the boys he'd made friends with. I relaxed back on the sunbed but after about 10 minutes noticed he wasn't back. So I then set about trying to find him – backwards and forwards around the pool, into the room (yo-yo on the bed – clearly not been in there), checked all the toilets, bar area, etc. I didn't think he'd have gone to the beach because the previous day he'd complained about how sandy it was!

After about half an hour, I was just on my way up to the hotel lobby to alert them when I saw Charlie sauntering along with the room key. I asked him where he'd been (I wasn't angry or shouting or anything because I was so relieved, but was very firm) and he burst into tears (he does this very easily) and said how he'd got confused about where the room was, then gone to the wrong room, then got lost, then found the room but couldn't use the key card thing properly, etc.

I comforted him and as we were walking back to the poolside, I noticed he had sand on his back and asked about it – he said he'd leaned against a sandy wall... then when he sat down on the sunbed, I noticed his feet were caked in sand...

It took a lot of questioning and lying and denying etc for him to tell the truth – and the only way I could get the truth out of him was to reassure him that I wouldn't be angry and wouldn't shout at him... It transpired that he had followed one of his football friends out of the hotel towards the beach and they had asked if he wanted to walk down with him after he'd told them his mum and brother were on the beach...

Imagine my horror initially when he said, in reply to my question about why did you go down to the beach – "Because someone asked me if I wanted to go" and then in reply to my follow-up question "Who?" – "I don't know; a Spanish man..."!

Obviously I was furious and wanted to kill him – but I amazed myself at how calm I stayed. In the end, the consequence was that he was not allowed to go anywhere on his own, not even to the loo, and had to be accompanied everywhere, which he hated. We obviously also had all the talks about the potential dangers of going with people he didn't really know (although it wasn't as bad as it had initially sounded), the importance of telling the truth and why, etc.

Their Moral World in a nutshell

☺ Morality develops along with cognitive development and alongside the development of empathy so we don't expect very young children to have a highly developed sense of right and wrong.

☺ As an understanding of right and wrong develops children are very black and white; rules are set by adults and cannot be altered. Whether or not an action is wrong is decided by reference to its outcome. As children get older they determine the rightness of an action by reference to the person's intention, they develop more flexibility about rules and they may begin to question the authority of adults.

☺ When teaching a child right from wrong parents need to avoid creating a sense of shame which is the feeling that 'I am a bad person' and may result in avoidance behaviour. If the child feels guilt then that leads to a desire to make amends. Use The Mistakes Process and encourage proper apologies, not hollow, hypocritical ones.

☺ All kids lie and smart kids lie better. The main thing is to call them out in a lie but not make them wrong for it. Don't punish but explain the impact on others. Descriptively praise any signs of honesty. And watch what you're modelling!

☺ Cheating is more likely in an environment where winning is everything. To counteract this make sure your focus is on process more than outcomes. Play games with your children to teach them how to play by the rules, win and lose graciously and to help them develop skills so they can win fairly.

☺ Consider the reasons why your child may be stealing so that you can respond strategically. Require them to make reparations. Descriptively praise any kind of honesty.

☺ Stay calm in the face of rude words. Explain what the words mean and why they are unacceptable. Help them vent their underlying feelings. Be aware of what comes out of your own mouth!

☺ Help your children develop healthy attitudes toward sex long before puberty by modelling a loving relationship and a nurturing, non-ashamed attitude toward bodies.

Further reading:

Brené Brown, *Daring Greatly: How the Courage to Be Vulnerable Transforms the Way We Live, Love, Parent, and Lead*, 2013

Po Bronson and Ashley Merryman, *Nurtureshock: Why Everything We Thought About Children is Wrong*, 2011

13

Their world of responsibility

"The willingness to accept responsibility for one's own life is the source from which self-respect springs."

– Joan Dideon

Aisha was worried about Saleem, aged 7. He had always been a good student but in the last few weeks had been reluctant to go into school. He had been slow getting ready in the mornings and fussing about little things and seemed down. His mother had asked him what was wrong many times and eventually he admitted that a couple of boys, Glen and Adam, would not let him join the daily game of football in the playground at break-time. And they had told other boys not to let him play either... This had been happening every day, and all Saleem's attempts to be included – including asking teachers, stealing the ball, offering to be in goal – had been to no avail. Aisha was furious with those horrible boys. She said to her son: "Don't worry about it – it's just football, it doesn't matter; they don't matter, find someone else to play with" but she resolved to take action. She thought she would speak to Saleem's teacher but when she got to the school she saw Glen and Adam's mums talking together and so went up to them and explained what was going on. She asked the mothers to speak to their boys and they agreed, apologetically.

Aisha thought the matter was settled when Saleem came home that day and said his day had been 'fine' but didn't want to play with his brother. He spent the afternoon in his room. Later she heard Saleem telling his brother that no-one in the playground would play with him now because he was a 'snitch'. His brother asked him what he was going to do and he said dejectedly "I don't know." Saleem was very unhappy.

Aisha was even more concerned when her husband asked Saleem whether he'd like to go ice-skating on the weekend and he said he didn't know how to skate and didn't want to learn. She recalled that when he was doing his homework that evening he hadn't tackled his sums with his usual enthusiasm but had kept asking her for the answers. Saleem's confidence was shot.

Responsibility

As parents we have a lot of responsibilities. We have to provide for our children and keep them safe; we have to look after them when sick, feed, educate and clothe them; we have to bring them up to be decent people of character. And we have to do all that while earning a living, looking after a home and taking care of our own physical and emotional wellbeing. So it's not surprising if responsibility seems like a heavy word. But taking responsibility for one's self can be very freeing and empowering.

"Responsibility begins with the willingness to be cause in the matter of one's life...
Responsibility is not burden, fault, praise, blame, credit, shame or guilt...
Being responsible starts with the willingness to deal with a situation from the view of life that you are the generator of what you do, what you have and what you are. That is not the truth. It is a place to stand.
No one can make you responsible, nor can you impose responsibility on another. It is a grace you give

> *yourself – an empowering context that leaves you*
> *with a say in the matter of life."*
>
> ## – Werner Erhard[100]

Can you remember how you felt when you first took responsibility for an aspect of your own life? I can remember the sense of freedom and being in charge of my life I had when I was first able to get around on public transport on my own. I also remember the huge pride I felt the first time I bought an item of clothing for myself (a lovely red jacket) from money that I'd earned. Can you recall moments of pride and confidence like that? We want to give our children that feeling that they can not just cope with the world, but flourish in it.

Our job as parents is not to be the cook, laundry person, chauffeur, entertainment director, bank and tutor, although we will do many things associated with those roles. **Our job is to raise our children to be independent, responsible adults.** We need to begin with that end in mind. When we train our children to be self-reliant we give them a great gift of freedom. We empower them.

Training children to be responsible for themselves

From the moment our babies take their first wobbly steps we help them to step away from us and to walk on their own. We need to teach our children to be responsible for themselves:

☺ to be self-reliant and

☺ to take responsibility for their own actions.

Self-reliance

Being self-reliant means:

---

[100] https://wernererhardquotes.wordpress.com/?s=responsibility

☺ **Doing things by themselves.** At different ages children can be learning to do things for themselves and for the household. By the age of 4 they will probably have already learnt to dress themselves (at least some clothing), go to the toilet (during the day) and feed themselves (not necessarily tidily). Throughout the primary school years they can learn to take more and more responsibility for their clothes (from putting things into the laundry basket to making sure they have what they need for the next day and operating the washing machine), their personal hygiene, taking care of their own environment (tidying their room and putting away toys and games), helping with meal preparation, doing homework and organising their own equipment. They can learn to manage money and to organise social events, arrange transport and keep themselves occupied. They will probably have chores to do which are about making a contribution to the family.

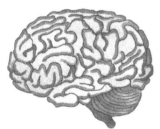

☺ **Thinking for themselves.** Parents encourage children to think for themselves when they ask them questions rather than issuing commands, when they invite input from the children into rules and other solutions to problems, when they don't automatically answer their questions but get them to think about it and maybe look it up, and when they listen to children's opinions, thoughts and ideas. It's an inconvenient truth for parents that you can't raise an adult with the ability to stand up for themselves and to question authority if you don't allow that in childhood!

☺ **Taking responsibility for their own feelings.** When parents are emotion coaches for their children they are teaching their kids to develop control over their emotional impulses so that their feelings are not always driving their actions. As we've seen this is something that develops over time and with good parental input. For  example: *if they feel angry, having a way of letting off steam without hurting others such as punching a pillow, going for a walk, or using breathing or visualisation exercises; if they feel sad knowing that it will pass, having a cry or talking to someone if they want and knowing how to cheer themselves up such as by listening to music they like, dancing or watching a funny video; if they feel inadequate, recognising this and knowing how to make themselves feel more capable; and if they feel stressed or overwhelmed, how to feel on top of things again such as by putting something in order or solving a puzzle or by listening to relaxation audio tracks.*

Why train children to be self-reliant?

Let's face it, it's quicker, easier, neater and sometimes safer for the adults to do things rather than let children do it themselves. Why? We're better at it, because we've had practice! Let's look at the benefits of investing time in training them to be responsible for themselves, and also consider the downsides if we do too much.

Advantages

For the child

When we train children to do things for themselves they learn some important life skills. But the most important benefit is the effect on the child's self-esteem.

A child who can do things for himself, who can tackle new challenges in his life, who has strategies for coping with life, is a self-confident child. When parents expect their children to do things for themselves they send them messages of faith in their capabilities. When we say *"be careful"* or *"I'll do that for you"* or we take over or we let them give up on things we unintentionally tell them that they can't manage.

We need to start when our children are young developing in them a positive, solution-oriented outlook on life, an approach that involves looking for solutions and strategies rather than giving up. When you believe you can find the answers you feel capable and competent.

> *"Character consists of what you do on the third and fourth tries."*
>
> *– James A. Michener*

When children are confident they are less likely to give up when faced with obstacles and less likely to be bullied or subject to peer pressure. As they grow older they are less likely to rely on substitutes for confidence like cigarettes, drugs and alcohol and less likely to seek approval through inappropriate relationships such as in gangs or through loveless sexual relationships.

For the parent

I'm guessing you'd love more time. Who wouldn't? Time for you to devote to the other children, to looking after your own wellbeing, to all the necessary things that need to be done in a family and to spending fun time with the children. That's what you get when kids are doing things for themselves, including occupying themselves.

When you know that your child can do things on her own you can trust her. When you tell your child this the relationship between you is strengthened and she develops pride in herself.

When kids are getting on with stuff on their own we nag less.

When children are being self-reliant there are many opportunities for us to descriptively praise and appreciate them more.

Parents unconsciously become resentful when much is done for the children and they don't appear to be grateful or they misbehave. When children do more for themselves they become more aware and more appreciative of what is done for them.

Training children to do more for themselves is a gift to them, not a burden.

Disadvantages of not training in self-reliance

Much has been written about parents becoming 'helicopter parents', hovering over their children all the time to make sure they are ok, saying *"Be careful. Don't climb too high. That's risky/dangerous/unsafe."* These children become tense and unable to look after themselves. They develop learned helplessness or even a victim mentality. They don't trust their own abilities or judgment. They certainly don't develop the competence that leads to confidence. *My brother in law is head of a Technical and Further Education College. He reports that he gets calls from parents complaining about their children (aged 18–22) not getting the grades they deserve. Some parents have even been known to try to negotiate salaries on behalf of their adult offspring with new employers.*

Children become fearful because they do not have faith in their own abilities to sort things out. They try less and give up easily. They expect everything to be done for them, not just by their parents but everyone else too.

It is not healthy for their future adult relationships if they equate doing things for them as a sign of love. They can develop the attitude that **life owes them a favour**. If they have never been expected to do anything for themselves then it's not surprising if they are resentful when finally they are called upon to do things on their own.

When parents do too much for their children, instead of being appreciative, children often take what is done for them for granted. **They become spoilt** and parents become resentful of the children and blame themselves for the unacceptable behaviour.

Many parents are concerned at the lack of respect shown by children towards their parents today. We have to show that we are worthy of respect by not putting ourselves in the role of slave. In no society in the world are slaves respected.

If children are over-protected they don't gain the confidence and resilience that comes from learning to handle things for themselves. But of course all parents want to protect their children – that's part of our job. We will have to make daily judgements differentiating between appropriate support and helicoptering.

In 2001 The Centre for Research into Parenting and Children at Oxford University published a report on bullying, *Bullying in Britain*, which found that young people who were the victims of bullying were more likely to have had over-protective parents who did too much for their children.

This report showed a connection between doing chores at home and the absence of bullying – because a child who has responsibilities at home has increased confidence.

When parents expect their children to do things for themselves they send them messages of their faith in their children's capabilities.

For example: *when my youngest started secondary school he was having a hard time settling into his new school. One of the things we did was to give him more responsibilities at home. This had the effect of boosting his self-esteem as his capabilities were demonstrated to him.*

Why do we do too much for our children?

☺ **It's quicker** to do it ourselves (and easier and neater). It's much quicker for us to tie their shoelaces, make their packed lunches and organise their sports equipment than teach them how to do it themselves. This is often because of the speed at which our lives operate, yet it can be really detrimental to our children's training to live life at this pace.

☺ **We anticipate resistance.** If we expect that our children won't want to do what we ask and will make a fuss and dig their heels in then we may avoid asking them to tidy their room in the first place. But with Descriptive Praise to encourage cooperation and Emotion Coaching to acknowledge how they feel about it we have tools to deal with resistance.

☺ **We believe that we show love by doing things for our children** but in fact it is more loving to prepare children to cope with adulthood. We don't like to see them struggle but in fact everyone has to struggle to move on to the next stage. Our parenting challenge is to allow our children to struggle. We can do it if we remember that that is the route to growth and that we can support our children.

☺ **We don't want to let go.** It is our job as parents to assist our children with the process of growing up and not to impede it. If we think of ourselves as a trainer and our task is to empower our children then that is the way we can be valued and needed.

"Keeping children helpless is one way of hanging on to our babies, even when they begin to tower over us."

– Cassandra Jardine[101]

☺ **We are afraid.** We feel anxious for our children's safety, particularly in big cities. These fears are often misplaced. We think the world is a more dangerous place than when we were children but in fact it's just that anxiety-inducing events such as the Madeleine McCann disappearance get 24/7 media coverage. However if we keep in mind our role of training our children to cope in the modern world, we will teach them how to deal with the things that concern us rather than trying to shield them from them. We need to teach our children how to use public transport or walk or cycle safely rather than keeping them at home or chauffeuring them everywhere (thus adding to the dangers on the roads).

We may teach them self-defence or street-wise behaviour just as we teach them about 'stranger

---

[101] *How to be a Better Parent: No Matter How Badly Your Children Behave or How Busy You Are*, 2003

danger'. We do need to educate them about being safe around alcohol, drugs and sex *before* they're teenagers just as we teach them about sharp objects, heights and electricity when they're small. We won't make them safe and they will resent us or become fearful if we 'cotton-wool' them. *I observed that of my daughter's friends the one who had been most cosseted at home was the one who really rebelled and engaged in risky behaviour once she escaped her parents' grip.*

☺ **We forget.** Sometimes we just get into habits of doing things for our children and we don't even think about whether they could be doing it themselves. It's just always been our job.

Victoria's son asked her if she would make him some jelly. To which she responded that he could learn to do it. "There are lots of things you can learn to do. I realise I haven't been letting you do things for yourself and I wonder what else you'd like to do independently." She was somewhat surprised when he replied that he'd like to learn to fold his clothes so that he could fit them all in his sports bag. (He had just come back from a school trip.)

The training tools

Remember the training tools you learnt about in Chapter 4, Setting up for Success? Well, we'll use the same tools to teach children to be responsible for themselves.

Have realistic expectations

What could your child be doing for himself? Here's a fascinating list of what British kids claim they can and can't do: http://www.npowermediacentre.com/r/4393/ knot_interested__only_one_in_five_young_brits_can_ tie_a (see our website – www.theparentpractice.com/book-resources#chapter-13).

In a recent survey of children's responsibilities over the years, sociologist Markella Rutherford[102] found that between the 1930s and 1970s children were expected to plan menus, shop and prepare meals for the family. They were involved in laundry, cleaning the house, caring for younger children, nursing sick family members, keeping household accounts, decorating or even helping to maintain the family car. In contrast, Rutherford says that the only real responsibility given to children today is schoolwork. By the 1980s if children were asked to shoulder more onerous chores, they were often done in exchange for toys, games or outings.

Psychologist Madeline Levine says letting kids off chores in favour of school work or because they need to practise a sport "sends your child the message that grades and achievement are more important than caring about others".[103]

Your turn

What could your child be doing for himself?

Consider whether he could be getting involved in food preparation, setting tables and cleaning up after meals. What about clothing? Could she be involved in deciding what to wear, laying out clothes, separating colours, putting clothes in the washing machine, hanging them up to dry and folding clean things? What about ironing? Children could be learning independence around personal hygiene according to age – running a bath, showering by themselves, brushing and washing their own hair, hanging up towels, rinsing out the sink after teeth-brushing etc. What chores could they be doing around the house or garden? Do you want them to be involved in tasks that go beyond looking after their own space? As early as

---

[102] 'Children's Autonomy and Responsibility: An Analysis of Child Rearing Advice' in *Qualitative Sociology*, Volume 32, Issue 4, 2009.
[103] Author of *Teach Your Children Well: Parenting for Authentic Success*, 2012, cited in http://www.wsj.com/articles/why-children-need-chores-1426262655

possible train your children to manage time and organise themselves and to look after their own kit for school. This could start with carrying their own school bag and include taking the right sports and music equipment and books to and from school. You can work up to them managing their own time around doing assignments. Other areas for learning responsibility are around managing emotions and resolving conflicts, thinking for themselves, managing money, learning to use public transport, arranging social events, etc.

What area will you focus on this week/month/year?

....

....

....

Train in small steps

If our children are not doing what we want them to do it means… they are not trained, yet. The desired behaviour comes at the *end* of the training process. (See our website – www.theparentpractice.com/book-resources#chapter-13 – for a compelling video by Carol Dweck on the power of the word 'yet' https://www.youtube.com/watch?v=J-swZaKN2Ic.)

We often say things like "*Mikhail should be doing his homework by himself – he's 9 years old!*" But the word 'should' is meaningless and gets in the way of proper training. It means that we have an expectation that a 9 year old could be doing his homework independently. Well, maybe he could. That would depend on his temperament and his experience of school work and his ability to do the task (which will vary from task to task) and how he feels about it. Change the word 'should' to 'could'. Example: *Mikhail could be doing his homework independently if I give him the support he needs, i.e.*

if I first explore how he is feeling about the work and we do a Chat Through beforehand.

Can you think of yourself as a trainer? Start from where your child is and think about what is effective to get him from point A to B. We usually want to go from A to Z in one step. The question to answer is what can I do to get my child from where he is now to where I'd like him to be? Concentrate on the process rather than the outcome.

Example 1: I want my child to be able to express upsets in words rather than hitting out when he's angry.
You will need to go through this in stages, moving away from hitting a person to perhaps hitting an appropriate object such as a pillow, to shouting or jumping on a trampoline or walking fast or another strategy for 'upset management' and then to using words which say how he feels. Descriptively praise every step on the way. You will need to give a lot of Emotion Coaching so that he develops a vocabulary for his feelings and so that his frontal lobes connect better with his emotional brain. You will need to do Take Twos when he does hit and ask him to make amends. Punishing would set the training back. Model using words yourself or walking away to cool down.

Example 2: I want to train my child to make her bed.
First show her how to do it – she may already know this. Then require her to do it, maybe in stages, starting with the easiest part – i) putting the pillow on the bed, then ii) teach her how to straighten the duvet. Then teach how to fold pyjamas in steps (first step – putting unfolded pjs on the bed). Descriptively praise each step and maybe invite her to tick it off her chart. A photo of the neatly made bed might help.

A useful way of thinking about training is:

☺ I do, you watch

☺ we do

☺   you do, I watch

☺   you do

We need to move from the co-pilot's chair to the back seat.

Plan

If you're training your children to be more organised about their own stuff for school then think about how to make that happen. Do you need a schedule for what needs to be taken into school each day? When should it be consulted? How will your child remember to consult it? Where does that schedule need to be posted? Who should make it? (Hint: your goal is your child's self-reliance.)

What things can be done in the evening to prepare for the next day? Clean clothes chosen, located and laid out? Shoes polished? Lunch boxes prepared? Homework/reading book/ any text books put in the school bag? Check if there are any forms to be signed? Do you need a checklist for these things?

What other sorts of reminders might work? (Not you!) A note above the towel rail/coat hooks/on the bathroom mirror/laundry basket? If the bins get collected on Friday mornings what will help them to remember to put them out on Thursday evenings? Would it help to schedule a regular time for everyone to do their household jobs?

Time

How much time will you set aside to train your child and where will you ~~find~~ make this time – will you need to get up earlier/start the going to bed/homework process earlier?

We can't expect the training process to be quick – we often give up too soon. If you want your child to eat healthily you probably know that you won't be able to stand back and let them choose whatever they want after a few weeks. It will take years of following rules and forming habits and maturing frontal lobes before they will choose salad over chips. (I'm not sure my own frontal lobes are fully mature yet.)

The best time to start getting children to contribute is when they're really young because they love to help. Don't do all the household chores when they're asleep or at school but do them with them. Make it fun by doing the vacuuming while dancing to your favourite upbeat dance tunes. My husband used to play Pavarotti and sing along while translating into outlandish lyrics.

Get their input

Chores – maybe ask them to choose from a list of jobs to take on as their contribution. Tell them you genuinely need their help and explain your values around everyone in the family supporting each other. Let them decide when and how to do it where possible. You can do this in a family meeting where there's a lot of Descriptive Praise and perhaps some nice things to eat as well!

Ask them for ideas about how they can do things on their own. If they want to go to a friend's house can they walk on their own or arrange a lift with someone else, or if you need to take them what needs to be done to free you up to make the trip? How can they remind themselves of things that need to be done? Will it be an old-school chart or a new-technology alert on a phone?

Involving them in little things will get them into the habit of thinking of solutions. Example: ask your daughter what she can do to make it less painful for her to brush her own hair after it's been washed. Get their suggestions on how to make the morning routine less stressful. What works for them may be different from how you'd do it. It's really important you give their way a try. Or if you can see a difficulty with it, ask questions to help them see its drawbacks. Example: if their solution to getting up on time is to have you wake them ask them what they could do to achieve the goal of getting up *independently*.

Don't do their thinking for them – when they ask questions don't rush to show off your knowledge but get them to think about it first – they may already know the answer. If not, direct them to where they can find out. Try books as well as Dr Google. Sometimes a question is a delaying tactic.

"Anyone who thinks the art of conversation is dead ought to tell a child to go to bed."

– Robert Gallagher

You can smile and respond, *"I think you know what you need to do, don't you?"* When someone else asks them a question don't answer for them and when there is a problem let them know you trust that they will come up with a solution. It doesn't mean you can't ever make suggestions or help your child solve his problems but let them have a go first. Remember your input is as a trainer and brain nurturer not as an encyclopaedia, or nag.

> You may recall the proverb: *Give a man a fish, and you feed him for a day; show him how to catch fish, and you feed him for a lifetime.*

When your child is faced with a problem:

- ☐ Listen and empathise. *"This is a tough problem."*
- ☐ Describe the situation to clarify the issues for your child. *"You really want to go to Amy's party but you're worried that Jessica wasn't invited… This is a dilemma for you as you're friends with both girls."*

☐ Ask questions that help your child think for herself. *"Are you thinking that Jessica will feel betrayed if you go to Amy's party?"*

☐ Wonder aloud. *"I wonder how Jessica would feel if...?"*

☐ Offer to help her prepare for something that's making her feel nervous. *"I hear you're nervous about making this call. Would it help if we ran through what you're going to say together?"*

☐ Use Descriptive Praise. *"You've really thought this through carefully and considered everyone's feelings..."*

Acknowledge any resistance

With children who are perhaps not yet in the habit of helping out let them know you understand that this is not a priority for them, that they would rather play with their Minions than be your minion! Don't make them wrong for not wanting to help – that's to be expected. If they're used to you doing things for them acknowledge that fact and that it's difficult to take on new responsibilities but that you realise that they are capable of it now. Acknowledge that it was easier for them when you used to carry the school bag!

"In the past I used to just jump in and sort things out for you but I realised that I was wasting a fantastic resource – your brain! Now I'm going to let you work out solutions for yourself as much as possible."

"You wish I'd do it for you, don't you? It was so much easier when Daddy did your shoes for you. Maybe it feels like you have so many responsibilities now. In a way that's true, because Mum and I think you're up to the task. We think you're very capable."

"When you were younger I cleaned out the hamsters' cage for you, even though they're your pets. Now we're going to do it together and soon I think you'll be able to look after them all on your own. Then your hamsters will know that you're their owner because you will be the one responsible for them."

"I'm guessing you don't want to pick up the fallen pears in the garden. It's not the most fun job, especially when they get all squishy. Will it help if you have some rubber gloves? And what about if I do my jobs alongside you? I need to rake up the leaves and mow the lawn. Then we'll both be carrying out our responsibilities together."

Use Descriptive Praise

You can acknowledge times when they have taken responsibility and appreciate them for the skills upon which you now want to rely. Descriptively praise any small steps in the right direction. Descriptively praising your children generally makes them more cooperative and more willing to please you. Younger children love to be told how grown up they're being but don't overdo it – you don't want them to associate being grown up with drudgery. Point out the behaviour that shows responsibility, self-reliance, helpfulness, good problem-solving, generosity and cooperation.

"Thank you so much for remembering to take your vitamins, Rochelle. You're really becoming responsible for your own health."

"You took your cup over to the dishwasher. And you used two hands. That way it didn't spill."

"*I noticed you took those plates and cups downstairs to the kitchen, Sam. That was considerate. Now there'll be plenty in the kitchen when we need them and we won't have to go searching the house with a hot piece of toast in hand!* "

"*I like the way you're brushing your teeth – you're really getting to the ones at the back, aren't you? I call that thorough.*"

"*You showed great attention to detail when you were making that model plane with Dad on the weekend. It was very painstaking work. Those skills will come in handy when it comes to organising your shelves in your room.*"

Don't nag

How can you bring it to their attention without nagging them? *Ask* them what they need to do or have written routines for regular tasks. Refer to how well they did it yesterday.

"You were really quick getting out of the bath when Mummy asked you to last night. I wonder if you can be just as quick tonight?"

Other words that don't help (don't feel guilty – we've all used them):

☺ Applying **labels** such as *lazy, stupid, weird, idiot, rude, naughty, clumsy, annoying, selfish, inconsiderate, bad, mean* or *slow* or even *silly* if it's said in a derogatory or demeaning way

☺ **Lecturing** (we think we're passing on pearls of wisdom…) *"If you don't brush your teeth properly you'll get holes in them and you'll have to have fillings and your breath will smell and…"*

☺ **Advising** – more pearls *"What you need to do here is…"* It can be disempowering – let them do their own thinking as this gives them the message we think they're capable of finding their own solutions.

☺ **Arguing** with them *"No, you're not hot. It's not hot in here at all. It's fine."* Remember you're the adult and the one in charge.

☺ **Negotiating** – this is not to say we can't listen to their point of view but make sure you're not giving in when your child says *"I'll only take out the bins if I can have another 15 minutes of TV."*

☺ **Explaining** – It's perfectly ok to give a reason for what you're asking them to do the first time but don't keep on giving the explanations and expect that to persuade a child who doesn't want to do what you're asking. Explaining the benefits of a tidy living room won't make your child feel like clearing up. *"You have to eat your broccoli because it's good for you. It's got vitamin A and K and Folic acid and..."*

☺ **Cajoling** and/or pleading *"Please, please will you just get your coat on!"*

☺ **Shouting** – no explanation needed!

☺ **Threatening** – especially if you don't then carry out your threat. *"If you don't get in the car now you won't be able to go to Tom's this afternoon."*

☺ **Bribing** *"If you get in the car now I'll let you sit in the front seat."*

☺ **Criticising** *"You never listen to anything I say."*

☺ **Being sarcastic.** *"That's right, you stay there. Your personal slave can vacuum around you."* This is an attempt to shame.

☺ Using **put downs** or personal attacks *"You're such a slob!"*

Don't pay your children to contribute

Pocket money is a great idea for teaching children the value of money. But keep that separate from the regular tasks that children do to contribute to the running of the household. Some families give a fixed amount of pocket money each week and there is no link to the set jobs that the children are expected to do. But there may be additional tasks that are optional for which they can earn some extra money.

Pocket money

Parents have the biggest influence on children's financial behaviour so in order to raise a generation of sound financial citizens here are four top tips to ensure your children become canny consumers, savvy savers, generous givers and insightful investors!

Start giving your children small amounts of pocket money whilst at primary school and for teenage children give them an allowance. It sends a very powerful message that parents trust them and feel they can be responsible for managing money. How much you give and what they can spend their money on will be personal to each family and age dependent. You might like to compare notes with other parents. Primary school-age kids are often interested in sweets, toys or comics whilst teenagers usually are motivated by mobile phone allowance and items of clothing.

Some families have set up a tripartite pocket money system whereby the allowance given is divided into three (not necessarily equal) parts and perhaps put into three jars. One is for the child to spend, the other for them to save, and the third to give away. This teaches the child to save and to value money as well as encouraging giving. Having your children wait and save teaches delayed gratification. If you want to teach compound interest you can even reward them by paying interest on the savings if they are not spent in the month.

Do talk to your children about the powerful consumer messages the media employ to entice you to buy goods. Discuss with older children the role of advertising and the manipulation involved. Most kids like the idea of not being conned by the conglomerates!

Don't do it for them

Work out what is your responsibility and what is your child's. This is not always easy.

Example: it is your responsibility to provide a healthy, balanced range of foods for your child. It is her job to decide what to eat and how much. When we force our children to 'clear their plates' we don't teach them to take responsibility for recognising when they have had enough.

It is your job to provide your child with the emotional and practical support they need for their learning but it is their job to do the work.

It is our job to set things up so that our children can be successful but sometimes our job is to support our children through failures. We can do lots of preparation and sometimes they'll still leave their school bag on the bus or forget about an extra choir rehearsal. Then we need to let them experience the natural consequences of their actions. This may mean supporting them as they arrange to get the bag back or as they apologise to the choir leader.

Example: setting and clearing the table (for an example of training your child to be self-reliant around homework see Chapter 9)

If this is a new task for your child then **give some notice** that it is going to happen. Let him know that you have confidence he is up to the job. Descriptively praise him for other areas where he is doing things on his own. "*You are getting so good at putting your dirty clothes in the laundry basket aren't you? What clever trick do you have for remembering? Oh, you look at your chart on the back of the bathroom door. Good thinking!*"

One 5-year-old girl so loved the Descriptive Praise she got for tidying up that when it was tidying up time she said "Goodie! I'm in charge of putting the cushions on the sofa."

Ask for his input – what will he need to do this task well? Practically, can he reach the cutlery and plates and glasses? Does he know how you like the table set? Would a photo help? Can he choose some elements of it? Does he know how to load things into the dishwasher? (This can take some training – my husband now knows how to stack for maximum efficiency, but it took a while.)

Can you make it fun? Can he pretend to be a waiter with a tea towel over his arm like in 'posh' restaurants? Would he like to choose a theme for decorating the table?

Acknowledge his feelings – that he would prefer to continue playing his game, or when he gets bored of the new job after a few days. Empathise if he feels hard done by because his younger sister is too little to do any jobs. Descriptively praise him for setting such a good example for her so she will be able to do her jobs when she's a bit older – maybe he will teach her?

Descriptively praise all small steps in the right direction. Don't give up too soon as it will take time to form this habit and Descriptive Praise is your most reliable tool here. How will you remember to keep praising? Have you got a pasta jar? How will you be able to vary your praise? Do you need to make a list of praises?

Keep it going. Remember it will take time and try not to get exasperated. Expect your child to forget or be resistant. Your job is to keep requiring it (and modelling it and praising it) until it becomes a habit. How do you remind without nagging? A photo of your child doing their jobs can be a great reminder.

Taking responsibility for actions

In Chapter 6 we looked at the Mistakes Process which gives us a tool for helping our kids to take responsibility when something goes wrong. When we approach mistakes calmly and without anger and blame and without punishment children are much more likely to take responsibility for their actions.

We can hold children accountable for breakages or loss of belongings or for hurting another physically or with words without damaging their self-esteem. When we require children to contribute to a window pane broken by their carelessly thrown ball or to the second school jumper lost this term or yet another broken pair of glasses we teach them to be responsible for those things. We don't have to make them wrong for it, just help them see how they can earn the money or live with a second-hand jumper from lost property. They thereby learn to appreciate the value of their possessions and those of others. We're also teaching them to alter their behaviour so that the jumper is less likely to get lost again.

When I was about eight I stole something from a shop and when my mother found out she made me return it and apologise to the shopkeeper. He was very kind and said that it didn't matter but it did matter to my mother and it mattered to me – I will never forget the feeling of guilt associated with taking something that didn't belong to me. My embarrassment was momentary but the lesson stayed with me forever.

When we use punishments children don't learn responsibility – they just learn that they are being controlled and the result is power struggles. Children also can't learn responsibility when the adults assume responsibility for a problem which is really their job to sort out. We want our children to become problem-solvers and to do this they need lots of experience and practice. For example: your child wants to play on the computer and the dog needs a walk. It is his responsibility to exercise the dog. *"You need to walk the dog and you want to play your game. What's the solution to this?"* or *"Here's a problem. The dog hasn't had his walk yet and that's your responsibility. How do you think you can solve it?"* Descriptively praise anything sensible in his answer. If he suggests you walk the dog you can calmly respond with something like this, *"You wish that you didn't have this responsibility. That doesn't work for me because I have my own jobs to do. I can see it's not going to be easy to figure out a solution but I think you're the man for the task. You have really good problem-solving skills. Yesterday you worked out how to share the TV programme choice with your brother in a way that was fair to both of you... Any ideas yet? Do you want to walk the dog first and then see if you have time for your game when you get back? Maybe you'd like to listen to those tracks you downloaded while you're walking."*

An obstacle to children taking responsibility is adult anger. We looked at this in Chapter 6 but it's worth reminding ourselves of it here. A child can't take responsibility for the things that are clearly his 'fault' if he can't deal with our anger on top of his own feelings of upset towards himself. To fend off those feelings he may turn them outwards, away from him, in making excuses or blaming others. Offence is the best defence!

The best way we can deal with this is to stay calm, not get upset and make him wrong but help him deal with the feelings so that he can begin to accept responsibility. If he says *"It's Jake's fault. He keeps bumping the table,"* when his drawing hasn't gone the way he wanted it to you can say *"You're really upset. I hear how disappointed you are that your drawing isn't working out the way you want. You've been working on it for ages."* Later, when he's calmer, you can help him see how his words wounded his brother and ask him how he can repair things with Jake.

Obviously this works best when you develop a culture in your family of a no-fault and solution-focused approach to mistakes and you model that attitude of kindness to yourself and to the children when mistakes happen.

Trip away

8-year-old Ethan was due to go to an adventure farm for a 2-night trip with his school. He had only spent 3 or 4 nights away from me since birth, and these had all been with his much-loved aunt and cousins, and he had always been accompanied by his younger brother. In addition, Ethan had always been anxious about new situations, finding the first day of term challenging, or being left at parties when he was younger.

Over the last few years I had used Emotion Coaching and many Chat-Throughs to help him in new situations. I had also taken every opportunity to encourage self-reliance – and at 8 years old he did many tasks for himself.

As the trip approached, I broached the subject of what he might want to take with him, and what he might do there, and how he might feel about being away from me for three days and two nights. He told me that he was a little bit 'worried' but mostly, he assured me, he was excited. "You see, Mummy, I don't need to be too worried, because I am the sort of boy who can do lots of things for myself..." he said.

As I breathed a sigh of relief, I reflected that all the effort I had put in was slowly but very surely paying off... With huge benefits for him, and great peace of mind for me!

Julie, mother of two

Adult feelings

An example of me taking responsibility for my upset feelings was when, for the 2nd year running, I managed to forget to attend my daughter's parent-teacher start of term talk. "NOOOOO!" I shouted and was just about to start blaming anybody and everybody else for not helping me remember when I instead remembered our 'Keeping Calm' tips. I explained to my family, in a tight voice, that I needed to go calm down. I went to the bottom step, sat down and had a mini tantrum! Yup, stamping feet, even swearing. It lasted all of 2 minutes. As my upset level came down, my thinking level rose – within 5 minutes I realised that this 'disaster' was actually a chance to arrange a private meeting with the teacher – ideal for Ella's last year before moving up to senior school. So instead of a poisoned evening at home, by taking responsibility for my own upset and venting it safely, I found a silver lining AND modelled great self-control for my children. Self-control is NOT about being perfect – it's about knowing how to deal with your strong feelings in a way that doesn't harm others or yourself.

Sue, mother of three

Responsibilities beyond the family

We've explored the idea that our children can take responsibility for doing day-to-day things for themselves and for the family. They can also learn with our help to be responsible for their emotions, recognising them and owning them rather than blaming others for them. We model this when we use 'I' statements such as "*When you ignore me and stare right past me, I feel disrespected,*" rather than "*You make me so angry,*" or "*You are so disrespectful.*" They can learn to manage them so that their actions are not always dictated by their feelings. They can learn to think for themselves, to voice opinions, share ideas and come up with solutions to problems. They can be responsible for their own actions and be accountable for wrongs done to others or for carelessness with belongings.

But beyond the boundaries of their world of family and school and sports is a much wider world that we can teach our children as the adults of tomorrow to take responsibility for. (For more on this see the next chapter, The World Beyond Them.)

Your turn

Training your child to do something independently – do they know HOW to do this task?

Does the task need to be broken down into smaller steps? Detail the steps you are going to take.

....

....

....

Would rules help?

Are there positive rules that would help them remember what to do, that could be supported by Descriptive Praise (and possibly some other reward) for following the rule?

....

....

....

How long will it take and when is the best time to do it?

....

....

What will help everyone remember to do this task/develop this habit?

Written checklist/routines, tick charts, putting what is needed within reach/where it will be seen?

....

....

What will you descriptively praise your child for during the training?

Write specific phrases here:

....

....

....

....

How will you offer support and empathy during the training?

Acknowledging reluctance, or accepting frustration, does not mean giving up on the goal! Write down some Emotion Coaching phrases:

....

....

....

Responsibility in a nutshell

- ☐ Teaching children to take responsibility for themselves is not a burden, but an empowering gift. There are huge advantages for a child's confidence when he develops competencies. There are many advantages for parents too when children can do things for themselves but it can be hard for parents to do the training as it takes time and it challenges our ideas about our role as parents.

- ☐ Children can learn to be responsible for:

  - ☐ Doing things for themselves and making a contribution to the family

  - ☐ Thinking for themselves

  - ☐ Recognising and managing their own feelings

- ☐ Use all the Setting Up For Success skills to train children to be independent

- ☐ Using the Mistakes Process helps children take responsibility for their actions without getting into power battles or loss of self-esteem.

14

The world beyond them

"There is no single effort more radical in its potential for saving the world than a transformation of the way we raise our children".

– Marianne Williamson

In a talk about parenting at the Aspen Ideas Festival in July 2012 this email, which was received from one of a Harvard Professor's students, was read out by Ericka Christakis, early childhood educator and Harvard College administrator:

Hi Prof,

I attended lecture yesterday and found out that we had an assignment due for the course last week. Until the lecturer mentioned it yesterday, I was oblivious to the fact that we had an assignment due! My attempt to notify you of this yesterday didn't pan out. Upon my subsequent re-inspection of the syllabus, I also noticed that there were two reading assignments due before the midterm. Those, too, I didn't know were due at any particular time.

I am completely astonished about these revelations and not sure how this happened. I'm also surprised you didn't notify me earlier of my failure to complete these assignments. What do you suggest that we do?[104]

While she was careful not to blame the parents Ms

---

[104] http://www.aspenideas.org/sites/default/files/transcripts/what-is-goal-parenting.pdf

Christakis said "to me this is a failure" – this young adult has failed to learn to take responsibility for himself and his studies.

Much has been written in recent years about how 'children these days' are being raised with a sense of entitlement leading to narcissistic, self-absorbed adults who are resentful, complaining, expecting others to do much for them and ultimately unhappy. This is in fact not a new claim. Previous generations have been accused of being spoiled too. Alfie Kohn, in his book *The Myth of the Spoiled Child*, asserts that there is no evidence that the dominant style of parenting today is permissive. Or that permissive parenting causes spoilt, narcissistic children. His view is that there is nothing unusual about today's children. *"Every Generation is Generation Me; that is until they grow up."*[105]

You may nonetheless want to be sure to avoid raising children whose world view does not extend beyond their front path, or who are cynical, indifferent, or self-absorbed. You may want to cultivate in your children an interest in something beyond their immediate world. You may want them not to be wrapped up in what are often referred to as 'first world problems'.

Caring

> *"Nobody cares how much you know, until they know how much you care."*
>
> **– Theodore Roosevelt, US President**

One of the many balancing acts for us as parents is to raise children who care, but not so much that they get paralysed with overwhelm. If your child is of a sensitive nature he will

---

[105] Alfie Kohn, *The Myth of the Spoiled Child: Challenging the Conventional Wisdom About Children and Parenting*, 2014

care, deeply, about many things. Other children let life wash over them, which is less dramatic but they can appear not to have compassion. What do we want them to care about? Well us of course, and their siblings and friends and extended family. There is a whole world beyond them that we may not have given much thought to but actually we do want our children to take an interest in and to care about. When your children become teenagers they may be deeply passionate about causes or you may be longing for them to get out of bed and care about something... anything. Now is your chance to foster these qualities of compassion and curiosity. Now is the time to help them connect with the world beyond them.

"Happiness is a by-product of being involved, being interested, caring about something beyond yourself."

– Ellen Galinsky[106]

What can adults do to help children perpetuate that sense of wonder that they have when very small? You may want to cultivate in your children openness to ideas and a sense of living in the present, mindfulness. Do explore with them what they are interested in and allow them to choose what they care about. But don't turn it into A Project as in the following anecdote reported by Larry Cohen at the Aspen Ideas Festival 2012: *"I got a panic call from a mother who said 'I'm really worried about my child, I'm really worried about my child.' I was like, 'what's the situation?' She's like, 'well, she's 4 and she hasn't found her passion yet.'"*

What would you like to encourage your child to care about? You may find something in the list below or think of

---

[106] Co-founder and president of Families And Work, Co-director, When Work Works Project, Author, *Mind In The Making: The Seven Essential Life Skills Every Child Needs,* 2010

something else. Choose something to help your child engage with the world beyond him, something that helps him feel part of something bigger.

Neighbourhood	Community	World issues
Current affairs	Democratic processes	The animal world
The natural world	The planet	The practice of faith/religion
Spirituality		

....

....

In this chapter we explore some practical age-appropriate ways of getting your children to think outside their day-to day-experiences.

Start by revisiting the list of qualities you looked at in chapter 2. Did you include ones like thankfulness or gratitude? What about compassion? Do you want your children to be people who can find, or at least seek, meaning and joy in the small things of everyday life? Do you want your children to be givers?

Of course parents can be modelling these qualities and without that example it would be a case of "do as I say, not do as I do" but we know that won't be enough. This chapter provides a number of ways you can purposefully foster these qualities in your children. Write down your values here (or on the form on our website – www.theparentpractice. com/book-resources#chapter-14) so that they can be at the forefront of your mind as we go through these examples.

....

....

....

....

> *"One of our greatest priorities should be to help young people learn life skills and attitudes that are conducive to living a flourishing life and making a positive contribution to society; to help them discover that bringing happiness to others leads to a much deeper sense of fulfilment than any A grade or iPhone ever could."*
>
> *– Anthony Seldon*[107]

Don't make them wrong

If your children appear self-absorbed don't make them wrong for it. It is to be expected – particularly in younger children and teenagers. It is also to be expected if children are experiencing a lot of stress in their lives, when they will move into self-preservation mode. Can you be brave and ask yourself do they have basic needs for love and structure that aren't being addressed?

We know that criticising them or labelling them as selfish will not create change. Punishing or lecturing them will make them resentful. Did any of you grow up with the refrain *"think of the poor starving children in Africa"* ringing in your ears when you didn't eat the food that was on your plate? I was quite happy for them to have my food! That reference to my ingratitude just made me feel guilty. I was raised as a Catholic and we do guilt well. But while I would want to raise my children as "[people] for others" (to paraphrase the Jesuit

---

[107] Former headmaster of Wellington College and author of *Beyond Happiness: The trap of happiness and how to find deeper meaning and joy*, 2015

goal) I know it doesn't work to make them feel that they are less important. At school I learnt that 'I' is the least important letter in the alphabet and I am still trying to shrug off that learning.

Instead it might be more productive to think of how you can cultivate habits of thinking beyond themselves and being appreciative of what they have.

Human beings are by nature social creatures. We have a deep desire to connect and to belong. We need communities to support and sustain us but if the community is to prosper it also needs us.[108]

Caring about...

Neighbourhood or community

The first step beyond our own households is our local community or neighbourhood. How can your children be involved? Of course that will depend on the physical structure of the neighbourhood, the local amenities, the permanence of the population and the attitudes of the inhabitants. When my children were growing up we lived on quite a busy road and there weren't many other families with children the age of ours so the opportunity for organic engagement with the neighbours was limited. It required adult involvement. Ann lives in a quiet street with a golf course at one end. Her daughter is the eldest in the group of neighbourhood children and 'looks after' several of the younger ones, which gives her a great sense of responsibility and pride. They all play together and don't need adults. Camilla's children live opposite a park where the local children hang out. They have neighbours with young children and her 12-year-old daughter loves to go and help out with the little ones. Jenny spends weekends and summers in a village by the sea where

---

[108] Hugh Mackay, *The Art of Belonging*, 2014

her children have forged links and developed a real sense of community through riding and sailing clubs. Her children are able to cycle around the village without adult supervision.

> *When Mike Lanza was looking for a house for his young family he purposefully chose a neighbourhood that would be conducive to community so that his kids could be independent and feel like they belonged to the neighbourhood. He cruised the streets looking for kids playing (very suspicious looking!) and talked to people. He and his wife also took steps to foster community by playing games or taking meals in their front garden, by walking the dog and talking to people and knocking on doors to introduce themselves. They also created a back yard wonderland for kids and invited the neighbourhood in.*[109]

If you live in an urban environment you may have concerns about allowing your children to play out in the street. You may need to be more involved in facilitating connections with others but it is worth the effort as connecting is so important for your children to understand that no man is an island, that we all depend on each other and that each person has something valuable to contribute. As social creatures we can only reach our potential when we engage with our communities.[110] You never do harm to someone you feel you belong to. We know that social exclusion is the reason behind the disaffection that causes radicalised young people to seek purpose with fanatical groups. Addressing the problem of social exclusion is everyone's responsibility.

---

[109] Mike Lanza, author of *Playborhood: Turn Your Neighborhood Into a Place for Play*, 2012, interviewed by Sarah Konowski on ABC Radio 702 Sydney, 25 June 2015
[110] Hugh McKay, *The Art of Belonging*, 2014

When our children are young, belonging to local clubs such as Brownies or Scouts fosters a sense of local community and these kinds of organisations are often involved in activities that benefit the community.

Parents can obviously model a neighbourly attitude and include the children in their endeavours. You may be looking out for an elderly person in your street, helping with shopping perhaps or dog-walking. We used to give our ancient and very frail next-door neighbour a lift to church on Sundays. You may be taking steps to look after your local environment such as by picking up litter or planting flowers on your verge or nature strip or around the trees alongside your street. There will always be volunteering opportunities in your local community.

If you want to get your children involved at this level look at notice boards in your local cafés, church, charity shops, library or other community centre. Your child's school will probably have initiatives from time to time that involve helping out in the local community. Many schools have some kind of charity effort before Christmas – if the children are asked to put together a donation box then consider getting them to fund it themselves or work to earn the money you spend on it or at least to go and make the purchases themselves.

If your neighbourhood does not have things like street fairs or community drives or the like perhaps you could organise one!

Ann's daughter and the other children in their neighbourhood collect up all the golf balls that land in their gardens and sell them back to the golfers. The children choose what charity they want to support and they donate the proceeds of their sales to it.

I recently became aware of the long-term effects of modelling in this sphere. When I was expecting Gemma I was visiting an elderly lady who lived on her own. After the baby was born she gave me a teddy bear that had belonged to her husband who had died many years previously. I used to tell Gemma about my old friend and the teddy bear was called 'Mr Mullens'. The other day I learnt indirectly (via my mother) that my now adult daughter was giving her time to visit the elderly in our neighbourhood.

Further afield....

Beyond your immediate community there may be issues in which you would like to involve your children. If you live in a big city the issue of homelessness and poverty will be ever present and on a trip into an urban centre you will doubtless come across people who are begging. We have choices about how to respond to this that our children will certainly pick up on.

If you do as Victoria did with her sons and stop and talk to some homeless people then your children will get the idea that these are real human beings with stories behind their current situation. Even if you just say 'good morning' as you pass rather than the more usual embarrassed avoidance of eye contact this treats the person as an individual rather than a nuisance. If your children show interest you may want to go further and either donate as a family to homeless charities or get involved on a personal level by helping out at soup kitchens. If you know of initiatives by businesses such as Prêt à Manger in the UK who give surplus food to homeless people then the next time you're in such a place mention it to the children. Maybe buy a copy of The Big Issue, the magazine sold by homeless people. Victoria's son is always keen to support the salespeople who come to the door by buying yet another cleaning product. It doesn't matter if you don't need 7 car cleaning mitts; if you can afford it buying one teaches your child that you can assist in a way that gives dignity.

Whatever you do **modelling isn't enough; you have to involve the children** if you want them to absorb your values and develop habits about giving. If you donate generously to charities that will be a wonderful thing but will not have much effect on your children unless you draw it to their attention, tell them about the cause and why it matters to you and maybe get them involved in choosing organisations to support.

"Belonging to good organisations and being part of something bigger than ourselves makes us feel connected and reduces isolation, which is such a potent source of happiness."

– Anthony Seldon

Beyond our shores....

There are many global charities which do wonderful work to support those in poverty and ill health and suffering from the effects of war, persecution, famine and other natural disasters. For a child under 10, giving to such organisations is likely to have most impact when they can understand to some degree what is going on in the countries affected and how their donation will work. So those charities that offer sponsorship programmes of children or communities or allow you to buy a sheep or goat or provide for a well are more easily understood by children than a simple monetary donation to medical research into malaria, worthy though that is. When you sponsor a child you get a photo and a bit of history and regular updates about your sponsee and your child can connect in some small way with this individual. This facilitates caring.

Your turn

What level of community engagement would you like to encourage in your children?

....

....

....

Current affairs or world issues

Taking an interest in people struggling beyond our shores starts to involve children in the causes of their dilemmas. Many families want to educate their children about issues that affect the world, not just tales of privation and distress but also about great inventions, sporting events, music, art, or amazing natural occurrences like the Aurora Borealis or a lunar eclipse or heart-warming tales about people or animals. How do you do this in your family in a way that doesn't overwhelm children or present them with material that they are too young to absorb? Just letting them watch the adult news or read the newspaper could be either boring or scary for this age group. But this doesn't mean that children as young as 5 can't have opinions about big ideas, and discussions with your children about current affairs can be very engaging, sometimes amusing and a great way to connect with them as you find out what they care about.

Many of the families we talked to read a weekly newspaper for kids in the UK called *First News*. This is pitched at 7–14 year olds and is in an engaging, colourful format with interesting, relevant and digestible stories. *"They love it and it sparks quite a bit of interesting conversation. I find that car journeys are a great time to chat about current affairs. We had lots of chats around the election so they understood the different parties, who stood for what, how many seats it took to win etc... We also ask general knowledge questions. The kids love us to ask them questions – so we try to ask them about geography, history, religion, current affairs, etc. We give some we know they will know but others that are harder and that they learn from. I think so often kids get into a car and they either play with their digital device or watch a movie... they are missing a really key time to interact with their parent."* – Jenny, mother of four.

In Australia there is the ABC's 'Behind the News' website, in the US *Time* magazine has a version for children called *Time for Kids* and the Pitara website originating in India also provides items of interest for children. There are also news programmes on TV designed for children such as the BBC's 'Newsround' in the UK aimed at 6–12 year olds.

Of course the dinner table is also a great place to have conversations about current affairs. Parents can start by saying something like, *"I heard this story on the radio about Cecil the lion, who was killed in Zimbabwe by a hunter... what do you think about that?"* This is a great opportunity for children to feel that their views matter as well as to become informed and to teach them conversational skills. But the primary purpose is engagement, not education. *My husband and his brothers were taught from an early age to make conversation with whoever was sitting next to them at a meal so Henry, aged 5, confidently turned to his neighbour and asked her if she knew Jemima Puddleduck. Fortunately she did, so the conversation went from there.*

Studies have found that family mealtime conversations play a huge role in language acquisition[111] and school

---

[111] Dr Catherine Snow, Harvard Graduate School of Education, http://www.cfs. purdue.edu/CFF/documents/promoting_meals/spellsuccessfactsheet.pdf

performance[112] as well as fostering a sense of belonging to the family which is essential for self-esteem and related to lower use of drugs in adolescence.[113]

Your turn

How can you encourage your children's interest in current affairs?

....

....

....

Civic life – taking responsibility

There are many levels of engagement in civic life and we can teach our children about it when they're young. If children learn to be involved in democratic processes they will live a richer life, be more responsible for what goes on in their community and be more likely to preserve the fundamental freedoms that are central to a democratic way of life. They will learn about the art of persuasion and discourse and the value of freedom of speech, not just for the advocates of the views we share but those with opposing views as well. A passionate life is a rich one, and sometimes a loud one!

Adults can talk to their children about their own civic participation and whenever possible involve the children directly. Can you take them along when you vote and explain the process and why it is important? Tell them about the candidates and their policies –it will ensure you

---

[112] Studies from the University of Illinois and Columbia University's National Center on Addiction and Substance Abuse

[113] Dr Blake Bowden, Cincinnati Children's Hospital, http://www.cfs.purdue.edu/cff/documents/promoting_meals/spellsuccessfactsheet.pdf

are well informed! You might volunteer for a political party or display bumper stickers on your car or posters in your windows. There are many ways of being involved apart from putting a cross on a ballot paper every few years. We may be involved in the judicial process by serving on a jury or taking part in public meetings, rallies or marches. We may sign petitions or attend lectures. Teach your child that her voice matters and she will be more likely to use it. Start by listening to the kids in family meetings as discussed in Chapters 4 and 8. If her school has some kind of student representative body perhaps your child would be interested in running for office. If the school has a debating team she may be more interested in that. Either way she would learn a lot about persuasive skills. Descriptively praise her when she makes a reasoned argument, backing up her opinion with facts. This will also help her in her school work.

At a local level you can demonstrate involvement in decision-making processes and taking responsibility for bodies in which you have a stake such as being a parent representative on the school council, parent/teacher association or board of governors. You could be involved in your local parish council or on committees of various kinds. Joining your local Neighbourhood Watch could be one way of caring for your community. Being informed and taking part are two crucial aspects of civic engagement.

The natural world

Today's families often have limited opportunities to connect with the natural environment. Richard Louv called this phenomenon 'nature-deficit disorder'.[114] Louv points to how

---

[114] Richard Louv, *Last Child in the Woods: Saving Our Children From Nature-Deficit Disorder*, 2005

modern family life has changed in the last twenty years with children spending more time viewing television and playing video games on computers than they do being physically active outside, with the attendant health difficulties that brings.

Spending time in nature has so many advantages for children. Apart from the physical benefits of being active, breathing fresh air and being in the sun, when children can run free and play with friends without too close adult supervision they get a tremendous sense of independence and freedom. Running and climbing, playing game upon imaginary game with their friends without any toys, exploring on the beach or in the woods, building dams, watching  crabs, fish and seals, observing tides and moon phases, seeing what the wind is doing, watching migratory birds, seeing baby birds or animals being born, watching amazing sunsets (plus getting blown over by gale force winds and soaked by torrential rain in the UK!) are all opportunities for bringing children close to nature and inspiring in them a sense of wonder. It also teaches them practical skills that enable them to feel confident and resilient. Geocaching (the world's largest treasure hunt) is also a great way to explore nature; see https://www.geocaching.com/play (or see our website – www.theparentpractice.com/book-resources#chapter-14).

I love that they come home after a holiday tousle-haired, freckle-faced and legs covered in bruises.

– Alison

Getting involved with animals stimulates caring that comes naturally to most children. If children have responsibility for animals at home they learn compassion and to respect life. They learn to take care of another creature and that this is not a momentary duty which can be given up when the initial excitement fades.

Children often like to get involved in protecting animals in the wild and may choose to support charities like World Wildlife Fund that promote animal conservation. As with human sponsorship programmes you can adopt an animal as a way of caring for it, but do explain what this means to your child.

Mattheo received an adoption present several years ago of a snowy tiger. But he didn't seem very grateful. In fact, he was very reluctant and tearful. After the generous godmother left, apologies and thanks having been given, I gently suggested he had seemed rather upset and not his usual polite self. "I'm very frightened," he said, "When does the tiger arrive, where does he live and how long do I have to feed him all by myself?" It was hard not to laugh, but the poor boy had not understood the adoption part and believed the offer to feed the tiger for 3 months involved him directly.

Rosanna, mum of two

When children spend time in the natural world they are more likely to want to protect it. *Alexander, who had been known to take only his own plate and put it in the dishwasher, surprised his dad when, coming across some rubbish on a beach, he said that it was wrong to leave rubbish on the beautiful beach and although it wasn't his rubbish he could clean it up.*

Their interest in the environment may mean that you get told off for not recycling properly or for leaving lights on! The evangelism of the newly converted can be a bit trying sometimes. But one of the great things about having children is that they allow you to look at the world with fresh eyes and with renewed enthusiasm.

Appreciating the natural world can be a spiritual experience. It can bring serenity, peace and calm. Being in nature forces you to slow down and allows you just to think and be creative. Creative surges don't usually come upon you when rushing around or keeping to a schedule. Taking in an amazing view from a mountain top or sitting by a calm lake or watching a raging sea or observing baby animals at play all serve to make us feel part of something bigger than ourselves. Even on a smaller scale learning about the industry of ants or the architecture of a termite mound or the complexity of bee society conveys a real sense of awe that dispels indifference.

Children who never get to explore environments like the bush or woodland can develop a fear of the outdoors. I recently took a group of 11–15 year olds bush walking and many of them were terrified that they were going to die when faced with having to descend a moderately steep rocky trail.

Your turn

What will you do to get your children out in and engaging with the natural world?

....

....

....

Back when my boys were 5 and 8 we had a particularly fun and laid-back summer family holiday. We'd bonded over long, lazy days on the beach, gorgeous sunsets and blissful freedom from busy schedules and running around.

I arrived back home to London with a bump. It was chilly and raining, we had no food in the fridge, and on the kitchen counter sat the kids' registration forms for the Autumn term's swimming and tennis lessons which I'd neglected to send off before I left.

Visualising what my afternoons were about to return to filled me with dread – dashing out the door with tennis shoes, rackets or the swimming bags, plus snacks for them or a book for my inevitable waiting times.

I longed to be back on holiday, away from this self-inflicted madness.

We'd spent a lot of time on the beach talking and laughing. My older son was beginning to ask me very profound questions about the meaning of life and I enjoyed exploring it with him.

Suddenly it occurred to me!

There are clubs for every sport, hobby, interest and activity – but one about one that promotes good ethics and values? A club where kids can learn about themselves and their relationship to the world around them? What if this club took place in the comfort of home? No driving around, no searching for parking. Snacks and drinks straight out of the kitchen.

I decided right there and then to create our own club, just the three of us. We freed up Tuesday afternoons to have our Special Day. We rotated through three different themes each week:

- *Family*
- *Community*
- *The World*

Before they got home from school I laid out some materials based on my idea for that week's theme. I'm not an artsy crafty type, so this was very basic.

For Family day, they'd make cards to send their grandmothers who lived far away. One day when dad was at home sick they made him funny cards and vouchers so they could be his slaves for the afternoon and bring him whatever he wanted in bed.

For Community day, we went to the local park and picked up litter. We baked banana bread for our elderly neighbour, or collected wood for her fire.

For World day, we sponsored a child in Ghana via ActionAid and drew her pictures and wrote letters about our life in England.

We became attracted to books aimed at kids about recycling and ecology and they started a Walk to School campaign to raise money for our local Common.

Our Special Day club only lasted about a year but now that they're teenagers, I can see the long-lasting effects. They have a deep awareness of their place in the family, community and the world. They've got strong ethics and values and good self-esteem.

Kelly, Mum to two boys

Spirituality

"Just as a candle cannot burn without fire, men cannot live without a spiritual life."

– Buddha

Spirituality may mean the following of a formal religion with attendance at services at church, mosque, synagogue or temple and observance of religious practices to do with dress, food and other customs and celebration of festivals. Attending religious services often has a community aspect to it as well as a spiritual dimension.

> *Our 8-year-old girls took their First Communion this summer in the local church which was a culmination of weekly sessions over 6 months, and a chance to make new friends in addition to undertaking the spiritual journey. I expected there to be reticence about attending every week, but there hardly was, and they always bounced in afterwards, full of what they had learned that day.*
>
> *Alison*

Or spirituality may take a more informal but no less profound expression. Many people describe themselves as 'spiritual but not religious', saying that science may be able to explain the world but not their place in the universe.[115]

Consider what spirituality means to you. Is it something that connects you with forces bigger than yourself? Is it to do with a search for meaning and purpose? It may be about mindfulness, being present and having a sense of wonder. For some the experience of meditation is a spiritual one.

---

[115] Tom de Castella, BBC news magazine, 3 Jan 2013 http://www.bbc.com/news/magazine-20888141

> *"Meditation is a fine-tuning device where we sit still and we tune and tune and tune until we get the most clear and still station on the dial, which is our soul."*
>
> **– Elizabeth Lesser**

There are various practical ways we can encourage children to develop their spiritual side to encourage contemplation of meaning, foster awareness and nurture a sense of wonder and connection.

Here are 6 spiritual practices that you can encourage in your children:

1.Gratitude

> *"We're not grateful because we're happy. We're happy because we're grateful."*
>
> **– Brother David Stendl-Rast**

Help your child become more appreciative by:

☺ **Modelling appreciation of things and people.** Say *thank you* of course but also talk about being grateful for what you have and the people in your lives. *"I love the way Daddy always checks with me if I need anything when he's going up to the shops – that's really thoughtful." "When you asked me if I was missing my mum and dad who are so far away I felt really cherished." "I love the way Auntie Sally makes my favourite dessert when we go there for Sunday lunch. That makes me feel very cared for." "This is my special watch that used to belong to Papa. I think of him when I wear it and I take very good care of it so I will always have it to remember him by." "These tools were expensive so I need to look after them carefully by* *oiling the blades so they don't rust and putting them away carefully."*

☺ **Having lower expectations.** David Brooks, columnist for the *New York Times*, writes that being thankful is a result of life exceeding our expectations.[116] He argues that people don't need to dampen their ambitions but will feel more gratitude if they have small anticipations. People who are usually grateful take nothing for granted. This is the opposite of feeling entitled.

☺ **Noticing when the children are appreciative and commenting on it** *"When you say thank you for the dinner I made I feel really appreciated." "I love it when you say thank you for driving you to Kim's house. Not only is it polite but it makes me feel that you don't just take the things I do for you for granted."*

☺ **Appreciating what *they* do with Descriptive Praise** (of course!) *"I really love it when you do what Daddy asks you to do quickly. Now we have time for two stories!" "That's sensible that you've put all the lids back on your felt pens. That way they won't dry out."* Or dropping a thank-you note into a lunch box or school bag or on their bedside table or pillow for them to find. Or maybe a text message for an older child.

☺ **Saying how you *feel* instead of criticising when they are not appreciative,** e.g. *"When you tell me you don't like your new action man I feel that you don't value the things I buy you." "I rearranged my schedule to be able to take you to the football trials. It was a long drive and a lot of effort so when you didn't thank me I felt taken for granted."*

---

[116] http://www.nytimes.com/2015/07/28/opinion/david-brooks-the-structure-of-gratitude.html

☺ **Requiring them to say thank you.** You probably have rules around this for everyday table manners and you may have rules about writing or calling a relative to say thank you when they've been given a gift. This may be obvious to many but in my own extended family there are some who do this as a matter of course and some from whom I've never received a thank you. G. K. Chesterton said that "*thanks are the highest form of thought,*" and that "*gratitude is happiness doubled by wonder.*"

☺ **Having them earn privileges or treats** rather than getting things just because they are alive. E.g. screen time is earned when responsibilities have been carried out.

☺ **Holding them accountable for breakages/losses.** If kids help pay from their own money (savings or earnings) for lost library books, toys and phones, windows broken by their balls, or paint-filled brushes left to dry out, they learn a valuable lesson about valuing what they have and what others have lent them, rather than assuming someone else will simply 'buy another'. This should never be done in an angry or blaming way. Example: *if your child has lost uniform sports kit for the second time this term, instead of you buying a replacement (while muttering) see if you can get a second-hand one from the lost property department or have him earn the money to replace it.*

☺ **Creating gratitude rituals.** Many families have a Golden Book in which they record Descriptive Praises for their child each evening. You can extend this to include more general things for which you are grateful or have a different book for it. In her book *The Blessing of a Skinned Knee*, Wendy Mogel mentions a Jewish tradition calling for 100 blessings of gratitude each day.[117] 100 things may be a tall order but you could develop a practice of sharing with your child each evening 3 things which made you happy that day. It doesn't have to be something very significant – it may be that you loved how big and yellow the moon looked this evening. This passes on to your children the things that you value. You might do this as a whole family from time to time – around Thanksgiving or Christmas perhaps or any time in your culture or religion when gifts are given. Or you might do it more frequently – some families make it a weekly practice.

You don't have to be religious to have a daily habit of saying thanks for the meal you share as a family.[118] It was a practice in my family that the children said thank you for their meal when they asked to get down from the table.

Another ritual for *savouring* things mentioned by Jeffrey Froh,[119] is that of using regular practices or props to remind your family of past occasions when you've been happy together such as looking at family photographs or videos or undertaking rituals around holidays or birthdays. This is something we've always done. My children love looking at the family albums – we find a physical album kept in a common place gets looked at more than photographs hidden away on a computer – and never wanted to change a single element of our putting-up-the-Christmas-tree ritual. But we never did it in a regular mindful way and I love the idea of making it into a practice

---

[117] Wendy Mogel, *The Blessing of a Skinned Knee: Using Jewish Teachings to Raise Self-Reliant Children*, 2008

[118] Sarah McElwain (editor), *Saying Grace: Blessings for the Family Table*, 2003

[119] Jeffrey Froh is a psychology professor at Hofstra University and co-author with Giacomo Bono of *Making Grateful Kids: The Science of Building Character*, 2014

for growing thankfulness. It also relates to the habit of being present and enjoying the moment which you may want to teach your children. Froh refers to it as *"Squeezing the juice from life. It's not about having more but how we extract as much as we can from what we already have."* Perhaps your Golden Book could be called a Juice book!

Professor Froh conducted a study in New York where middle-school students were asked to count their blessings for two weeks by listing five things they were grateful for. The control group listed complaints about hassles in their lives. The kids who focused on blessings for just two weeks reported feeling more gratitude, more life satisfaction, more optimism and were more positive even months later.

☺ **Showing gratitude through service or giving back,** as above. Can they give to others less fortunate? Can you organise a toy tidy-out and donate old toys or books to the local hospital? Can they arrange to bake some Christmas goodies and take them to a local children's or aged care home?

"If the only prayer you said in your whole life was, 'Thank you,' that would suffice."

– Meister Eckhart

---

2. Openness and listening

Openness to ideas, people and experiences means accepting what comes without expecting predetermined outcomes. Some temperaments will find this easier than others.

Cautious children like to know in advance what is going to happen. But being receptive to new possibilities increases the chances of learning. Being open to others means practising empathy or putting yourself in the other's position and trying to understand their perspective, their feelings. We encourage empathy in our children when we use Emotion Coaching with them.

Parents can model listening to other points of view at home with members of the family. When reading the paper or watching the news how do we respond to points of view that are different to our own? We don't have to agree with others but accepting that there are different ways of looking at things encourages openness.

3. Compassion and nurturing

Involving the children in caring for animals, younger children and the elderly encourages compassion and nurturing. Helping children sow and care for plants also teaches nurturing in a very real way. Providing a living thing with the optimal conditions for growth is a great metaphor for how to live a caring life.

Our children are more likely to be compassionate if they have received compassion from us. That means considering the intention behind the behaviours we don't like and thinking about what caused it. What was this child trying to achieve? Can we help them get what they want a different way? Can we teach them to make amends without anger and blame? Do we listen to their feelings, thoughts and opinions? If so we are telling them that we care about them and are nurturing their emotional self. We can develop compassion in all the ways discussed in Chapter 3. One of the ways mentioned there is to watch TV or read books with children and pause the action to ask how they think the characters are feeling and what they might do next. This helps them step into the shoes of that person.

Notice examples of compassion in your children and descriptively praise it. *"You saw that Chin was feeling sad and you gave him your Yu-Gi-Oh cards to play with."*

4. Silence, attention and wonder

You can encourage your children to spend time in silence, becoming aware of what is around them to cultivate a sense of wonder. Young children are full of wonder about everything they see and experience – we can encourage this by marvelling at their discoveries. Join with them in star-gazing, cloud-watching and admiring the industry of ants or the velvety texture of rose petals. You might like to lie on your back in the grass being fully attuned to the five senses and observe the wind in the trees and the sun on your face. Encourage being present to all those sensations by getting your child to describe them to you in as much detail as possible. Comment on her receptivity to what's around her. Sensitive children will appreciate a positive use of this temperamental trait. You may rediscover an appreciation for small things yourself. **Wonder is an antidote to indifference.**

Encourage silence by having quiet periods at the end of the day when all electronics are off, the story has been read and the conversation finished. Stroke your children if they like that and speak to them about the value of finding a still, calm place inside themselves. Touching is a great way to communicate love. Get them to concentrate on their breathing. This is a great tool to teach children to combat stress in their lives.

Paying attention to what we feel and think is another aspect of mindfulness. Adults find this hard as we go about our day at full speed and trying to do several things at once. Concentrating fully on one thing at a time is not only more efficient but you are less likely to miss something important. You might like to train yourself and your children by reducing the distractions of digital devices. Make sure no one brings them to the table when you are connecting as a family. If you're spending time with your child be present and turn off your phone. Introverts will find this easier than extroverts. It can be hard to train our attention on things to wonder at rather than sensationalism or trivia.

5. Finding meaning

We seek meaning by observing our experiences and watching for patterns to help us understand the world. We then describe those patterns with labels, metaphors, symbols and stories. Young children do this through fantasy play – it is a key tool for understanding their world and therapists use it to help understand the child's experience. You can encourage your children to make sense of their world through stories, whether verbal, written or pictorial.

As adults we may have eschewed the idea that things happen with purpose and believe that the world is a capricious place of chance. But for children that is a frightening prospect. They need to believe that there is direction and a point to their lives. Help them to see that their lives are important by your appreciation of them.

6. Beauty and connection

Adults can help children see beauty by providing them with opportunities for beautiful sights and experiences and by pointing out the wonder of them. We can also help them see connections by simple practices such as making a family tree so they can see how they are related to others. If you have called your children by a family name tell them where that name came from and who had it before them. *My son Sam feels a real sense of connection with all the other Samuels who have come before him.*

You may have family sayings or jokes. Every time I woke my sons up in the morning I would ask them *"How's my bonny boy today?"* because that is what my grandfather used to do. I felt connected to him in that moment. He called me 'tuppence' because I was the second child in the family and now my brother calls his second child 'tuppence'. These are family rituals that connect members of the family to each other. Talk about how things are connected in nature, how one change in habitat affects the creatures which live there, how if one creature disappears that affects the whole ecosystem. Talk about similarities between people even if they come from different cultures or backgrounds. All of this encourages holistic thinking.

Paying it forward

On our camping trip a few weeks ago I walked past a family who were just setting up and the mum was pumping up an airbed with a foot pump. I asked her if she wanted to borrow my fully charged electric airbed pump. She followed me back to our camping area and I gave her the pump. Once she had walked away our friend's child Lewis (aged 9) asked if I had made a new friend and my daughter Lucie immediately just said: "That was just a random act of kindness." Lewis asked what that meant and Lucie proceeded to explain the knock-on effect of random acts of kindness and that they take nothing from us but give so much and if everyone just did a little something to help others the world would be a better place.

I was so proud of the way she explained it to someone younger than her. She really went into detail and explained the good feelings involved in doing something nice for someone else just to be kind.

Gaelle, mother of one

Your turn

What would you like your child to engage with beyond their world?

. . . .

. . . .

. . . .

What practice will you set up in your family to encourage this engagement?

. . . .

. . . .

. . . .

. . . .

. . . .

. . . .

What qualities would you like to encourage in your child?

. . . .

. . . .

. . . .

What practices can you adopt as a family to cultivate these qualities?

. . . .

. . . .

. . . .

....

....

....

Beyond their world in a nutshell

☺ Consider what you would like your children to be engaged with beyond their world. Put opportunities before them to expand their horizons and let them choose. Will it be getting them involved in the local community or looking further afield to people who need assistance beyond our shores?

☺ Can they be involved by donating toys, books or money or by baking or giving time?

☺ Think about ways of getting your kids interested in current affairs or world issues. Would a subscription to a children's newspaper or website be beneficial? How can you create opportunities for discussions about issues?

☺ What are you modelling around civic engagement? Tell the children why these issues matter to you. Ask their opinions. Can you involve the children directly in marches or signing petitions?

☺ When you plan your next holiday think about spending time with the kids in nature. Can you take them somewhere where they can get up close and dirty (literally) with the natural world?

☺ Even if you can't own a pet of your own in what ways could your children be involved in caring for an animal? Can you grow some plants with your children?

☺ Cultivating spiritual practices makes for a holistic approach to and a richer experience of life. You may like to consider family practices or rituals to nurture a sense of gratitude, openness and listening, compassion, wonder, meaning and connection.

Further reading:

Mike Lanza, *Playborhood: Turn Your Neighborhood Into a Place for Play*, 2012

Hugh McKay, *The Art of Belonging*, 2014

Alfie Kohn, *The Myth of the Spoiled Child: Challenging the Conventional Wisdom About Children and Parenting*, 2014

Richard Louv, *Last Child in the Woods: Saving Our Children From Nature-Deficit Disorder*, 2005

Jeffrey Froh and Giacomo Bono, *Making Grateful Kids: The Science of Building Character*, 2014

Wayne W. Dyer, *It's Not What You've Got!: Lessons for Kids on Money and Abundance*, 2007

Anthony Seldon, *Beyond Happiness: The trap of happiness and how to find deeper meaning and joy*, 2015

What next?

Well, here we are at the end of the book. I'm really hoping that *Real Parenting for Real Kids* answered many of your questions about how to bring out the best in your own children. I trust you have been putting into practice the ideas and techniques you've been learning about here and I really hope you're seeing some changes in your family. Are you using the Pasta Jar, the Golden Book, the Mistakes Process? Are you holding family meetings and getting your children's input on family issues? Are you looking underneath the surface behaviour and considering what's causing it? Have you organised some Special Time? Maybe you've re-thought how you discipline and how you use rewards and consequences. Maybe you're using some of the calming techniques when your kids are pushing your buttons.

If so, good for you. I really want to acknowledge you, and you to acknowledge yourself, for that. The real skill in parenting is to take the resources at your disposal and put them to use for you in creating a happy family life. Keep using all the tools in the book and on our website book resources page (www.theparentpractice.com/book-resources) as you keep developing your parenting practice and build mastery.

Do you want more? Do you want some personalised support? Do you like the ideas but struggle to apply them to your situation? Or maybe you're struggling to achieve results in some areas as yet. Are you thinking you could do with a bit more support?

Often people who are very successful are the ones who recognise the value of support. **No one succeeds alone. No one.**

☐ Max Talmud was the mentor to Albert Einstein who gave him books on science, maths and philosophy.

- [ ] George Martin was as instrumental in the success of the Beatles as any of the band members and in fact he was responsible for many of the arrangements and instrumentation on the early records.

- [ ] Sam Walton borrowed $20,000 from his father-in-law L. S. Robson to start his first retail business. It was Robson's belief in him as well as the cash which allowed Walton to build Walmart.

- [ ] Oprah Winfrey says that without her father she would have "gone in another direction".[120]

- [ ] Even Usain Bolt has a coach!

If you'd like a little more input or hand-holding we'd love to meet you.

Face to face
If you can access our work **in London** this is what's available:

- [ ] One-day, five-week or ten-week courses
- [ ] In-house workshops on various topics
- [ ] Seminars in schools and in the workplace
- [ ] Individual consultations
- [ ] Parenting Facilitation training for professionals

If you're too far away for that or too busy for face-to-face work, don't worry! We have designed a solution just for you.

Online
Our Positive Parenting Academy is an online course with videos, worksheets and exercises and membership of an interactive private Facebook group as well. Busy parents can access the courses in their own time, with their partners and/

---

[120] quoted in Gary Keller, *The One Thing*, 2013

or other child carers, in their own home, without worrying about babysitters, and even in their pyjamas! The Academy is a great way to reinforce the skills in 'Real Parenting' and also to involve a partner.

For more information on any of these options go to www.theparentpractice.com/programmes (or www.theparentpractice.com/professionals for our professional training). For free weekly tips and articles, as well as information about what we're doing, sign up for our newsletter: http://www.theparentpractice.com/signup .

As children get older, of course, the issues you're facing in your family will change. Stay with us and let us support you in your parenting journey.

Wishing you joy and ease in your parenting,

Melissa

Acknowledgements

Without the following people my parenting journey would never have begun:

- ☐ My darling husband John, my best friend and my best supporter in all I do. Without him there would be no team Hood.

- ☐ My three guinea pigs, Gemma, Christian and Sam. They have been very forgiving of my mistakes and very kind in their acknowledgment of my parenting efforts.

- ☐ My first parenting coaches, Noël Janis Norton and Gillian Edwards.

Without Camilla McGill I would never have had the courage to share what I learnt with others and The Parent Practice would not have been born.

Without this amazing team The Parent Practice would not be able to bring to hundreds of families every year the gold that transforms their family life:

- ☐ My business partner and dear friend, the indefatigable Elaine Halligan. She gave me the kick up the backside I needed to get this book underway and has been hugely encouraging throughout the process of writing.

- ☐ My wonderful team of facilitators, Sue Kumleben, Juliet Richards, Ann Magalhaes, Jenny Eastwood, Victoria Markou and Kristina Valeix who generously contributed many thoughts and stories during the book-writing process but who have also been contributing to the collective knowledge of The Parent Practice for years.

☐ I'm particularly grateful to Juliet for her careful editing eye – she helped me find my voice again when I was lost amongst the words. Although she was no earthly use when it came to reducing the word count!

This is a truly collaborative work, as is everything we do at The Parent Practice.

Without Caroline Ferguson, amazing mindset coach, there would still be mindset obstacles preventing me from having realised my vision and getting this book out of my head and on to paper.

Thank you to Suzanne Dibble and the Fab 5 Mastermind group who have helped me acknowledge our expert authority and have supported this book's inception and progress. Thank you especially to Sherry Bevan for leading the way with her own book, *The Confident Mother*, and for generously sharing its hatching with us.

Without Alison Jones, my writing coach and publisher, I would not have had the courage or the clarity to get writing. She has given extraordinary support and inspiration. She is a still, calm presence in the whirlwind of the writing experience.

Thank you also to Siobhan Barlow, mother and illustrator, who has done such lovely sympathetic drawings with such enthusiasm. She never complained even when I added to her brief without extending her deadline! I hope you really enjoy her illustrations and agree that they bring the pages to life. It was a moment of serendipity when Elaine met Siobhan while they were both walking their dogs on Wimbledon Common.

Thank you so much to all the masters of parenting, the families we've worked with over the years and my friends and family who are parents, who have contributed their wisdom, their tips, their strategies and their experiences (and even especially their Low Parenting Moments) to make this book real. Thank you for sharing your joys and heartaches with me to benefit others.

Thank you also to my own parents who did a really good job bringing me up and giving me a very happy childhood. Special thanks to my grandfather (on his cloud) who gave me a little notebook and asked me to write down a new word every day. There are some of them here Grandpa!

Index

Lightning Source UK Ltd.
Milton Keynes UK
UKOW06f2101010416

271323UK00001B/1/P